Microcomputer Applications for Business Series

AN INTRODUCTION TO
WordPerfect® 6.0

S. Scott Zimmerman Brigham Young University
Beverly B. Zimmerman Brigham Young University

Course Technology, Inc. One Main Street, Cambridge, MA 02142

An Introduction to WordPerfect 6.0 is published by Course Technology, Inc.

Editorial Director	Joseph B. Dougherty
Product Manager	Katherine T. Pinard
Print Production Manager	Myrna D'Addario
Senior Production Editor	Robin M. Geller
Production Assistant	Christine Spillett
Desktop Publishing Supervisor	Debbie Masi
Desktop Publishing	Lois Auger
Cover Design	Darci Mehall
Copyeditor	Karen Palmer
Proofreader	Nancy Kruse Hannigan
Indexer	Margaret Holloway
Technical Specialist	Jeff Goding
Student Testers	Joshua Merritt
Manufacturing Manager	Elizabeth Martinez
Print Buyer	Charlie Patsios

An Introduction to WordPerfect 6.0 © 1994 by Course Technology, Inc.

Trademarks

Course Technology and the open book logo are registered trademarks of Course Technology, Inc.
WordPerfect is a registered trademark of WordPerfect Corporation.
Some of the product names used in this book have been used for identification purposes only and may be trademarks or registered trademarks of their respective manufacturers and sellers.

Disclaimer

Course Technology, Inc. reserves the right to revise this publication and from time to time make changes in its content without notice.

ISBN 1-56527-155-6

Printed in the United States of America.
10 9 8 7 6 5 4 3 2 1

From the Publisher

At Course Technology, Inc., we are very excited about bringing you, college professors and students, the most practical and affordable technology-related products available.

The Course Technology Development Process

Our development process is unparalleled in the higher education publishing industry. Every product we create goes through an exacting process of design, development, review, and testing.

Reviewers give us direction and insight that shape our manuscripts and bring them up to the latest standards. Every manuscript is quality tested. Students whose background matches the intended audience work through every keystroke, carefully checking for clarity, and pointing out errors in logic and sequence. Together with our own technical reviewers, these testers help us ensure that everything that carries our name is error-free and easy to use.

Course Technology Products

We show both how and why technology is critical to solving problems in college and in whatever field you choose to teach in or pursue. Our time-tested, step-by-step instructions provide unparalleled clarity. Examples and applications are chosen and crafted to motivate students.

The Course Technology Team

This book will suit your needs because it was delivered quickly, efficiently, and affordably. In every aspect of our business, we rely on a commitment to quality and the use of technology. Every employee contributes to this process. The names of all of our employees, each equity holders in the company, are listed below:

Tom Atwood, David Backer, Stephen M. Bayle, Josh Bernoff, Erin Bridgeford, AnnMarie Buconjic, Jody Buttafoco, Jim Chrysikos, Susan Collins, John M. Connolly, David Crocco, Myrna D'Addario, Lisa D'Alessandro, Ann Deluca, Howard S. Diamond, Kathryn Dinovo, Katie Donovan, Joseph B. Dougherty, Mary Jane Dwyer, Don Fabricant, Robin M. Geller, Suzanne Goguen, Eileen Gorham, Michael Greene, Andrea Greitzer, Tim Hale, Roslyn Hooley, Tom Howes, Nicole Jones, Matt Kenslea, Wendy Kincaid, Suzanne Licht, Elizabeth Martinez, Debbie Masi, Dan Mayo, Kathleen McCann, Mac Mendelsohn, Laurie Michelangelo, Kim Munsell, Paul Murphy, Amy Oliver, Kristine Otto, Jim Palmer, Debbie Parlee, Kristen Patrick, Charlie Patsios, Jim Pelis, Darren Perl, Kevin Phaneuf, George J. Pilla, Katherine T. Pinard, Christine Spillett, Kathy Sutherland, Sheila Tobio, Michelle Tucker, David Upton, Mark Valentine

Preface

An Introduction to WordPerfect 6.0 is designed for any first course on how word processing is used in business.

The Textbook

This textbook presents a unique approach to teaching how to use WordPerfect. Students learn to plan before they press keys. They learn to analyze the business problem and design their documents. Then they solve the problem by following a distinctive step-by-step methodology, frequently referring back to their original plan. From this process students learn that word processing is not just a sophisticated method of typing, but is a valuable tool to help make them more productive and successful in business.

The New Edition

An Introduction to WordPerfect 6.0 covers many of the exciting new features of WordPerfect 6.0 including the Button Bar, Grammatik, Drag and Drop, Bookmarks, the Outline Bar, Multiple Document Windows, and Tiled Windows.

Each step in the text lists all available methods of executing WordPerfect commands: Pull-Down Menu (using the mouse or the keyboard), Function Key, and the Button Bar. Instructors and students can choose the desired method of executing each command.

All of the end-of-chapter Tutorial Assignments and Case Problems are completely revised and expanded. They now involve less typing and more problem-solving by the student.

Approach

An Introduction to WordPerfect 6.0 employs a problem-solving approach to teach students how to use WordPerfect 6.0. This approach is achieved by including the following features in each tutorial:

Objectives

A list of objectives orients students to the goals of each tutorial.

Tutorial Case

This case presents a business problem that students will solve in the tutorial and that they could reasonably encounter in an entry-level job. The business problem is geared to what the typical student taking this course is likely to know about business. Thus, the process of solving the problem using WordPerfect will be meaningful to the student. All of the key business areas — accounting, finance, marketing, production, and management — are represented.

Planning Section

Each tutorial's case also includes discussion about planning the document. Students learn to analyze the business problem and then set clear goals for the solution before they press keys. Outlines are introduced as basic tools.

Step-by-Step Methodology

The unique methodology integrates concepts and keystrokes. Students are asked to press keys always within the context of solving the problem. The text constantly guides students, letting them know where they are in the problem-solving process and referring them back to their original plan.

Page Design

Each page is designed to help students easily differentiate between what they are to *do* and what they are to *read*. In addition, the numerous screen shots include labels that direct students' attention to what they should look at on the screen.

Exercises

Each tutorial concludes with meaningful, conceptual questions that test students' understanding of what they learned in the tutorial.

Tutorial Assignments

These assignments provide students with additional practice on the individual WordPerfect skills that they learned in the tutorial. Students practice these skills by modifying the business problem that they solved in the tutorial. All of the Tutorial Assignments are new in this edition of *An Introduction to WordPerfect*.

Case Problems

Each tutorial concludes with several additional business problems that have approximately the same scope as the Tutorial Case. Students are asked to use the skills they learned in the tutorial to solve these case problems.

Command Reference

This helpful quick reference card lists common WordPerfect commands and function keys, pull-down menu choices, and button bar options used to execute each command.

Data Disk

A Data Disk containing all of the document files needed to complete all of the Tutorial Cases, Tutorial Assignments, and Case Problems is provided for the instructor. Instructors may freely distribute copies of the Data Disk either on disk or over a network to all students who purchase a copy of this book.

The Supplements

Instructor's Manual

The Instructor's Manual is written by the authors and is quality assured. It includes:

- Answers and solutions to the all of the text's Exercises, Tutorial Assignments, and Case Problems
- A 3½-inch disk containing solutions to all of the text's Tutorial Assignments and Case Problems
- Transparency Masters of key illustrations in the text selected by the authors

Test Bank

This supplement contains approximately 50 questions per tutorial in true/false, multiple choice, matching, and short answer formats. Each question has been quality-assurance tested by students for accuracy and clarity.

Electronic Test Bank

This Electronic Test Bank allows professors to edit individual test questions, select questions individually or at random, and print out scrambled versions of the same test to any supported printer. In addition, technical support is available from Delta Software at (402) 496-9344.

Acknowledgments

Creating this book was a team effort. Many people deserve a hearty thanks for shepherding the text through its many stages of production.

We want to thank the reviewers: Mel Martin, ETON Technical Institute; Marilyn Meyer, California State University at Fresno; Leonard Presby, Patterson State University; and Dennis Shafer, Cuyahoga Community College. Their comments and suggestions were most helpful in improving the content and readability of the text.

We appreciate our long, enjoyable, and successful association with the people at Course Technology. With their dedication, professionalism, and good humor, they were able to perform miracles in the face of impossibly tight deadlines. We would especially like to acknowledge the following: Jeff Goding and his coworkers for carefully working through all the step-by-step procedures and end-of-chapter problems, tutorial assignments, and case problems; Karen Palmer for her able copyediting; Nancy Hannigan for her careful, detailed proofreading; and Robin Geller for her wonderful job of managing the production of the text.

A special thanks goes to Joe Dougherty whose patience and dedication have provided strong leadership in making this project possible. We cherish our long association and friendship with Steve Bayle whose vision, knowledge, and hard work have initiated this and many other important projects. We have the deepest admiration for John Connelly who, against many odds, created not only a new and exciting company but also a new concept in publishing.

To Susan Solomon we owe a debt of gratitude for developing the basic model on which this text is based. Her dynamic leadership in overseeing this project has been invaluable.

Finally, we would like to acknowledge our product manager, Katherine Pinard, who has been a joy to work with. Her constant guidance, encouragement, and support, her many perceptive suggestions, and her attention to detail have improved the quality of this book in numerous way and ensured that it was completed on schedule.

To all of you we give our heartfelt thanks.

S. Scott Zimmerman
Beverly B. Zimmerman

Brief Contents

Table of Contents

Your Data Disk for the WordPerfect Tutorials

To complete the tutorials and exercises in this book, you must have a Data Disk. The Data Disk contains all the practice files you need for the tutorials, the Tutorial Assignments, and the Case Problems. Before continuing, obtain a copy of the Data Disk from your instructor.

Disks can be damaged. To avoid losing data, one of the first things you should do when you get a disk with data or programs on it is copy the original disk onto another diskette or onto your hard drive and store the original disks in a safe place. That way, if the working copies are ever lost or damaged, you can always make new working copies from the stored originals.

In this section, you will copy the Data Disk that you received from your instructor. Find the description of your computer system below and follow the appropriate instructions.

- If your computer system has a hard disk and you are permitted to save files on the hard disk, turn to the section "Copying the Data Disk to a Hard Disk" on the next page.
- If you plan to load and save your files to a floppy disk, continue reading the section "Copying the Data Disk to a Blank Disk" below.

Copying the Data Disk to a Blank Disk

Before you begin, make sure you have the Data Disk labeled *An Introduction to WordPerfect 6.0* that you received from your instructor and one blank, formatted disk of the same size. Using a felt-tip pen, write the words "WordPerfect 6.0 data disk" on the label of the blank, formatted disk. Before putting the original Data Disk in the disk drive, make sure that it is write-protected.

To make a working copy of the Data Disk:

1   If your computer does not have a hard drive, insert your computer's Systems Disk into a disk drive and make that drive current. For example, if your Systems Disk is in drive A, type **A:** to make A the current drive. If your computer has a hard drive, go to the next step.

2   If the size of your Data Disk matches drive A, type **diskcopy a: a:** and press **[Enter]**. If the size of your Data Disk matches drive B, type **diskcopy b: b:** and press **[Enter]**.

3   Your computer prompts you to insert the Source disk in the drive you specified. If your Systems Disk is in that drive, remove it. Insert your Data Disk in the specified drive and press **[Enter]**.

After a few moments, your computer will prompt you for the Target disk.

4   Replace the original Data Disk with the blank, formatted disk and press **[Enter]**.

5   Continue swapping Source and Target disks as instructed until you see a message that asks if you want to copy another disk. Type **n** to answer no.

6   Remove the working copy from the disk drive. Store the original Data Disk in a safe place and use your working copy from now on.

Continue with Tutorial 1, "Creating a Document," on page WP 3.

Copying the Data Disk to a Hard Disk

Before you begin, make sure you have the Data Disk labeled *An Introduction to WordPerfect 6.0* that you received from your instructor. Before putting the original Data Disk into the disk drive, make sure that it is write-protected.

To create a directory on your hard disk for the Data Disk:

1   At the C:\WP prompt, type **md data** and press **[Enter]** to create a directory.

2   Type **cd data** and press **[Enter]** to make \WP\DATA the current directory.

Now you are ready to copy the Data Disk to the hard disk.

3   If the size of the Data Disk matches drive A, insert the Data Disk in drive A. If the size of the Data Disk matches drive B, insert the Data Disk in drive B.

4   Be sure C:\WP\DATA is the current directory.

If the Data Disk is in drive A, type **copy a:*.*** and press **[Enter]** to copy the Data Disk to your hard disk.

If the Data Disk is in drive B, type **copy b:*.*** and press **[Enter]** to copy the Data Disk to your hard disk.

5   After the copying is complete, remove the Data Disk from the disk drive.

6   Store the original WordPerfect Data Disk in a safe place.

Continue with Tutorial 1, "Creating a Document," on page WP 3.

WordPerfect 6.0 Tutorials

■   ■   ■

Tutorial 1

Creating a Document
Writing a Business Letter

Case: Clearwater Valve Company

Andrea Simone recently received a degree in business management with a specialty in operations and production. She has been hired as the executive assistant to Steve Morgan, the operations manager for Clearwater Valve Company. Clearwater designs and manufactures specialty valves for industrial sprinkler, cooling, and plumbing systems.

One of Steve's responsibilities is to train Clearwater's production plant employees on safety procedures. He decides to purchase training videos so he can conduct safety training easily and inexpensively. After looking through several catalogs, Steve determines that Learning Videos, Inc. publishes a video that seems appropriate. Steve asks Andrea to write a letter to request further information. He gives her a handwritten note with his questions.

In this tutorial you'll complete Andrea's assignment. You'll learn how to plan a letter and then how to use WordPerfect to write it.

OBJECTIVES

In this tutorial you will learn to:

- Plan a document

- Start WordPerfect

- Use pull-down menus, function keys, and button bars to execute WordPerfect commands

- Use word wrap

- Save, open, and edit a document

- Preview and print a document

- Exit WordPerfect

- Get help on WordPerfect features

Writing with WordPerfect

Before you begin, you need to learn three key terms: document, document window, and document file. In WordPerfect terminology, the letter that you'll write is called a document. A **document** is any written item, such as a memo, letter, or report. You use the document window to create and edit documents. The **document window** is the visual display on the computer monitor where you see the text you type and the changes you make to your document. You save your WordPerfect documents in a **document file**, which is stored on the computer's hard disk or on a 3½ or 5¼ inch disk. The document file contains the text itself, as well as formatting information about your document (Figure 1-1).

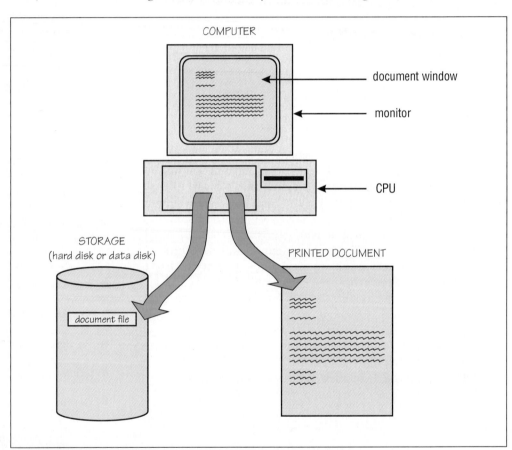

Figure 1-1
Document window on the monitor, document file on disk, and printed document

Let's begin now with the first step in writing with WordPerfect — planning a document.

Planning a Document

Planning a document before you write it improves the quality of your writing, makes your document more attractive and readable, and, in the long run, saves you time and effort. You can divide your planning into four parts: content, organization, style, and format.

Content

Begin your planning by determining what you want to say in the document, that is, the content. The content should clearly convey your purpose in writing and be appropriate to your reader. Include enough information to achieve your objective, but not so much that your reader becomes overwhelmed or bored.

As Andrea considers her purpose and her reader, she focuses on the handwritten note from Steve (Figure 1-2). The note lists Steve's questions and contains the catalog information about the training video. Andrea decides that the questions will be the primary content of her letter and that the catalog information will help her reader identify the correct video. She knows that she should limit the letter to a few short paragraphs.

Andrea, please write and find out the following:

Does the video cover the most recent OSHA, HAZCOM, and EPA regulations on chemical safety?

What instructor materials are available?

The video is catalog number LV18427, "Safety in the Work Place." Our customer service rep is Peter Argyle. His address is Learning Videos, Inc., 862 Pinewood Road, Suite #210, Pecos, TX 79772.

Figure 1-2
Handwritten note
from Steve Morgan
to Andrea Simone

Organization

After you have determined the content of your document, you should organize the information so that your ideas appear in a logical and coherent sequence. For a short letter or memo, you can organize the information in your head or make a few quick notes on paper. For a longer document, you should create a complete outline before you begin writing.

Andrea decides to use the standard organization for a business letter, which begins with the date, the inside address, and the salutation, then presents the body or text of the letter, and concludes with a complimentary closing and the writer's name and title.

Style

After you have settled on the content and the organization of your document, you should begin writing, using a style that satisfies your purpose and meets the needs of your audience. In business documents the style should be simple and direct. You can achieve this style by using simple words, clear sentences, and short paragraphs so your reader can easily grasp the meaning of the text while reading at a brisk, natural pace.

In addition to being direct, Andrea makes the tone of her letter positive and pleasant, to encourage a quick response from Learning Videos.

Format

Finally, you should make your document visually appealing. An attractive document is a readable document. Formatting features, such as ample white space, sufficient line spacing, and appropriate headings, make your document readable and your message clear. Your reader will spend less time trying to understand your message and more time acting on it. Usually the longer and more complex a document is, the more attention you'll need to pay to its format.

Since Andrea's letter to Learning Videos is short and simple, she decides to use the standard business letter format provided by WordPerfect. This format includes single-spaced lines and one-inch margins around all four edges of the page.

Having planned what she's going to write, Andrea is ready to use WordPerfect to write the letter to Learning Videos. In this tutorial, you'll create Andrea's letter, as shown in Figure 1-3.

CLEARWATER
VALVE
1555 North Technology Ave., Nutley, NJ 07110
Phone (201) 347-1628   FAX (201)374-8261

September 2, 1994

Mr. Peter Argyle
Learning Videos, Inc.
862 Pinewood Road, Suite #210
Pecos, TX 79772

Dear Mr. Argyle:

I have read the catalog description of your training video number LV18427, entitled "Safety in the Work Place." The video seems appropriate for our training needs at Clearwater Valve Company, but I would like additional information.

Specifically, please answer these questions:

1. Does the video cover the most recent OSHA, HAZCOM, and EPA regulations on handling hazardous chemicals?

2. What instructor materials are available for testing and documenting student performance?

Your attention to this matter is appreciated. I hope to hear from you soon.

Sincerely yours,

Andrea Simone

Andrea Simone
Executive Assistant, Operations

Figure 1-3
Letter from Andrea
Simone to Learning
Videos, Inc.

Before you start this tutorial, make sure WordPerfect is installed on your computer system. If you're using a computer in a lab, check with your instructor or technical support person. If you're using your own computer, install WordPerfect by following the installation instructions that came with your copy of the software.

Starting WordPerfect

To use WordPerfect to create documents, you have to start the WordPerfect software. Let's do that now.

To start WordPerfect:

① Make sure you have the WordPerfect data disk ready. If you haven't already created the WordPerfect data disk, follow the instructions at the beginning of this book or see your instructor.

② If necessary, turn on your computer.

If a menu of programs appears on the screen and WordPerfect is listed as one of those programs, you can run WordPerfect simply by choosing that menu item. If the menu doesn't list WordPerfect, exit from the menu. (If you don't know how to exit from the menu or how to select WordPerfect, consult your instructor or technical support person.) Steps 3 through 6 assume that your computer can't start WordPerfect directly from a menu of programs.

③ Make sure the DOS prompt and the cursor appear on the screen.

④ If necessary, change the default disk drive to the drive where WordPerfect is installed by typing the letter of the disk drive and a colon (:) and then pressing **[Enter]**.

For example, if WordPerfect is installed on drive C, type **C:** and press **[Enter]**. If WordPerfect is installed on drive F, type **F:** and press **[Enter]**. Check with your technical support person if you are not sure where WordPerfect is installed on your system.

⑤ Change the default directory to where WordPerfect is installed. For example, if your WordPerfect program was installed in the subdirectory WP60, you would type **cd\wp60** at the DOS prompt and press **[Enter]**. This changes the current default directory to the subdirectory called WP60.

If the message "Invalid directory" appears on the screen, WordPerfect is probably installed in a different directory, in which case you have to change the default directory to the one on which WordPerfect is located. If necessary, check with your instructor or technical support person to find out which directory contains WordPerfect.

⑥ Type **wp** and press **[Enter]**.

This starts WordPerfect. First you'll see the WordPerfect title screen, then you'll see the WordPerfect screen with a blank document window. The WordPerfect screen will appear in one of two modes: text mode (Figure 1-4) or graphics mode (Figure 1-5). You'll learn how to choose between these two modes later. In this tutorial we'll use the graphics mode to display WordPerfect screens, but you can use either mode you want.

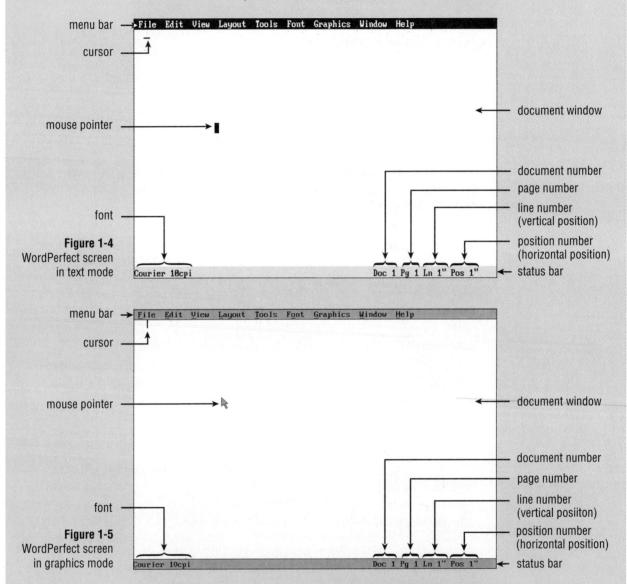

menu bar
File Edit View Layout Tools Font Graphics Window Help
cursor
mouse pointer
document window
document number
page number
line number
(vertical position)
font
position number
(horizontal position)
Courier 10cpi
Doc 1 Pg 1 Ln 1" Pos 1"
status bar

Figure 1-4
WordPerfect screen in text mode

menu bar
File Edit View Layout Tools Font Graphics Window Help
cursor
mouse pointer
document window
document number
page number
line number
(vertical posiiton)
font
position number
(horizontal position)
Courier 10cpi
Doc 1 Pg 1 Ln 1" Pos 1"
status bar

Figure 1-5
WordPerfect screen in graphics mode

You have now completed the procedure for starting WordPerfect.

The WordPerfect Screen and the Status Bar

Figure 1-5 shows the blank document window in which you create and edit WordPerfect documents. As you type words and phrases, they become part of the document that appears in the document window. Notice the blinking cursor in the upper-left corner. The cursor marks the spot where the next character you type will appear in the document.

The top line is the **menu bar**, which contains a list of nine items that correspond to the various functions WordPerfect can perform. You'll learn more about the items in the menu bar later.

The bottom line of the screen is the **status bar**, which tells you the font, the document number, the page number, the line number, and the exact position of the cursor.

Font

The **font** is the style and size of the text in your document. The status bar lists the name of the font, such as Courier, Times, or Univers. Depending on the printer you're using, you may select any of several different fonts. (You'll see how to change the font in Tutorial 2.)

Document Number

WordPerfect allows you to have up to nine documents in your computer memory at a time. *Doc 1* on the status bar means that the cursor is currently in document 1; *Doc 2* would mean that the cursor is currently in document 2. (You'll see how to use the various document windows in Tutorial 5.)

Page Number

Pg 1 means that the cursor is currently on page 1 — the first printed page — of your document. If your document has more than one page, this indicator will change as you move the cursor to other pages of the document.

Line Number

The **line number** is the distance in inches or fractions of inches from the top of the page to the current location of the cursor. *Ln 1″* means that the text you type will be one inch from the top of the page when you print the document. As you add lines of text to the document, the cursor moves farther down on the screen and the line number increases.

Unless you specify otherwise, your document will automatically have a one-inch margin at the top and bottom of each page.

Position Number

The **position number** is the distance from the left edge of the page to the current location of the cursor. *Pos 1″* means that the text you type at Pos 1″ will be one inch from the left edge of the printed page when you print the document. As you type each character along a line of text, the cursor moves to the right and the position number increases.

Unless you specify otherwise, your document will automatically have a one-inch margin along the left and right edges of the page.

The word "Pos" on the status bar also gives information about the keyboard and the appearance of the characters at the cursor. For example, if Caps Lock is on (so that typed letters appear in uppercase), "Pos" appears as "POS." If Num Lock is on, "Pos" appears with a colored or gray background (text mode only).

The status bar also indicates other WordPerfect features you'll learn about later.

The Keyboard

You'll use the keyboard to type text into your document and to execute WordPerfect commands. A **command** is an instruction you issue to WordPerfect to tell it to perform a specific task. For example, you may want to reset the size of the margins, change the line spacing, or underline a word. You can execute these commands by pressing the right sequence of keys.

The Mouse

If your computer has a mouse, WordPerfect also allows you to use the mouse to execute commands and to position the cursor. (If your computer doesn't have a mouse, go to the next section.)

The **mouse pointer** is an object on the screen that you control by moving the mouse along a hard surface. In text mode, the mouse pointer appears as a rectangular box on the screen. In graphics mode, it appears as an arrow.

To use a mouse, you need to know how to position the mouse pointer, click one of the mouse buttons, and drag the mouse. To position the mouse pointer, move the mouse until the mouse pointer is at the desired location. To **click** an item, move the mouse pointer to the desired item and then press and immediately release the left mouse button. (When you're instructed to click the mouse, always click with the left mouse button.) To **double-click**, move the mouse pointer to the desired location and then press the left mouse button twice in quick succession. To **drag** the mouse pointer, move it to the desired location on the screen, press the left button, and hold it down. Then, while still holding down the button, move the mouse pointer to a new location on the screen and release the button.

The Default Settings

Part of planning a document is deciding its format, including the width of the margins, the line spacing, and the justification (how the text is aligned along the left and right margins). WordPerfect provides a set of standard format settings that you can use with most documents. These standard settings are called the **default** format settings because they automatically specify a format for your document unless you purposely change them. Figure 1-6 lists common WordPerfect default format settings. Your setup of WordPerfect may have different default settings. Some of these settings may not make sense to you now, but they will become clear as you work through the tutorials. You won't change any format settings in this tutorial.

Default Format Settings

Left margin	1 inch
Right margin	1 inch
Top margin	1 inch
Bottom margin	1 inch
Justification	Left
Line spacing	1 (single)
Paper size	8.5" x 11"
Tabs	Every 0.5"
Page numbering	None
Hyphenation	Off
Repeat value	8
Date format	Month, Day, Year
Widow/orphan	Off
Units of measure	" (inches)

Figure 1-6
Some WordPerfect
default format
settings

Using Pull-Down Menus

Now that you have learned how to plan a document and load WordPerfect, you're ready to learn how to execute a few commands. Perhaps the easiest way to issue a WordPerfect command is to use a pull-down menu.

A **pull-down menu** is a list of commands that appears to be "pulled down" from one of the items on the menu bar at the top of the screen. Figure 1-7 shows the File pull-down menu. Each of the nine items on the menu bar has a pull-down menu associated with it. Once the menu has been "pulled down," you can choose the command you want from the list.

pull-down menu →

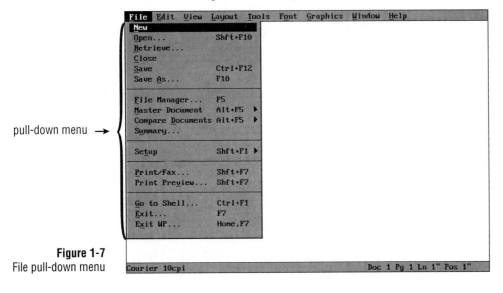

Figure 1-7
File pull-down menu

In the steps that follow, you'll use a pull-down menu, with and without a mouse, to insert the date into the text.

Using the Keyboard with Pull-Down Menus

To pull down a menu using the keyboard, hold down [Alt] and press the letter key that corresponds to the underlined letter (in text mode, the highlighted letter) of the menu item you want. The underlined or highlighted letter is called the **mnemonic letter** because it is usually the first letter of the command and is easy to remember. In this book, we'll show the mnemonic letter in boldface type (as in **T**ools). This letter is usually shown uppercase, but you can press an uppercase or lowercase letter to execute the command.

To use the keyboard to pull down a menu:

● Press **[Alt][T]** to pull down the **T**ools menu. This key combination means that you press and hold down **[Alt]**, press **T**, then release both keys simultaneously. This menu lists the various Tools options. See Figure 1-8.

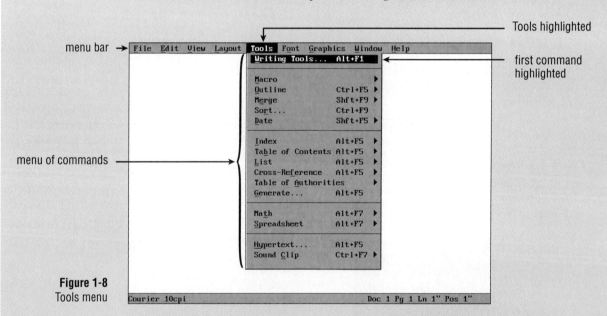

menu bar →

menu of commands —

Figure 1-8
Tools menu

Tools highlighted

first command
highlighted

Once a pull-down menu is open, you can move from one pull-down menu to another by pressing [←] (Left Arrow) or [→] (Right Arrow).

② Press [→] to pull down the **F**ont menu, then press [←] to return to the **T**ools menu.

To close a pull-down menu without executing a command, you press [Esc].

③ Press **[Esc]** to close the current pull-down menu, and press **[Esc]** again to return the cursor to the document window.

You also could have pressed [Spacebar] twice to close the menu, but don't do so now — you have already closed the pull-down menu and the menu bar. [Esc] and [Spacebar] work the same way in closing menus.

Now that you know how to pull down a menu, move from one menu to another, and close a pull-down menu, you are ready to execute a WordPerfect command. In the following steps, you will use the Date Text command, which automatically inserts the current date into a document. Using the Date Text command saves you the keystrokes of typing the date and ensures that the date is accurate.

To execute the Date Text command using the keyboard and a pull-down menu:

1 Press **[Alt][T]** to choose the **T**ools pull-down menu from the menu bar.

   The Tools menu appears on your screen.

2 Press **[↓]** five times to highlight **D**ate.

   Several of the commands in each pull-down menu have sub-menus. Commands having sub-menus are marked with an arrowhead character (▶). You can open a sub-menu from the keyboard by pressing [→] or by pressing the letter key that corresponds to the mnemonic letter in the name of the menu item.

3 Press **[→]**.

   The Date sub-menu opens to the right of the Date command. See Figure 1-9. Instead of using [→] to open the Date sub-menu, you could also have pressed the mnemonic letter D.

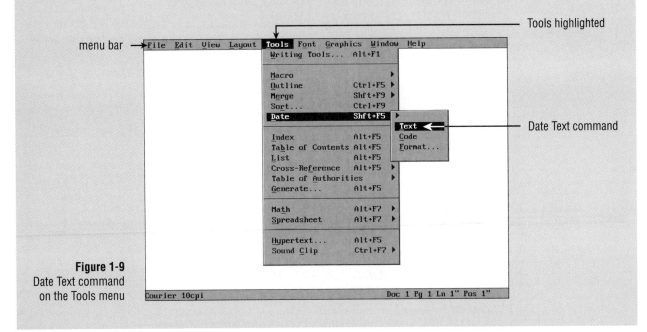

Figure 1-9
Date Text command
on the Tools menu

④ Make sure that the word **T**ext (in the sub-menu) is highlighted and press **[Enter]**.

The Tools menu disappears from the screen, and the current date appears in the document window. See Figure 1-10. The document you are creating now contains the current date (assuming your computer's clock is set to the current date).

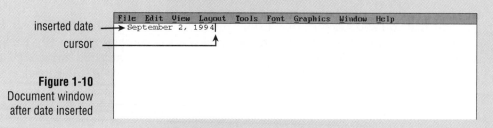

inserted date

cursor

Figure 1-10
Document window
after date inserted

⑤ Press **[Enter]** to move the cursor to the next line.

Using the Mouse with Pull-Down Menus

In this book, we assume that you are using the mouse to pull down menus and to choose menu options. Feel free, however, to use the keyboard if you like or if you don't have a mouse attached to your computer.

Let's insert the date into the document again, only this time we'll do it using the mouse. If your computer does not have a mouse, go to the next section.

To use the mouse to pull down a menu:

① Move the mouse pointer to the word **T**ools in the menu bar and click the *left* mouse button. (If you're unsure about how to use the mouse, refer to the section entitled "The Mouse" earlier in this tutorial.)

You can move the mouse pointer to any letter in the word Tools and then click the left mouse button. The Tools menu appears on the screen.

② Click the **D**ate command.

The Date sub-menu opens to the right of the Date command.

③ Click **T**ext.

This operation chooses the Date Text command and inserts today's date into the sample document once again.

④ Press **[Enter]** to move the cursor to the next line.

Using the Function Keys and the Template

In addition to using the pull-down menus, you can execute WordPerfect commands by pressing function keys. A **function-key command** is a command you issue by pressing a function key, sometimes alone and sometimes in combination with a modifier key ([Shift], [Ctrl], or [Alt]). The commands available with the function keys are listed on the function-key template (Figure 1-11).

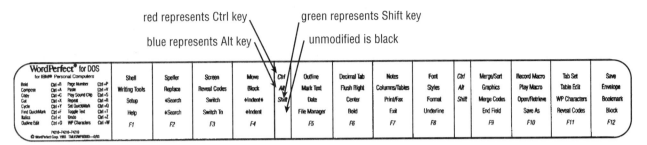

Figure 1-11
WordPerfect function-key template

The **template** is a plastic strip that sits on the keyboard over the function keys and lists the names of the WordPerfect function-key commands, also called **WordPerfect keys**. The names of the WordPerfect keys are color-coded to indicate which modifier key, if any, you must press with the function key to issue the command. A command name in black indicates no modifier key; green indicates [Shift]; blue indicates [Alt]; and red indicates [Ctrl]. Thus, to execute the command for Date, which appears in green next to the function key [F5], you would press [Shift][F5]. In these tutorials, when you are told to issue any WordPerfect command using the function keys, the modifier and the function key will be in boldface and in separate brackets, for example, **[Shift][F5]**. Following the modifier and the function key will be the name of the WordPerfect key in parentheses. In the following steps you'll use the template and the function keys to insert the current date into the document for the third time.

To insert today's date using the function keys:

● Press **[Shift][F5]** (Date). The Date dialog box appears in the center of the screen. See Figure 1-12.

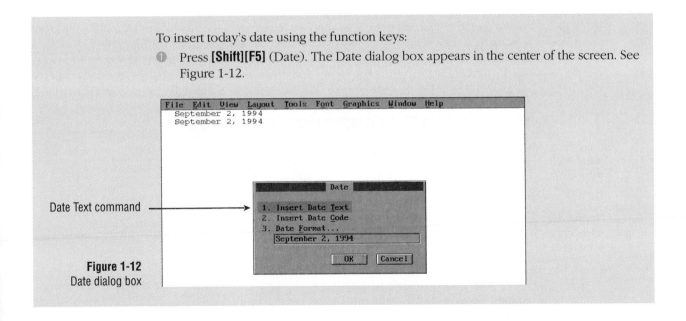

Date Text command

Figure 1-12
Date dialog box

A **dialog box** is a small window that appears on the screen and contains messages, warnings, options, and commands. You can execute commands or select options by choosing the appropriate buttons, check boxes, or listed items.

❷ Choose **1** (Insert Date **T**ext) from the Date dialog box.

You can choose this option by pressing 1, which is the option number, or by pressing T, which is the option's mnemonic, or by clicking the command. WordPerfect inserts today's date into the document. At this point, if you have followed all the previous instructions, including those with mouse commands, the current date appears three times in your document window. If you skipped the section "Using the Mouse with Pull-Down Menus," the current date appears twice in your document window.

❸ Press **[Enter]** to move the cursor to the next line.

In most cases, when you press a function key with one of the modifier keys, WordPerfect displays a dialog box, such as the one shown in Figure 1-12. You can then choose an option from the dialog box by pressing the number that corresponds to the menu item you want, by pressing the corresponding mnemonic letter, or by clicking on the command with the mouse.

Using the Button Bar

In addition to using the pull-down menus or the function keys to execute WordPerfect commands, you can also use a button bar. A **button bar** is a set of commonly executed commands that you can choose "at the click of a button." You must have a mouse to use the button bar. If you don't have a mouse, go to the next section.

In text mode, a button bar is displayed on the screen as a list of descriptive words that represent individual commands, as shown in Figure 1-13. In graphics mode, each button bar command is represented by a small picture called an **icon**, as shown in Figure 1-14. The Tools button bar and other button bars have more commands than can fit on the screen; therefore, on the left side of the button bar are up and down arrows. By clicking these arrows with the mouse, you can shift the button bar to display the other buttons that aren't currently visible.

scroll arrows
to scroll through
Tools buttons

Figure 1-13
Tools button bar in
text mode

Tools button bar

WordPerfect provides seven predefined button bars that contain different sets of commands. You can display only one button bar at a time.

In the steps that follow, you'll select a button bar, execute commands using the button bar, learn how to turn the button bar off, and customize the button bar.

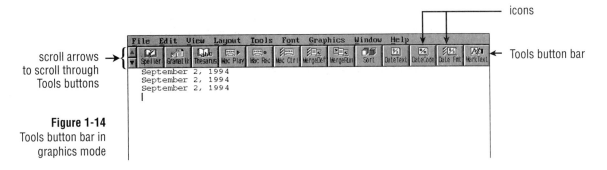

icons

scroll arrows → to scroll through Tools buttons

← Tools button bar

Figure 1-14
Tools button bar in graphics mode

Selecting and Displaying a Button Bar

The best way to decide which button bar to use is to determine what commands you will use most often. If you find yourself frequently using commands from the Tools pull-down menu, for example, you might want to display the Tools button bar. It contains a set of the most frequently used commands from the Tools pull-down menu. Figure 1-15 lists the seven predefined button bars provided by WordPerfect. You can customize any of these button bars or create your own.

Figure 1-15
WordPerfect predefined button bars

PREDEFINED BUTTON BARS	
Button Bar	**Contents**
Fonts	Frequently used commands from the Font menu
Layout	Frequently used commands from the Layout menu
Macros	Predefined macros
Outline	Commands to create and edit outlines
Tables	Commands to create and edit tables
Tools	Frequently used commands from the Tools menu
WPMain	Frequently used general WordPerfect commands

Let's select and then display the Tools button bar.

To select and display the Tools button bar:
1 Choose **V**iew, then choose Button Bar **S**etup.
Remember, to execute this command click View to open the View pull-down menu, and then click Button Bar Setup.

② Choose **S**elect. See Figure 1-16.

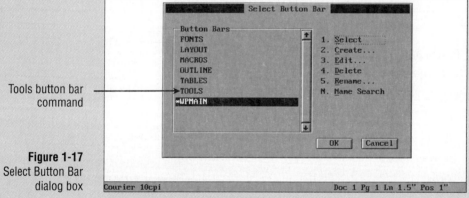

View highlighted

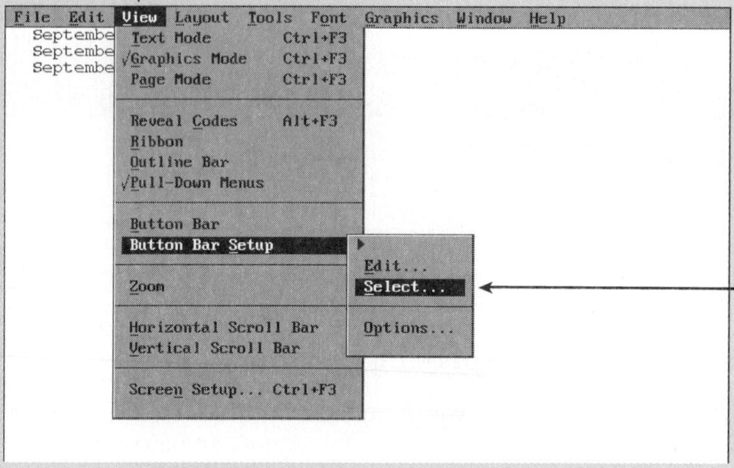

Button Bar Setup
Select command

Figure 1-16
Button Bar Setup
Select command on
the View menu

The Select Button Bar dialog box appears on the screen. It shows a list of the
button bars available to you. See Figure 1-17.

Tools button bar
command

Figure 1-17
Select Button Bar
dialog box

The Select Button Bar command allows you to choose from among the different
button bars.

③ Highlight TOOLS in the button bar list by clicking on it or by moving the highlight
bar with [↑] or [↓].

④ Choose **1** (**S**elect) by clicking on it or by pressing **1** or **S** to select and display the
tools button bar.

You now see the Tools button bar on the screen. It contains a set of commonly used
commands that are found in the Tools pull-down menu, as shown in Figure 1-13 or Figure 1-14.

Executing Commands Using the Button Bar

Now that you have selected and displayed a button bar, you can use it to execute commands. You do this by moving the mouse pointer to the desired button and clicking the left mouse button. Let's use the button bar to execute the Date Text command that we used earlier.

To execute the Date Text command using the button bar:

❶ Click the Date Text button on the button bar.

WordPerfect inserts the date once again into your document. As you can see, executing a command with the button bar is fast and easy.

❷ Press **[Enter]** to move the cursor down to a new blank line.

At this point, if you have followed all the previous instructions, the current date appears four times on your screen.

Although it takes a few steps to select and display a button bar, you can now use any of the commands on it with one click of the left mouse button.

Turning the Button Bar On and Off

Since the button bar takes up room in the document window, there may be times when you want to turn it off. The Button Bar command in the View pull-down menu is a toggle switch that turns the button bar alternately on or off. A toggle switch is like a light switch: if a feature is on, choosing the toggle switch turns it off; if the feature is off, choosing the toggle switch turns it on. Let's use the Button Bar command to turn off the button bar.

To turn the button bar off:

❶ Choose **V**iew from the menu bar. See Figure 1-18.

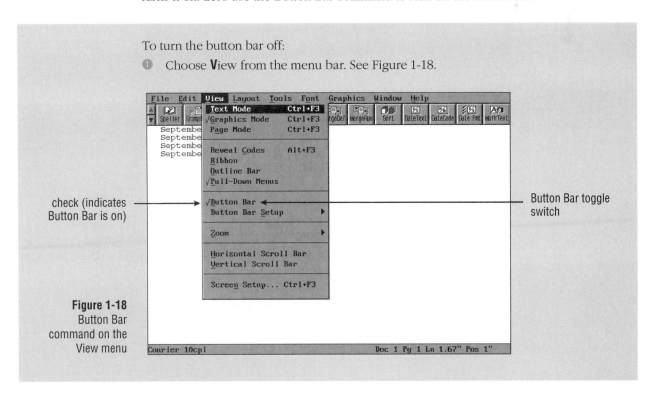

check (indicates Button Bar is on)

Button Bar toggle switch

Figure 1-18
Button Bar command on the View menu

Notice that the Button Bar command appears on the pull-down menu with a check mark in graphics mode or an asterisk in text mode. This means that the button bar is on and that choosing that command will turn the button bar off.

❷ Choose **B**utton Bar.

The button bar disappears from the screen.

❸ Choose **V**iew again.

Notice that the Button Bar command doesn't have a check mark or an asterisk next to it. This means the button bar is off.

❹ Choose **B**utton Bar.

The button bar is once again displayed on the screen.

WPMain is the most commonly used button bar. It will be more useful than the Tools bar in completing the tutorials in this book. Let's select the WPMain button bar.

To select the WPMain button bar:

❶ Choose **V**iew, Button Bar **S**etup, **S**elect.

This means choose the View menu, then choose the Button Bar Setup command from the View menu, then choose the Select command from the Button Bar Setup sub-menu. WordPerfect displays a list of the available button bars.

❷ Choose WPMAIN by highlighting it and then choosing **1** (**S**elect).

WordPerfect displays the WPMain button bar, as shown in Figure 1-19.

Figure 1-19
Document window
with the WPMain
button bar

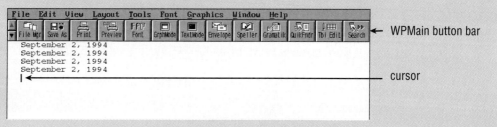

Changing the Button Bar Options

WordPerfect allows you to change certain features of the button bar. For example, you can place the button bar at the left, right, top, or bottom of the document window. For the rest of the figures in this book, the button bar is displayed at the left of the document window. With the button bar on the left, the document window can display more lines of text.

To display the button bar on the left side of the screen:

① Choose **V**iew, Button Bar **S**etup.

② Choose **O**ptions.

The Button Bar Options dialog box appears on the screen, as shown in Figure 1-20.

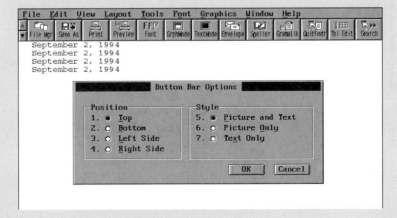

Figure 1-20
Button Bar Options
dialog box

③ Choose **3** (**L**eft Side) and then choose OK.

You can choose OK by clicking the OK button or by pressing [Enter]. The Left Side command tells WordPerfect to position the button bar along the left side of the screen. The Button Bar Options menu disappears and your screen looks like Figure 1-21 below if you are using graphics mode or Figure 1-22 on the following page, if you are using text mode.

Figure 1-21
WordPerfect screen
in graphics mode
with the button bar
on the left

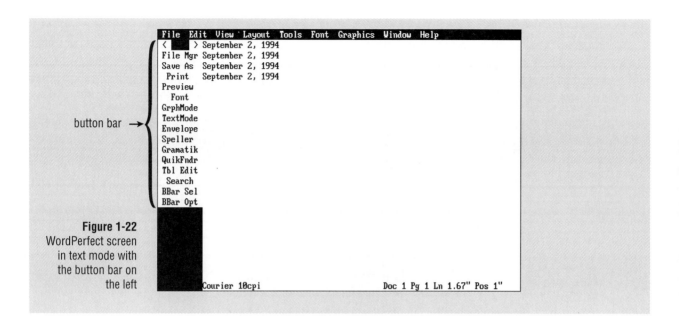

Figure 1-22
WordPerfect screen
in text mode with
the button bar on
the left

Using Pull-Down Menus, Function Keys, or the Button Bar

You've seen that WordPerfect offers you several ways to execute the same commands: pull-down menus, function keys, or the button bar. Which method is best?

The answer depends on your level of experience and your personal preference. Most commands require fewer keystrokes if you use the function keys rather than the pull-down menus. However, many people find the pull-down menus easier because they can simply choose from the menu instead of memorizing the function-key commands.

In these WordPerfect tutorials, you can use whichever method you prefer or whichever method your instructor requires. In most cases, when we ask you to execute a command, we first instruct you to issue the command from a pull-down menu, which you can select using the keyboard or the mouse. We then tell you how to issue the same command using a function key. For example, an instruction to execute the Date Text command would be "Choose **T**ools, **D**ate, **T**ext or press **[Shift][F5]** (Date/Outline) and select **1** (Date **T**ext)." To execute this command using pull-down menus, you would press [Alt][T] or click the left mouse button on the word Tools in the menu bar to pull down the Tools menu. Then you would choose Date from the Tools menu, then Text from the Date sub-menu. To execute this command using the function keys, you would press [Shift][F5] (Date) and then either press 1 (or T) or click the mouse pointer on Text. In those operations where you can use only the keyboard but not the mouse, or where the keyboard is much simpler to use, we'll just tell you what keys to press.

If you have a mouse, the button bar is often the easiest and fastest method of executing commands. In these tutorials, we will assume that the standard button bar, named WPMain, appears in the document window. We will list the button bar option in those cases where a button bar command is available.

Switching Between Text Mode and Graphics Mode

As mentioned earlier, WordPerfect allows you to display and edit your documents in either text mode or graphics mode. **Text mode** displays your document on the normal computer-text screen, which can't display fonts in different styles or sizes, can't show graphic images, and can't display certain formatting features. The computer's response time is faster in text mode and text mode takes less memory than graphics mode. **Graphics mode**, on the other hand, displays your document close to how it will appear when you print it. Fonts of different sizes and styles appear true-to-form on the screen. Most of the formatting features also appear on the screen. The computer responds more slowly in graphics mode and graphics mode takes more memory than text mode.

Let's use the pull-down menus to switch between text mode and graphics mode so that you can see the difference.

To switch between text mode and graphics mode:

① Choose **V**iew from the menu bar to display the **V**iew pull-down menu.

You will see that one of the commands — Text Mode, Graphics Mode, or Page Mode — is marked with an asterisk or a check mark on the View menu. The marked mode is the currently active mode. (We will not be using Page Mode in these tutorials.) You will next choose Text Mode or Graphics Mode, whichever one is not currently active.

② If WordPerfect is in text mode, choose **G**raphics Mode, if WordPerfect is in graphics mode, choose **T**ext Mode.

WordPerfect switches from text mode to graphics mode or vice versa. (If you switched to graphics mode, you may see a message that WordPerfect is autoselecting a graphics screen type.) Figure 1-4 and Figure 1-5 show the difference between the two modes. If your computer lacks the necessary memory to use graphics mode, you'll see a message indicating that there is insufficient memory. WordPerfect will then simply stay in text mode.

③ Switch back to the previous mode.

As you can see, WordPerfect allows you to switch between the two modes at any time.

④ Set WordPerfect to the desired mode.

As we mentioned earlier, the figures in this book show graphics mode. If your instructor permits it and your computer has the power, we recommend that you use graphics mode.

Closing the Document Window

Having completed this introduction to WordPerfect commands and to text and graphics mode, you're ready to begin typing Andrea's letter to Learning Videos. But before you can type the letter, you must be sure that the WordPerfect document window is empty. If it isn't, all the text that now appears in the window will be part of the document when you print it. Let's clear the screen now by closing the document window.

To close the document window:

① Choose **F**ile, **C**lose.

Remember, this instruction means to choose the File menu from the menu bar, then choose Close from the File menu. WordPerfect displays a dialog box with the prompt "Save Changes to (Untitled)?" and then pauses for you to choose "Save As," "Yes," "No," or "Cancel." See Figure 1-23.

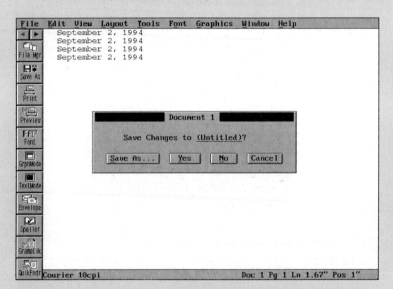

Figure 1-23
Dialog box after
Close command

If you executed the Close command by accident, you would choose Cancel. You could also press [Esc] to close the dialog box without taking any action. Remember, any time you accidentally open the wrong menu or press the wrong function key, you can return to the previous step by pressing [Esc].

In this case, you want to close the document window without saving the document.

② Choose **N**o. This indicates that you don't want to save the document.

You have now closed the current document window without saving its contents. You are still in WordPerfect, but now you have a new, blank document window.

Entering Text

With a blank document window on the WordPerfect screen and the cursor at Ln 1" Pos 1", you're ready to type Andrea's letter (Figure 1-3). Let's begin by typing the date, the inside address, and the salutation of the letter.

To type the date, the inside address, and the salutation:

❶ Press **[Enter]** six times.

This moves the cursor down one inch from the top margin, giving a total of about two inches of space at the top of the page and allowing room for the Clearwater Valve Company letterhead. The line number on the status bar should read Ln 2" (or a decimal number close to 2), indicating that the cursor is two inches from the top of the page. See Figure 1-24.

cursor

Figure 1-24
Document window
after you clear
window and press
[Enter] six times

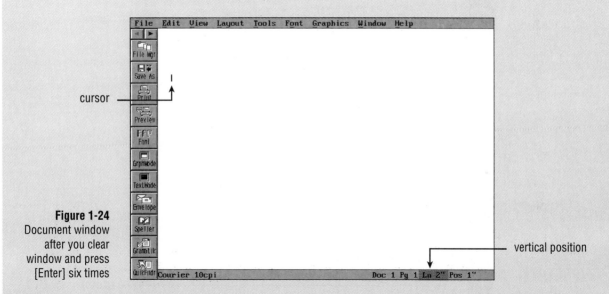

vertical position

If you pressed [Enter] too many times, just press [Backspace] to delete the extra blank lines. If the line number on your screen has a slightly different value, such as Ln 1.95 or Ln 2.12, don't worry. Different printers produce slightly different measurements when you press [Enter].

You are now ready to insert today's date.

❷ Select **T**ools, **D**ate, **T**ext or press **[Shift][F5]** (Date) and choose **1** (Date **T**ext). The date appears in your document.

❸ Press **[Enter]** four times to insert three blank lines between the date and the inside address.

The status bar should now display Ln 2.67" (or some number close to that value).

Next enter the inside address, shown on Steve's note (Figure 1-2).

❹ Type **Mr. Peter Argyle** and press **[Enter]**. Type **Learning Videos, Inc.** and press **[Enter]**. Type **862 Pinewood Road, Suite #210** and press **[Enter]**. Finally, type **Pecos, TX 79772** and press **[Enter]** twice — once to end the line and once to add an extra blank line. See Figure 1-25. Don't worry if you have made typing errors. You'll be able to fix them later.

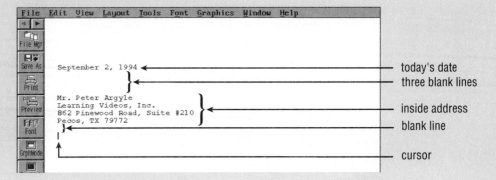

Figure 1-25
Document window after you insert the date and type the inside address

❺ Type **Dear Mr. Argyle:** and press **[Enter]** twice to double-space between the salutation and the body of the letter.

You have now completed the date, the inside address, and the salutation of Andrea's letter, using a standard format for business letters. See Figure 1-26.

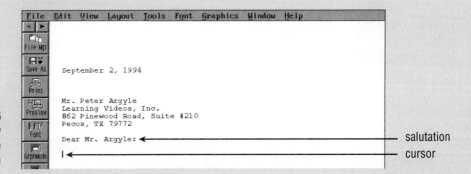

Figure 1-26
Document window after you type the salutation

Saving a Document

The letter you're typing is currently stored in your computer's memory, but not on a disk. If you were to exit WordPerfect without saving your letter, turn off your computer, or experience an accidental power failure right now, the information you just typed would be lost. You should get in the habit of frequently saving your document to a disk. Unless a document is very short, don't wait until you've typed the whole document before saving it. As a rule, you should save your work about every 15 minutes.

Although Andrea hasn't been working on this letter for 15 minutes yet, she decides, just to be safe, to save the document now.

To save a document:

① Insert the WordPerfect data disk into drive A and close the drive door.

This tutorial assumes that you have a hard disk (drive C) and at least one disk drive (drive A).

② Choose **F**ile, **S**ave. See Figure 1-27. Alternatively, you can press **[Ctrl][F12]** (Save) or click the Save As button on the button bar.

File highlighted —

Save command →

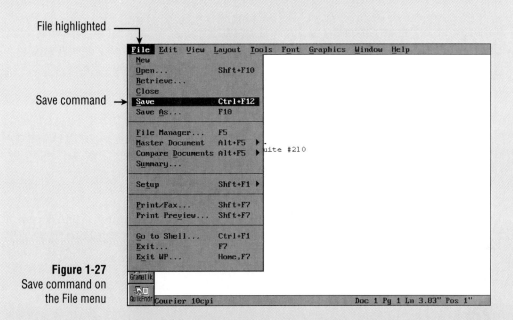

Figure 1-27
Save command on
the File menu

WordPerfect displays the Save Document 1 dialog box and waits for you to type a name for the document.

③ Type **a:\s1file1.dft**. See Figure 1-28. Choose OK by clicking the OK button or by pressing **[Enter]**.

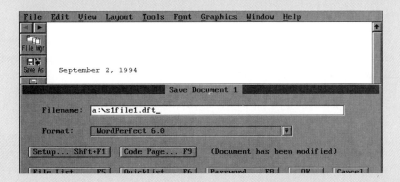

Figure 1-28
Save Document
dialog box

WordPerfect saves the document file to the disk in drive A.

If the error message "Drive A not ready 1 Retry; 2 Cancel" appears at the bottom of the screen, make sure the disk in drive A is positioned properly. Then select 1 (Retry). If the error message "Disk error on drive A. 1 Retry; 2 Cancel" appears, your disk is probably not formatted. Remove it from the drive, insert a formatted disk, close the drive door, and select 1 (Retry).

Figure 1-29 shows the process that occurs when you save a document. WordPerfect copies the file in the computer's memory to your computer's disk storage. Now identical copies of the file exist, both in the computer's memory and on the disk.

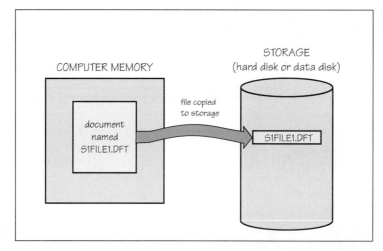

Figure 1-29
Saving a file to a
disk

After you save the document to the disk, the path and filename of the document, "A:\S1FILE1.DFT," appear at the bottom of the document window on the status bar (Figure 1-30).

document name

path

Figure 1-30
Status bar after you
save the document

status bar

Document Filenames

Besides saving your documents frequently, another good habit to get into is to use descriptive filenames that help identify the contents of your files. Document filenames can be any legal DOS filename and may contain the path (such as "a:\" or "c:\wpfiles\"). The filename may contain from one to eight characters and may include a filename extension of one to three characters. In S1FILE1.DFT the filename extension DFT stands for "draft," indicating that this is the first draft of Andrea's letter.

Eight characters in the filename and an additional three in the extension often don't allow you to use complete names, but you can at least create meaningful abbreviations. For example, since Andrea is writing a letter to Learning Videos, she could save the final version of her letter with the filename LVI.LET, where LVI is an abbreviation of the name of the company, and LET reminds her that the document is a letter. If she were to write a memo to Clearwater employees about the 1994 budget, she might name the memo 94BUDGET.MEM, where the filename extension MEM stands for memo.

In this book, the six tutorials on WordPerfect involve many files. Therefore, we use filenames that will help you and your instructor recognize the origin and content of the various documents. To name these files so you can recognize their contents, we have categorized them as follows:

File Category	Description
Tutorial Cases	The files you use to work through each tutorial
Tutorial Assignments	The files that contain the documents you need to complete the Tutorial Assignments at the end of each tutorial
Case Problems	The files that contain the documents you need to complete the Case Problems at the end of each tutorial
Saved Document	Any document you have saved

Let's take the filename S1FILE1.DFT, for example. At first glance this filename might appear to have no meaning, but it does contain meaningful abbreviations. The first character of the filename identifies the file as one of the four categories given above, as shown here:

If the first character is:	The file category is:
C	Tutorial **C**ase
T	**T**utorial Assignment
P	Case **P**roblem
S	**S**aved Document

Thus, S1FILE1.DFT is a document that you have saved.

The second character of the document filename identifies the tutorial from which the file comes. Thus, S1FILE1.DFT is a file you saved from Tutorial 1. The remaining six characters of the filename identify the specific file. All documents in the tutorials are named FILE, followed by a number. Each time you save a file, you will increase the number after FILE by 1. The filename extensions also help identify the file. A letter has the filename extension LET, a memo MEM, a report REP, and a draft document DFT. Thus, the filename S1FILE1.DFT tells you that this is the first draft that you saved in Tutorial 1.

Applying these same rules, the file T1FILE1.LET is the first document (a letter) found in the Tutorial Assignments from WordPerfect Tutorial 1, and C4FILE1.REP is the report you will use in a Tutorial Case for WordPerfect Tutorial 4. Files that you open (load from the disk into a document window) or save in the Tutorial Assignments and the Case Problems have a word or an abbreviation (other than FILE) to help identify them. For example, P1IBM.LET is the filename of the Case Problem "Letter to IBM" from Tutorial 1.

Word Wrap

Having saved the first part of your document, you are now ready to complete the letter. As you type the body of the letter, do not press [Enter] at the end of each line. Instead, allow WordPerfect to determine where one line ends and the next one begins. When you type a word that extends into the right margin, WordPerfect automatically moves the cursor and the word to the next line. This automatic breaking of a line of text is called word wrap. Word wrap ensures that each line of text fits between the left and right margins and eliminates the need for you to press [Enter] at the end of each line, as you would on a typewriter. If you happen to press [Enter] before word wrap occurs, press [Backspace] until the cursor moves back to the previous line, then continue typing.

Let's see how word wrap works as you type the body of the letter.

To observe word wrap while you are typing a paragraph:

① Be sure the cursor is at the left edge of the screen and two lines below the salutation of the letter.

② Type **I have read the catalog description of your training video number**, press **[Spacebar]**, and then slowly continue to type **LV18427**. As you type, notice that the cursor and "LV18427" automatically jump to the next line. See Figure 1-31.

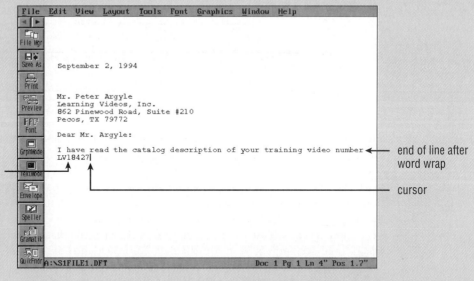

word wrapped down
to next line

end of line after
word wrap

cursor

Figure 1-31
Document window
after you type the
first line of the first
paragraph

(Because different fonts have different letter widths, the word or letter at which word wrap occurs in your document may be different from our example.)

③ Type the rest of the first paragraph of the body of the letter. See Figure 1-32.

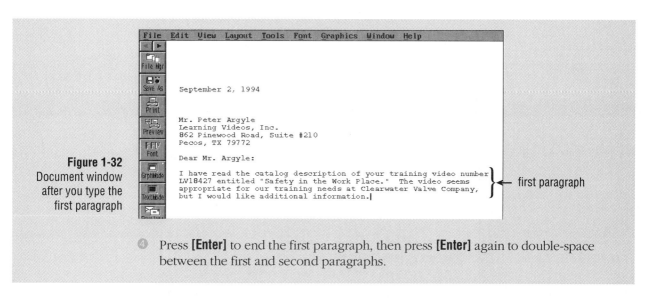

Figure 1-32
Document window
after you type the
first paragraph

first paragraph

④ Press **[Enter]** to end the first paragraph, then press **[Enter]** again to double-space between the first and second paragraphs.

When you press [Enter], WordPerfect inserts an invisible code called a **hard return** into the document to mark the end of a line or the end of a paragraph. The word or punctuation mark immediately preceding a hard return always ends a line, regardless of how long or short the line is.

When a line ends with a word wrap, WordPerfect inserts an invisible code called a **soft return** into the document to mark the end of the line (Figure 1-33). The words before and after a soft return are not necessarily permanent — if you later add text to or delete text from the line, the word at which word wrap occurs may change.

Remember the following rule: As you type, press [Enter] only at the end of a paragraph or where you definitely want a line to end. This allows WordPerfect to automatically insert soft returns so that each line of a paragraph fits between the left and right margins.

Let's continue with our sample letter.

To enter the rest of the body of the letter:

① Type the first line of the second paragraph. See Figure 1-33.

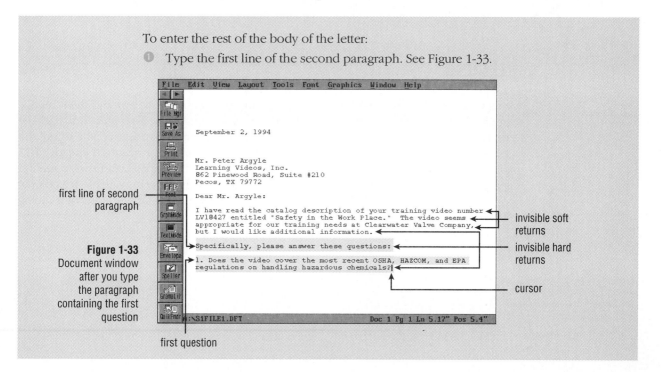

first line of second
paragraph

invisible soft
returns

invisible hard
returns

cursor

Figure 1-33
Document window
after you type
the paragraph
containing the first
question

first question

❷ Press **[Enter]** at the end of the line.

❸ Press **[Enter]** again to double-space between that line and the first question.

❹ Type **1. Does the video** and continue typing the text shown in Figure 1-33. Complete question number 1, then press **[Enter]** twice to double-space between paragraphs.

❺ Type question 2, as shown in Figure 1-34, and press **[Enter]** twice to insert a double space.

Figure 1-34
Document window
after you complete
the body of the
letter

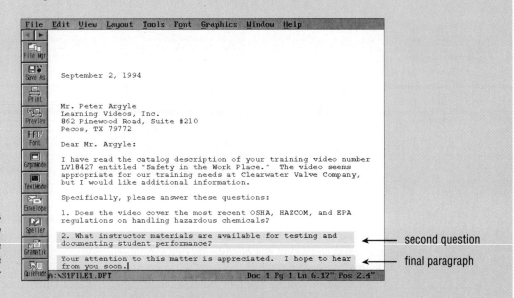

❻ Now type the final paragraph of the body of the letter. If you're working in graphics mode, your screen should now look like Figure 1-34. If you're working in text mode, your screen may be different.

Scrolling

As you can see in Figure 1-34, the cursor is at the bottom of the screen and the screen is almost filled with text. As you continue to add text at the end of the document, the text that you typed at the beginning of the document will shift up and disappear off the top of the document window. If you are working in text mode, this will have occurred already. This shifting up or down of text, called **scrolling**, allows you to see a long document one screenful at a time. The entire document is still in the computer's memory and available for editing; you just can't see it all at once (Figure 1-35). Let's watch more carefully the effect of scrolling as you insert the final lines of Andrea's letter.

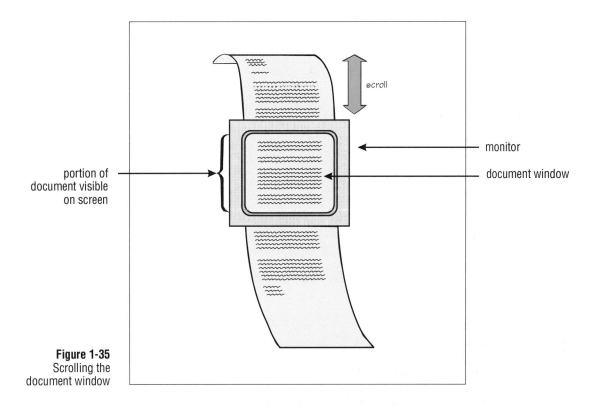

Figure 1-35
Scrolling the
document window

To observe scrolling while you are entering text:

① Make sure the cursor is at the bottom of the screen, at the end of the body of the letter, as shown in Figure 1-34.

② Press **[Enter]** twice to double space between the body of the letter and the complimentary close. As you press [Enter], watch the document scroll upward.

③ Type **Sincerely yours,** (including the comma).

④ Press **[Enter]** four times to allow space for the signature. Again watch how the text scrolls up the screen as you add lines to the end of the document.

⑤ Type **Andrea Simone**, press **[Enter]**, and type **Executuve Assistant, Operatiosn**. Make sure you type *"Executive"* and *"Operations"* as shown here, with the typing errors. You'll correct these errors later.

As you can see in Figure 1-36 on the following page, the date (and possibly the inside address) no longer appears in the document window. When you pressed [Enter] at the bottom of the screen, the text above the cursor scrolled up so that the date is no longer in view.

date has scrolled off screen

text continues to scroll up

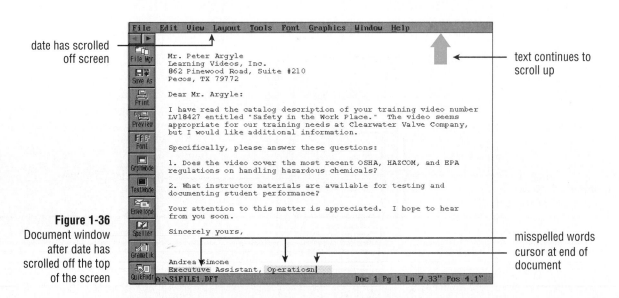

misspelled words
cursor at end of document

Figure 1-36
Document window
after date has
scrolled off the top
of the screen

To see the beginning of the letter, you can use the arrow keys to scroll the text back into view.

To scroll the text using arrow keys:

① Press and hold down [↑] (Up Arrow) until the cursor is at the beginning of the letter and the line number reads Ln 1".

Notice that as you press [↑] when the cursor is at the top of the screen, the text of the letter scrolls down, so that the lines at the end of the letter disappear from the screen and the lines at the beginning reappear. When the cursor gets to the beginning of the document, scrolling stops because the cursor can't go any higher.

② Press and hold down [↓] (Down Arrow) until the cursor is at the end of the letter, on or below the line "Executive Assistant, Operations."

As you can see, the arrow keys allow you to scroll the document so you can move the cursor to any part of the document that doesn't currently appear on the screen.

Correcting Errors

Novices and experienced WordPerfect users alike make mistakes. One of the advantages of using a word processor is that when you make a mistake, you can correct it quickly and cleanly. The following steps show you several ways to correct errors when you're entering text or executing a command.

If you discover a typing error as soon as you make it, you can press [Backspace] to erase the characters to the left of the cursor, back to and including the error, and then type the correct characters. The Backspace key may be a left-facing arrow. It is located in the upper-right corner of the main set of keys. You can also eliminate unwanted space. For example, if you accidentally press [Enter] or [Spacebar], you can use [Backspace] to return the cursor to where you want it.

If you typed the last line of the letter exactly as shown, the word "Operations" is misspelled. Let's correct that error now.

To correct the typing error:

❶ Make sure the cursor is positioned immediately after the word "Operatiosn."

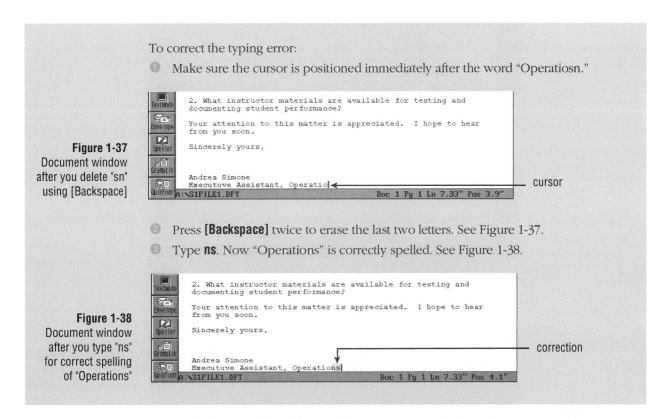

Figure 1-37
Document window after you delete "sn" using [Backspace]

cursor

❷ Press **[Backspace]** twice to erase the last two letters. See Figure 1-37.

❸ Type **ns**. Now "Operations" is correctly spelled. See Figure 1-38.

Figure 1-38
Document window after you type "ns" for correct spelling of "Operations"

correction

If you make an error and discover it some time later, you can use the arrow keys ([←], [→], [↑], and [↓]) to move the cursor to the error, delete the error, and type the correct characters. The word "Executive" is also misspelled. Let's correct it now.

To use the Left Arrow key to correct a typing error:

❶ Press [←] until the cursor is immediately to the left of (in graphics mode) or under (in text mode) the second "u" in "Executuve." See Figure 1-39.

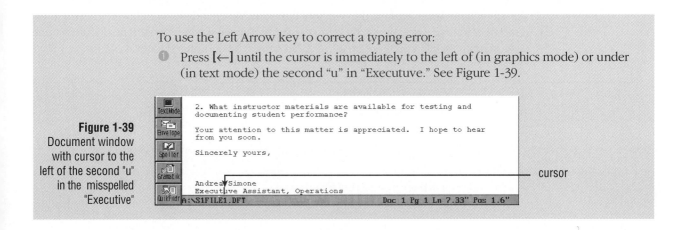

Figure 1-39
Document window with cursor to the left of the second "u" in the misspelled "Executive"

cursor

❷ Make sure that the message "Typeover" does *not* appear in the lower-left corner of the screen. If it does, press **[Ins]** or **[Insert]**.

❸ Press **[Del]** or **[Delete]** to delete the character at the cursor. See Figure 1-40.

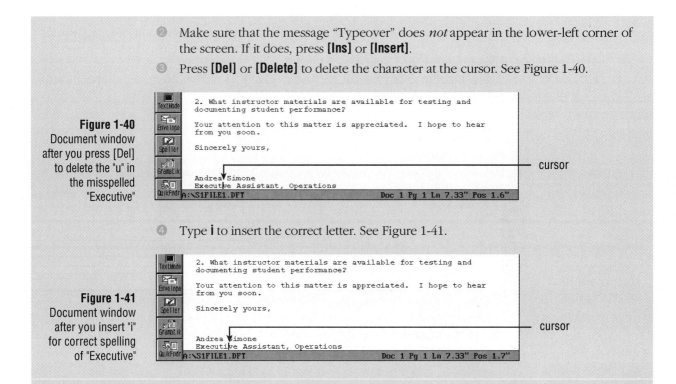

Figure 1-40
Document window
after you press [Del]
to delete the "u" in
the misspelled
"Executive"

cursor

Figure 1-41
Document window
after you insert "i"
for correct spelling
of "Executive"

cursor

❹ Type **i** to insert the correct letter. See Figure 1-41.

You'll learn other methods of correcting typing errors later in this tutorial and in future tutorials.

Take a few minutes to read over the letter you've just typed and compare it with Figure 1-3. Your letter should have the same text, but yours won't include the Clearwater letterhead, probably won't have the same date, and may have a different number of words on each line. Use the arrow keys ([↑], [↓], [←], and [→]) to move the cursor to various locations within the letter. If you find any errors, make the necessary corrections now.

Saving the Completed Letter

Now that she has completed her letter, Andrea wants to save the document to a disk. Although she saved the letter earlier, the version currently on her disk is incomplete. You must remember to save a document after you complete it, even if you've saved the document one or more times while you were creating it. Let's save the completed letter now.

To save the completed letter:

❶ Make sure the disk you used earlier to save the incomplete letter is still in drive A.

It doesn't matter where the cursor is in the document window when you save a document.

❷ Choose **F**ile, **S**ave or press **[Ctrl][F12]** (Save).

WordPerfect briefly displays the prompt "Saving A:\S1FILE1.DFT." Since you've saved the file previously, WordPerfect knows the filename and saves the document without prompting you for information.

Previewing a Document

Andrea has completed her letter and is pleased with its content, organization, and style, but she really can't see the overall format. The document window displays the text, but it doesn't show the margins or how the letter will fit onto the printed page.

Before Andrea prints the letter, she wants to make sure it has the proper format. WordPerfect provides a method for her to preview the letter before she prints it. Let's preview the letter you've just typed.

To preview a document:

● Choose **F**ile, Print Pre**v**iew, or press **[Shift][F7]** (Print) and choose **7** (Print Preview), or click the Print Preview button on the button bar. WordPerfect displays the Print Preview screen.

A picture of the document appears on the screen just as it will appear when it is printed on paper. If your monitor doesn't support graphics mode, WordPerfect displays an error message, since the Print Preview command works only with graphics monitors.

Notice that the WPMain button bar has disappeared and the Print Preview button bar is at the top of the window.

❷ If you can't see the entire page of the letter, choose **V**iew, **F**ull Page or click the Full Page button bar at the top of the screen. You can now see the layout of the entire page. See Figure 1-42.

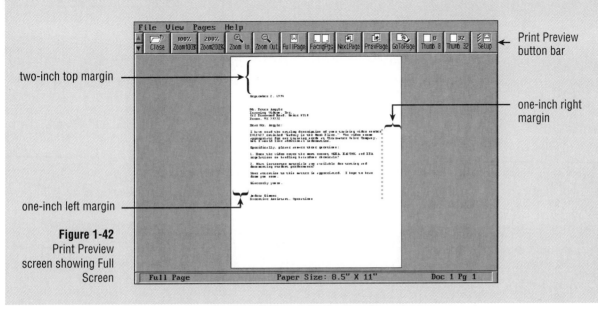

two-inch top margin

Print Preview button bar

one-inch right margin

one-inch left margin

Figure 1-42
Print Preview screen showing Full Screen

③ To see the letter in actual size, choose **V**iew, **1**00% View or click the Zoom 100% button. See Figure 1-43.

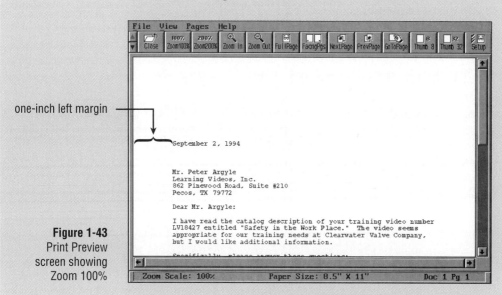

Figure 1-43
Print Preview
screen showing
Zoom 100%

one-inch left margin

Now you can see the one-inch margins on the left and right edges of the page. You can also see that the body of the letter will be printed ragged right (unjustified); that is, the right edge of the text lines is not aligned along the right margin. Don't worry about this. When you print the document, it will be very readable.

④ Slowly press [↓] several times and [↑] several times to see how the page scrolls on the screen.

If you press the arrow keys too fast, you may have to wait while WordPerfect redraws the document.

⑤ Choose **F**ile, **C**lose, or press **[F7]** (Exit) or **[Esc]**, or click the Close button when you are ready to exit the Print Preview option and return to the normal document window.

Andrea is satisfied with the format of the letter.

Printing a Document

Having typed, saved, and previewed the document, Andrea is now ready to print it.

To print a document currently in a document window:

① Make sure your printer is turned on and the paper is properly inserted in the printer. If you have questions about setting up your printer for use with WordPerfect, see your instructor or technical support person.

② Choose **F**ile, **P**rint/Fax, or press **[Shift][F7]** (Print), or click the Print button on the button bar.

WordPerfect displays the Print/Fax dialog box. See Figure 1-44.

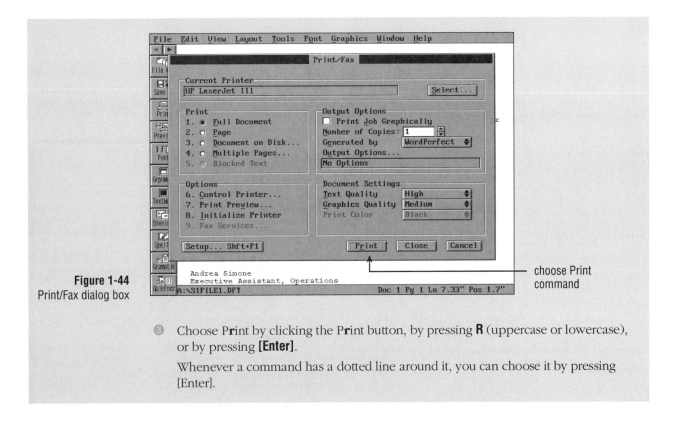

Figure 1-44
Print/Fax dialog box

choose Print
command

❸ Choose P**r**int by clicking the P**r**int button, by pressing **R** (uppercase or lowercase),
or by pressing **[Enter]**.

Whenever a command has a dotted line around it, you can choose it by pressing
[Enter].

WordPerfect prints the letter. Your printed letter should look similar to the one shown in
Figure 1-3.

Exiting WordPerfect

Andrea has now finished typing and printing her letter to Learning Videos, so she is ready to
exit WordPerfect. She knows that she should never just turn off the computer without first
exiting WordPerfect. Let's see how to exit WordPerfect properly.

To exit WordPerfect:

❶ Choose **F**ile, E**x**it WP or press **[Home]** and then **[F7]** (Exit).

WordPerfect displays the Exit WordPerfect dialog box and waits for you to choose
among various options.

❷ Since you've already saved the completed document to disk, choose **E**xit. (If you
hadn't saved your document yet the Save check box next to your document number would be checked, and WordPerfect would prompt you to type a filename.)

You have now exited WordPerfect. The cursor returns to the DOS prompt if you entered
WordPerfect from DOS or to a menu program if you entered WordPerfect through a menu.

Opening a Document

After Andrea types, saves, and prints the draft version of the letter to Learning Videos, she gives the printed draft to her supervisor, Steve Morgan. Steve reads the letter and makes a note to Andrea to include a question about volume discounts (Figure 1-45). After she adds this question, Andrea will print the letter again and mail it.

```
September 2, 1994


Mr. Peter Argyle
Learning Videos, Inc.
862 Pinewood Road, Suite #210
Pecos, TX 79772

Dear Mr. Argyle:

I have read the catalog description of your training video number
LV18427 entitled "Safety in the Work Place."  The video seems
appropriate for our training needs at Clearwater Valve Company,
but I would like additional information.

Specifically, please answer these questions:

1. Does the video cover the most recent OSHA, HAZCOM, and EPA
regulations on handling hazardous chemicals?

2. What instructor materials are available for testing and
documenting student performance?

Your attention to this matter is appreciated.  I hope to hear
from you soon.

Sincerely yours,

Andrea Simone

Andrea Simone
Executive Assistant, Operations
```

Andrea, please add this question.

3. Do you provide a discount for volume purchases? If so, what is the pricing structure for the volume discount?

Figure 1-45
Andrea's draft with Steve's addition

To do this, Andrea must start WordPerfect again, open the document file from the disk into computer memory, add a third question to the letter, save the revised letter, and print the final version.

To open a document file into a document window.

1 Start WordPerfect as you did earlier in this tutorial, in the section entitled "Starting WordPerfect."

2 Make sure the document window is blank.

If necessary, clear the screen, as explained in the section entitled "Closing the Document Window."

③ With a blank document window, choose **F**ile, **O**pen or press **[Shift][F10]** (Open/Retrieve).

WordPerfect displays the Open Document dialog box and waits for you to type the document name. See Figure 1-46.

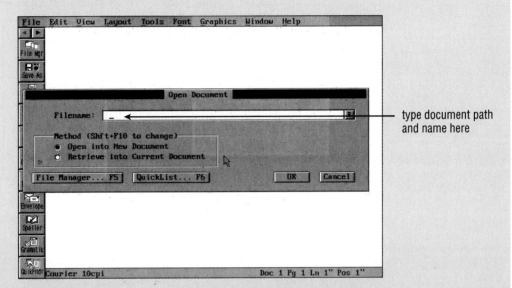

type document path and name here

Figure 1-46
Open Document dialog box

④ Make sure the disk on which you saved the letter is in drive A.

⑤ Type **a:\s1file1.dft** and press **[Enter]**.

WordPerfect opens the document from the disk into the document window. See Figure 1-47.

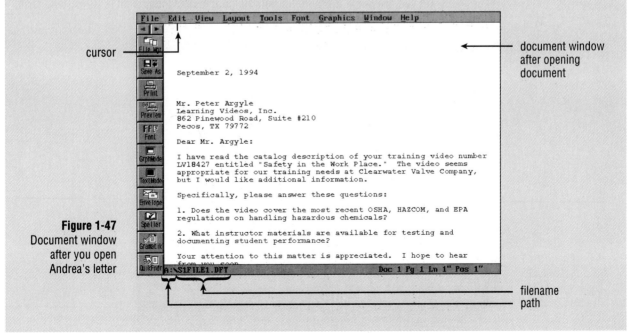

cursor

document window after opening document

Figure 1-47
Document window after you open Andrea's letter

filename
path

When you open a document from the disk, WordPerfect copies the document file into the computer's memory (Figure 1-48). A copy of the document file remains on the disk.

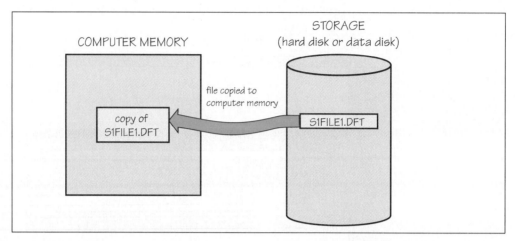

Figure 1-48
Opening a
document file

Now that she has opened the file, Andrea is ready to make the addition Steve requested.

To modify the letter:

1. Press [↓] and [→] to move the cursor to the end of question 2, immediately after the phrase ". . . documenting student performance?"
2. Make sure "Typeover" doesn't appear in the lower-left corner of the screen. If it does, press **[Ins]**.
3. Press **[Enter]** twice to insert a double space after question 2.
4. Type **3. Do you provide a discount for volume purchases? If so, what is the pricing structure for the volume discount?.** See Figure 1-49.

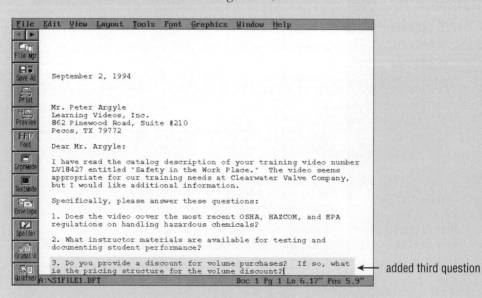

Figure 1-49
Document window
after you add the
third question

The letter is now modified the way Steve wants it. Andrea looks over the letter one last time for any errors. She is ready to print the final version. But before she prints the letter, she has to save this new, final version because the letter on the screen is different from the one on the disk. Let's save the final version now.

To save the final version of the letter with a new filename:

① Choose **F**ile, Save **A**s, or press **[F10]** (Save As), or click the Save As button.

WordPerfect displays a dialog box with the prompt: "Filename: A:\S1FILE1.DFT." The filename of the document on the screen automatically appears in the prompt. But because this is the second time you're saving the letter and because you want to keep the previous version of the letter for instructional purposes, now saved in S1FILE1.DFT, you'll use a new filename.

② Type **a:\s1file2.let** and press **[Enter]**.

Now a copy of the final letter is saved on the disk as S1FILE2.LET. See Figure 1-50.

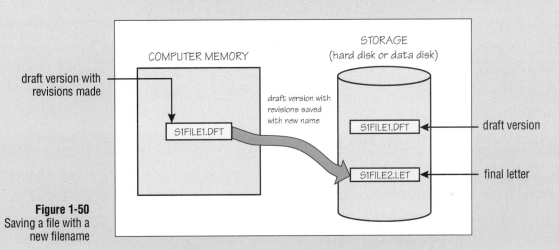

Figure 1-50
Saving a file with a
new filename

This completes Andrea Simone's letter to Learning Videos. You can now print the final copy of the letter.

③ Print the document. See Figure 1-51 on the following page.

CLEARWATER
VALVE
1555 North Technology Ave., Nutley, NJ 07110
Phone (201) 347-1628   FAX (201)374-8261

September 2, 1994

Mr. Peter Argyle
Learning Videos, Inc.
862 Pinewood Road, Suite #210
Pecos, TX 79772

Dear Mr. Argyle:

I have read the catalog description of your training video number
LV18427 entitled "Safety in the Work Place." The video seems
appropriate for our training needs at Clearwater Valve Company,
but I would like additional information.

Specifically, please answer these questions:

1. Does the video cover the most recent OSHA, HAZCOM, and EPA
regulations on handling hazardous chemicals?

2. What instructor materials are available for testing and
documenting student performance?

3. Do you provide a discount for volume purchases? If so, what is
the pricing structure for the volume discount?

Your attention to this matter is appreciated. I hope to hear
from you soon.

Sincerely yours,

Andrea Simone

Andrea Simone
Executive Assistant, Operations

Figure 1-51
Final version of
Andrea's letter

Getting Help

How do you know which menu item to select or which function key to press in order to change the margins, number pages, or perform any other WordPerfect command? The best way is through training and continued experience in using WordPerfect. These WordPerfect tutorials will give you the training and the experience you need to perform the most important WordPerfect operations.

But WordPerfect provides another way for you to learn what commands are available and how to execute them: the WordPerfect Help feature. Both the main menu bar and the template list the Help feature. When you choose Help, Contents ([Alt][H], C) or press [F1] (Help), WordPerfect displays a Help screen that lets you choose one of the following:

- Index of WordPerfect Features — an alphabetic list of features
- How Do I — a list of common WordPerfect tasks
- Glossary — a list of definitions of WordPerfect terms

- Template — a display of the function-key template and the actions of the function-key commands
- Keystrokes — a list of special keystrokes and their actions
- Shortcut Keys — a list of special keys that quickly issue commands equivalent to pull-down menu commands.
- Error messages — a list of causes and solutions for the most common error messages

Let's use two of these commands, Index and Template, to get help on some WordPerfect features.

Getting Help with a List of Features

Suppose you forget how to execute the WordPerfect command for inserting the date into a document. You can use the Help feature to get information on "Date" by using the alphabetical list of features. Let's do that now.

To see an alphabetical list of features that start with the letter D:

1 Choose **H**elp, **C**ontents or press **[F1]** (Help). WordPerfect displays the Help window. See Figure 1-52.

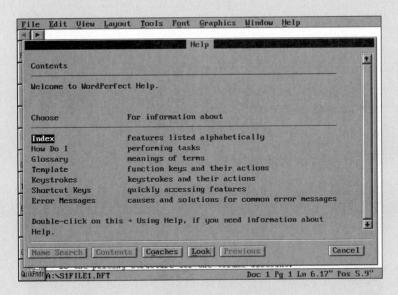

Figure 1-52
Help window with
the Help Contents

Note: Your copy of WordPerfect may be configured so that [F3] is the Help key. If [F1] doesn't display the Help window, try [F3].

② Make sure Index is highlighted, then choose **L**ook to look at the Index. You can choose Look by clicking the Look button, by pressing L, or, because the dotted line is around the Look command, by pressing [Enter]. WordPerfect displays information about each command in alphabetical order. See Figure 1-53.

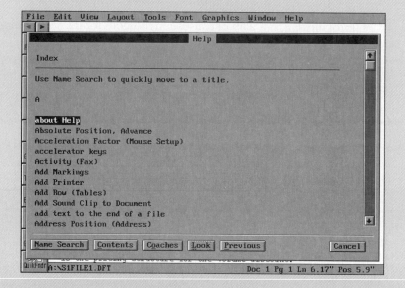

Figure 1-53
Help window with
the Help Index

③ Choose **N**ame Search. A box appears, prompting you to enter the name of the feature on which you want help.

④ Type **date** and press **[Enter]**.

As you type each letter, WordPerfect displays a list of the features starting with the letters you've typed to that point. After you finish typing the entire word, the Date command is highlighted. See Figure 1-54.

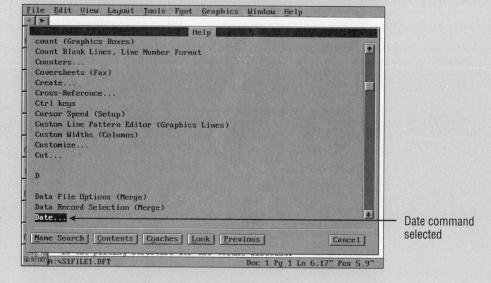

Figure 1-54
Help window with
Date command
highlighted

Date command
selected

⑤ Choose **L**ook. WordPerfect displays a list of various Date commands.

⑥ With Date highlighted, choose **L**ook again. WordPerfect displays an explanation of the Date command. See Figure 1-55.

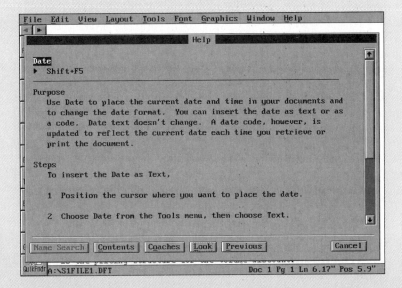

Figure 1-55
Help window with information on the Date command

⑦ Press [↓] several times to scroll down through the explanation of the Date command. As you can see, the Help dialog box explains how to place the date in the document as you have done in previous examples.

⑧ After viewing the Help explanation, choose Cancel by pressing **[Esc]** or by clicking the Cancel button to close the Help dialog box and return the cursor to the main document window.

Getting Help with the Function-Key Template

If you don't have a WordPerfect function-key template on your computer keyboard, or if you want information about a template command, you can use Help to see the template.

To use Help to display the function-key template:

① Choose **H**elp, **C**ontents or press **[F1]** (Help) to display the Help dialog box.

② Highlight Template by clicking on it or by pressing [↓] three times, then choose **L**ook.

This screen shows the function keys you would press to execute WordPerfect commands. See Figure 1-56 on the following page.

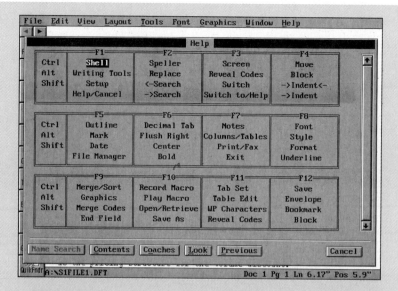

Figure 1-56
Help window with
the function-key
template

③ Highlight the word Date in the box labeled F5.

To highlight the word, you can click on it or press [↓] until the highlight bar is on the word Date.

④ Choose **L**ook again to see the explanation of the Date command.

⑤ Choose Cancel or press **[Esc]** to close the Help dialog box.

You could use this same procedure to get help on any template command.

You have completed Tutorial 1. Remember to exit WordPerfect before turning off your computer.

Exercises

1. If the cursor is at the DOS prompt and in the directory where the WordPerfect program is located, what do you type to start WordPerfect?

2. What does the status bar message Doc 3 mean?

3. What is the difference between Pos and POS on the status bar?

4. What does the status bar message Ln 4.5" mean?

5. List three ways you can execute a command to automatically insert today's date into a WordPerfect document.

6. How would you find out information about using the Backspace key in WordPerfect?

7. How would you find information about the Print command in WordPerfect?

8. What are the default margin settings in WordPerfect?

9. With the cursor in the document window, how would you do the following using the keyboard? Using the mouse?
   a. Display the button bar
   b. Change the button bar from WPMain to Layout
   c. Close the WordPerfect document window
   d. Double-space between paragraphs
   e. Move the cursor one line down
   f. Print the document that is in the document window
   g. Exit WordPerfect

10. Define the following WordPerfect terms:
    a. Word wrap
    b. Pull-down menu
    c. Button bar
    d. Icon
    e. Dialog box
    f. Open (a document)
    g. Scrolling
    h. Default format settings
    i. Mnemonic letter (in a pull-down menu or dialog box)
    j. Function-key template
    k. Hard return
    l. Soft return
    m. Document window

11. Describe each of the following mouse-related items:
    a. Mouse pointer
    b. Click (as in "click the Open button")
    c. Double-click
    d. Drag

12. Name and describe the four steps in planning a document.

13. Why should you save a document to your disk several times, even before you finish typing it?

14. What is the purpose of Print Preview?

Tutorial Assignments

Be sure your WordPerfect data disk is in drive A and that a blank document window is on the screen. Then open the file T1FILE1.DFT and do the following:

1. Delete the current date at the beginning of the letter, then use WordPerfect's Date Text command to insert today's date into the document.

2. Save the letter as S1FILE3.LET.

3. Preview the document to see what it will look like before you print it.

4. Print the document.

Clear the document window, open the letter T1FILE2.DFT from your data disk, and do the following:

5. In the body of the memo, insert a space between "Work" and "place" in the word "Workplace."

6. Delete the lowercase "p" in "place" and type an uppercase letter, so that the phrase reads "Work Place."

7. Correct the error in the word "Valev" to make it "Valve."

8. Correct the error in the word "traiming" to make it "training."

9. Save the document as S1FILE4.MEM.

10. Print the document.

Clear the document window, then use Figure 1-57 to complete Assignments 11 through 15.

Figure 1-57

> MEMORANDUM - Clearwater Valve Company
>
> Date: February 17, 1995
>
> To: Andrea Simone, Executive Assistant, Operations
>
> From: Megan Lui, Human Resources Manager
>
> Re: Safety Training
>
> Thanks, Andrea, for the great job you did in setting up safety training for our employees. Everyone I talked to thought the training was great. That's a real compliment given the fundamentally boring nature of the subject matter!
>
> Keep up the good work.
>
> cc: Steve Morgan, Operations Manager

11. Type the memo, pressing [Spacebar] twice after "Date:," "To:," "From:," and "Re:."

12. Use WordPerfect's Date Text feature to insert today's date.

13. Save the memo as S1FILE5.MEM.

14. Preview the memo before printing it.

15. Print the memo.

Case Problems

1. Letter to Request Information About Copier Machines

Ivan Janetski is the equipment manager for the public accounting firm of Hofstetter, Inouye & Pilling. One of his responsibilities is to purchase office copiers for the company. After reading an advertisement for Mita copiers, he decides to write for more information on copier models and prices. He has already written the body of the letter and now needs only to insert the date, the inside address, the salutation, the complimentary close, and his name and title.

Open the document P1MITA.LET from your WordPerfect data disk into a document window, and do the following:

1. Move the cursor to the beginning of the document and press **[Enter]** six times to insert sufficient space for a letterhead.

2. Use WordPerfect's Date Text command to insert today's date.

3. Insert four blank lines after the date and, using the proper business letter format, type the inside address: **Mita Copystar America, Inc., P.O. Box 3900, Peoria, IL 61614**.

4. Insert a blank line after the inside address, type the salutation **Dear Sales Representative:**, then insert another blank line.

5. Move the cursor to the end of the document, insert a blank line, and type the complimentary close **Sincerely,** (including the comma).

6. Add four blank lines to leave room for the signature and then type the name and title: **Ivan Janetski, Office Equipment Manager**.

7. Save the letter as S1MITA.LET.

8. Preview the letter.

9. Print the letter.

2. Memo to Congratulate the Head of a Sales Team

One of your co-workers at Clearwater Valve Company, Leslie Homen, is head of a sales team. Her team recently received a company award for having the highest sales for the quarter.

Do the following:

1. Write a memo to Leslie Homen congratulating her on receiving the award. Remember to use the four-part planning process. You should plan the content, organization, and style of the memo, and use a standard memo format similar to the one shown in Figure 1-57.

2. Save the document as S1HOMEN.MEM.

3. Preview the memo.

4. Print the memo.

3. Letter of Introduction to a Distributor

Suppose you're a sales representative for Clearwater Valve Company. You have a list of distributors through whom you would like to sell your product. One of the distributors is Mr. Dale Chow of Energy Ventures, 891 Second Street, Los Altos, CA 94002, a company that distributes equipment for oil rigs.

Do the following:

1. Write a letter introducing yourself to Mr. Chow and requesting the opportunity to visit him to discuss the possibility of having Energy Ventures distribute Clearwater Valve Company products.

2. Save the letter as S1ENERGY.LET.

3. Preview the letter.

4. Print the letter.

Tutorial 2

Formatting and Editing a Document

Writing a Product Information Memo for an Ad Launch

Case: Decision Development Corporation

David Truong is an assistant product manager at Decision Development Corporation (DDC), a company that specializes in software tools for business. David reports to Liz Escobar, the product manager. One of David's responsibilities is to write product description memos to the DDC advertising group to explain the key features and benefits of new products.

The advertising group uses these memos to help them prepare for the launch meetings, at which they plan the advertising campaigns for new products.

Liz has just stopped by David's office and asked him to write a product description memo to the ad group about DDC's newest product, InTrack, an investment tracking program. Liz reminds David that she wants him to submit his first draft to her for comments and corrections. After she returns the draft to him, he should make the necessary changes and print three copies of the memo — one for the advertising group, one for her, and one for the InTrack product file.

In this tutorial you'll plan, write, and edit David's memo to DDC's advertising group.

OBJECTIVES

In this tutorial you will learn to:

- Make large-scale cursor moves and use the scroll bars

- Change fonts

- Change margins

- Justify text

- Boldface, underline, and italicize text

- Reveal hidden format codes

- Delete words, sentences, and paragraphs

- Use the speller, thesaurus, and grammar checker

- Print multiple copies of a document

Planning the Document

First, David plans the four components of the document. He considers content, organization, style, and format.

Content

David has kept notes on the key features of InTrack and has a copy of the program specifications produced by DCC's software design team. He distills this information so the advertising group will understand the product and still have the necessary details to write the text of the advertisements, commonly called ad copy. He knows that the ad group is familiar with computer software, so he feels free to use technical terminology.

Organization

Because the product description is a memo, David knows that his document will begin with the standard memo heading. He decides that the body of the memo will be a numbered list of the key features of InTrack.

Style

David assumes that the ad group will adapt and edit his information to a style that suits the needs of the ad campaign. His style, therefore, will be clear and straightforward.

Format

David decides that in his first draft he will use WordPerfect's default format settings, which include one-inch margins and text aligned along the left margin but ragged along the right margin. He knows that Liz might suggest format changes, but for now he'll use the defaults.

■   ■   ■

Having planned the document, David writes the rough draft. He submits it to Liz, who later returns the draft with her editing marks and notes (Figure 2-1). David looks over her comments and is ready to create the final draft of the InTrack product description memo.

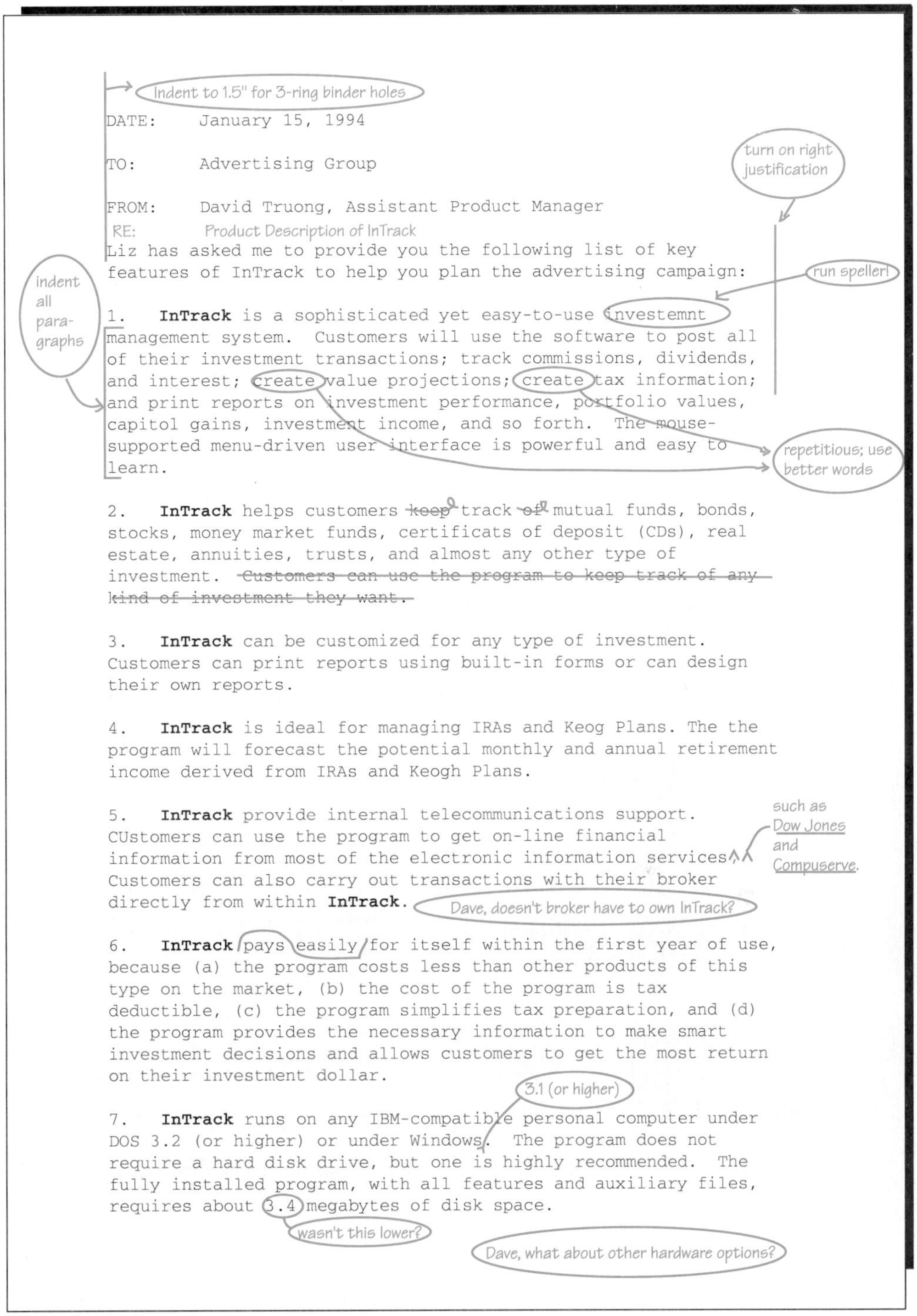

Indent to 1.5" for 3-ring binder holes

DATE: January 15, 1994

TO: Advertising Group

FROM: David Truong, Assistant Product Manager

RE: *Product Description of InTrack*

turn on right justification

Liz has asked me to provide you the following list of key
features of InTrack to help you plan the advertising campaign:

indent all para-graphs

run speller!

1.   **InTrack** is a sophisticated yet easy-to-use *investemnt*
management system. Customers will use the software to post all
of their investment transactions; track commissions, dividends,
and interest; create value projections; create tax information;
and print reports on investment performance, portfolio values,
capitol gains, investment income, and so forth. The mouse-
supported menu-driven user interface is powerful and easy to
learn.

repetitious; use better words

2.   **InTrack** helps customers ~~keep~~ track ~~of~~ mutual funds, bonds,
stocks, money market funds, certificats of deposit (CDs), real
estate, annuities, trusts, and almost any other type of
investment. ~~Customers can use the program to keep track of any kind of investment they want.~~

3.   **InTrack** can be customized for any type of investment.
Customers can print reports using built-in forms or can design
their own reports.

4.   **InTrack** is ideal for managing IRAs and Keog Plans. The the
program will forecast the potential monthly and annual retirement
income derived from IRAs and Keogh Plans.

5.   **InTrack** provide internal telecommunications support.
CUstomers can use the program to get on-line financial
information from most of the electronic information services∧
Customers can also carry out transactions with their broker
directly from within **InTrack**.

such as Dow Jones and Compuserve.

Dave, doesn't broker have to own InTrack?

6.   **InTrack** pays easily for itself within the first year of use,
because (a) the program costs less than other products of this
type on the market, (b) the cost of the program is tax
deductible, (c) the program simplifies tax preparation, and (d)
the program provides the necessary information to make smart
investment decisions and allows customers to get the most return
on their investment dollar.

3.1 (or higher)

7.   **InTrack** runs on any IBM-compatible personal computer under
DOS 3.2 (or higher) or under Windows. The program does not
require a hard disk drive, but one is highly recommended. The
fully installed program, with all features and auxiliary files,
requires about 3.4 megabytes of disk space.

wasn't this lower?

Dave, what about other hardware options?

Figure 2-1
Memo with Liz
Escobar's
suggested changes

In the instructions on editing the memo, you'll be given a choice, when appropriate, of whether to use pull-down menus (with the keyboard or with the mouse), the function-key template and the function keys, or the button bar to execute WordPerfect commands.

Opening the Document

David begins by opening the first draft of his memo, which has the filename C2FILE1.DFT. Remember, the filename extension .DFT stands for "draft."

To open the document:

① Start WordPerfect (if you haven't done so already) and make sure a blank document window is on the screen. If necessary, refer to Tutorial 1 to see how to clear the document window.

② Insert your WordPerfect data disk into drive A.

③ Choose **F**ile from the main menu bar and then choose **O**pen, or press **[Shift][F10]** (Open/Retrieve). The Open Document dialog box appears on the screen.

④ Type **a:\c2file1.dft** and choose OK. The rough draft of David Truong's memo appears on the screen. See Figure 2-2.

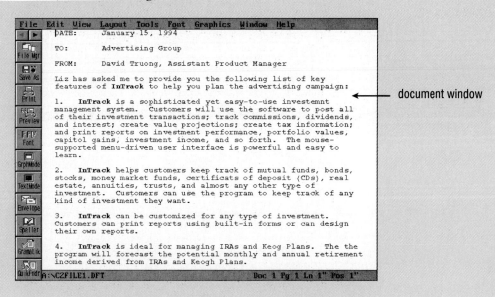

← document window

Figure 2-2
Draft of memo in
document window

Making Large-Scale Cursor Moves with the Keyboard

You already know how to use the arrow keys ([→], [←], [↑], [↓]) to move the cursor one character to the right or left or one line up or down. Now you'll see how to move the cursor more than one character or one line at a time. These large-scale cursor moves will save you considerable time and energy when you have to move the cursor around to different parts of your documents.

As you work through the following steps, you may notice several typographical and spelling errors in David's memo. Leave them for now. They appear in the document to help you learn various ways of editing the text and correcting the spelling — two skills we'll cover later in this tutorial.

To make large-scale cursor moves:

① Press **[Home]**, **[Home]**, and **[↓]**.

When a sequence of keystrokes is separated by commas, you should press each key separately, but don't type the commas. Notice that pressing these keys moves the cursor to the end of the document. See Figure 2-3.

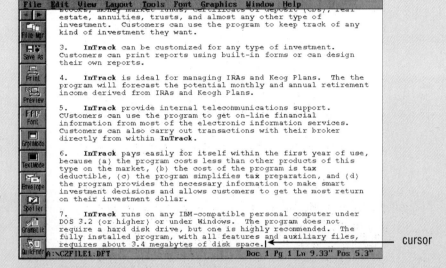

Figure 2-3
Document window
after moving cursor
to end of document

② Press **[Home]**, **[Home]**, and **[↑]** to move the cursor to the beginning of the document.

③ Press **[↓]** enough times to move the cursor to the "1" in the first numbered paragraph of the memo.

④ Press **[End]** to move the cursor to the end of the current line. This method is much faster in moving the cursor to the end of the line than if you repeatedly press [→].

⑤ Press **[Home]** and **[←]** to move the cursor to the beginning of the current line.

⑥ Press **[Ctrl][→]** (Word Right) three times to move the cursor to the word "a," then press **[Ctrl][←]** (Word Left) three times to move the cursor back to the "1."

As you can see, [Ctrl][→] moves the cursor one word to the right, and [Ctrl][←] moves the cursor one word to the left.

⑦ With Num Lock off, press **[+]** (Screen Down) on the numeric keypad once to move the cursor to the bottom of the screen. Press it again to move the cursor down another screen. See Figure 2-4. If you're using WordPerfect in text mode, the cursor may be in paragraph 6 instead of paragraph 7. Your screen may be different due to differences in font size.

cursor

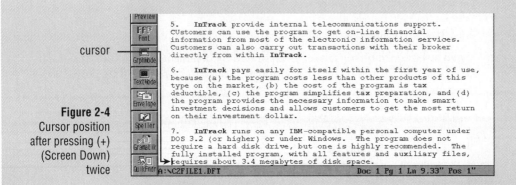

Figure 2-4
Cursor position
after pressing (+)
(Screen Down)
twice

Pressing [+] on the keypad (with Num Lock off) moves the cursor to the bottom of the current screen. When you press it again, the cursor moves to the bottom of the next screenful of text. You must remember to use the plus-sign key [+] *on the numeric keypad* and to have Num Lock off. If you press the plus key on the typewriter keyboard or on the numeric keypad with Num Lock on, a plus character will be inserted into the document.

⑧ Press **[-]** (Screen Up) on the numeric keypad twice.

Pressing [-] once on the numeric keypad moves the cursor to the top of the current screen. Pressing it again moves the cursor up another screenful. See Figure 2-5. Your cursor might be in a different position due to differences in mode or font size.

cursor

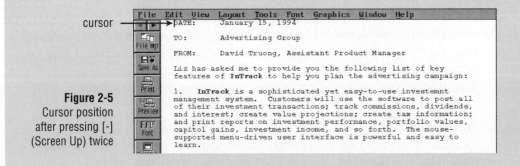

Figure 2-5
Cursor position
after pressing [-]
(Screen Up) twice

The cursor-movement keys demonstrated in the preceding steps are only a few of the many ways you can move the cursor in WordPerfect. Figure 2-6 lists most of the WordPerfect cursor-movement commands. You'll use some of the other cursor-movement keys in later tutorials.

CURSOR - MOVEMENT KEYS	
Cursor Key	**Movement**
[←]	Left one character
[→]	Right one character
[↑]	Up one line
[↓]	Down one line
[Ctrl][←]	Left one word
[Ctrl][→]	Right one word
[Home], [←]	Far left side of screen
[Home], [→]	Far right side of screen
[Home], [Home], [←]	Beginning of line
[Home], [Home], [→] or [End]	End of line
[Home], [↑] or keypad [-]	Top of screen, then up one screen at a time
[Home], [↓] or keypad [+]	Bottom of screen, then down one screen at a time
[PgUp]	First line of previous page
[PgDn]	First line of next page
[Home], [Home], [↑]	Beginning of document (after any formatting codes)
[Home], [Home], [↓]	End of document

Figure 2-6
Cursor-movement
keys

You can also move the cursor to any location in the document window simply by clicking the mouse pointer on that location. If you're using a mouse, this is often the easiest way to move around a page. In the next section, you'll learn how to use the mouse to make large-scale cursor moves through your document. Throughout these tutorials, when we give instructions to move the cursor to different places in a document, we will give only the keyboard instructions. Feel free to use the mouse instead if you like.

As you move the cursor through a document, you'll discover that the cursor won't move to any region of the screen unoccupied by text. If the cursor is at the end of a document, for example, and you press [+] (Screen Down), the cursor won't move, since it can't go lower than the end of the document. Similarly, if the cursor is at the end of a short line of text and you press [→], the cursor won't go any farther to the right. Instead, it will move to the first character of the next line.

Sometimes as you move the cursor through a document, you'll see WordPerfect reformat the screen by shifting text left or right, wrapping words from one line to another, and so forth. This happens because some format changes don't actually appear on the screen until you move the cursor through the affected text.

Using the Scroll Bars

Another way of moving the cursor through your document is with the vertical scroll bar. A **scroll bar** is a bar located along one edge of the document window or along an edge of a list in a dialog box. The scroll bar has arrow buttons on each end of it and a scroll button that slides along its length. Clicking the arrow buttons or dragging the scroll button up or down moves the cursor through the document, scrolling the text as it moves.

To use the scroll bar, you need a mouse. If your computer doesn't have one, skip to the next section.

Let's first display WordPerfect's vertical scroll bar in the document window. Then we'll use the scroll bar to move the cursor through the document.

To display and use the vertical scroll bar:

❶ Choose **V**iew, **V**ertical Scroll Bar. See Figure 2-7.

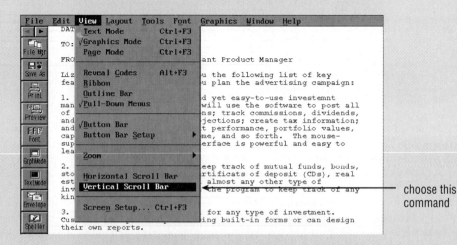

Figure 2-7
Vertical Scroll Bar
command

choose this
command

The vertical scroll bar appears along the right edge of the document window. See Figure 2-8.

scroll up arrow

scroll button

scroll bar

Figure 2-8
Vertical Scroll Bar in
the document
window

scroll down arrow

② Click the down arrow button at the bottom of the scroll bar. Click it several times, and as you do so, watch how the cursor moves down the screen.

As you can see, the cursor moves down the screen until it gets to the bottom, and then the text begins to scroll up as the cursor moves toward the end of the document.

③ Position the mouse pointer on the up arrow button and hold down the left mouse button until the cursor gets to the beginning of the document.

④ Finally, drag the scroll button down to the bottom of the scroll bar. To drag, position the mouse pointer anywhere in the scroll button, press and hold down the left mouse button, move the mouse pointer down the screen, and then release the mouse button.

The cursor moves to the last line of the document. See Figure 2-9.

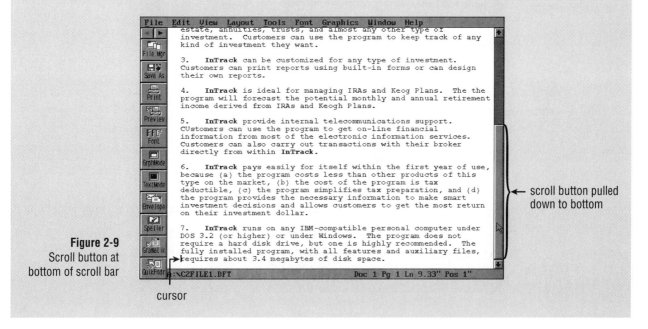

Figure 2-9
Scroll button at
bottom of scroll bar

cursor

scroll button pulled
down to bottom

WordPerfect also provides a horizontal scroll bar. You display this the same way you displayed the vertical scroll bar, by choosing Horizontal Scroll Bar from the View menu.

Changing Fonts

David's first task in editing the memo is to change the font from Courier to Times Roman, as requested by Liz. Courier and Courier-like fonts give the appearance of a typewritten document, while Times Roman and Times-like fonts give the appearance of a typeset document. Liz wants the memo to look as professional as possible so she prefers Times Roman.

To change the font of the document:

1. Press **[Home]**, **[Home]**, **[↑]** to move the cursor to the beginning of the document.

   As with almost all WordPerfect formatting commands, a font change in a document takes effect from the location of the cursor to the end of the document. Since David wants the font change to affect the entire document, he moves the cursor to the beginning of the document. Format changes stay in effect until another change is made.

2. Choose Font, Font on the main menu, or press **[Ctrl][F8]** (Font), or click the Font button on the button bar.

   WordPerfect displays the Font dialog box, as shown in Figure 2-10. Notice that the name of the current font appears in the font box. At the bottom of the dialog box, in the Resulting Font box, WordPerfect displays an example of what the selected font will look like.

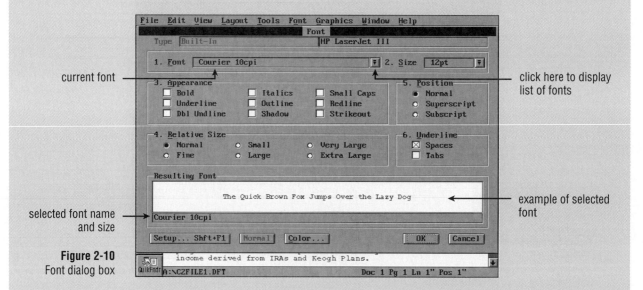

current font

click here to display
list of fonts

example of selected
font

selected font name
and size

Figure 2-10
Font dialog box

3. Choose 1 (**F**ont) from the Font dialog box or click the mouse pointer on the down arrow to the right of the current font name.

   The available fonts appear in a list (with a scroll bar at the right), with the current font highlighted. See Figure 2-11. Your list of fonts may be different depending on which ones are installed on your system. You can use the scroll bar or the arrow keys to look through the list of fonts.

cursor

list of fonts (yours
may be different)

current font

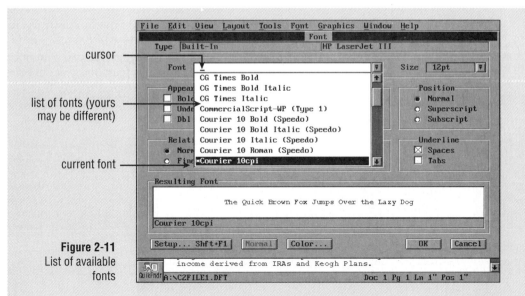

Figure 2-11
List of available
fonts

④ Scroll through the list of fonts until you see Times Roman or one of its variations. The font name variations could be CG Times, Dutch 801 Roman, Roman-WP, or Times. You may see one or more of these fonts in the font list. The font name may include a font size, such as "10cpi" or "12pt." The abbreviation **cpi** means "characters per inch," so 10cpi means a font size that prints ten characters per inch horizontally. The abbreviation **pt** means "point" or "points." A point is a measure of the height of a font, where one point is 1/72 of an inch, so that 12pt is 1/6 of an inch, or six lines per inch vertically. If the font name doesn't include a size, you can select the size from the Size box that appears to the right of the Font box.

⑤ Highlight the desired font (preferably a Times Roman-style font of 10cpi or 12pt) by clicking its name or by using the arrow keys to move the cursor to its name, and then press **[Enter]**.

   If you can't find Times Roman or any of its variations, choose some other font. The name of the font now appears in the box to the right of the Font command. See Figure 2-12.

new font

Figure 2-12
New font selected
from list

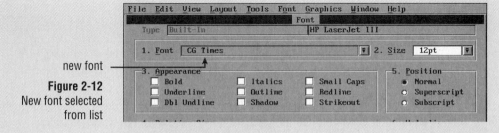

⑥ Choose OK by clicking the OK button at the bottom of the Font dialog box or by pressing **[Enter]**.

   The cursor returns to the main document window.

In text mode, the document window doesn't show the new font, but more words are displayed on each line of text because Times Roman fonts are narrower than Courier. In graphics mode, the document window displays the new font, as well as the increased number of words per line of text, as shown in Figure 2-13. Even if you are using graphics mode, your screen may look different from Figure 2-13 if you chose a font other than 12pt CG Times.

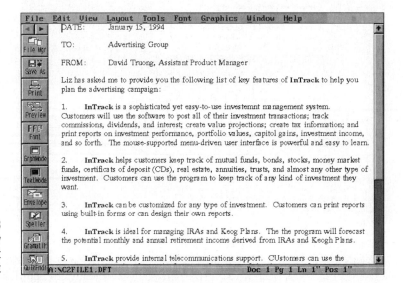

Figure 2-13
Document window
showing document
in new font

Changing Margins

David's next task in editing the memo is to increase the left margin to 1.5 inches. Because changing the left margin affects page layout, WordPerfect's margin command is found on the Layout menu.

To change the left margin:

❶ Press **[Home]**, **[Home]**, **[↑]** to make sure the cursor is at the beginning of the document.

Remember, format changes take effect from the location of the cursor to the end of the document, so if you want to change the margin for an entire document, you must move the cursor to the beginning of the document before you set the new margin value.

❷ Choose **L**ayout, **M**argins, or press **[Shift][F8]** (Format) to display the Format dialog box. See Figure 2-14. If you use the function-key command, choose **2** (**M**argins) from the Format dialog box.

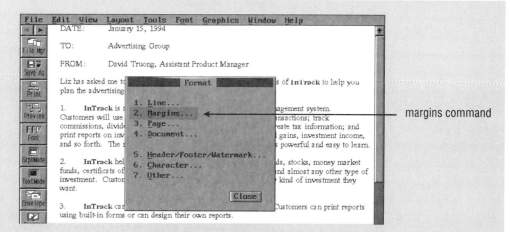

margins command

Figure 2-14
Format dialog box

WordPerfect displays the Margin Format dialog box. See Figure 2-15. The current left, right, top, and bottom margin settings (as well as information about paragraph margins) appear in the dialog box. David's goal is to make the left margin 1.5 inches, as suggested by Liz in Figure 2-1.

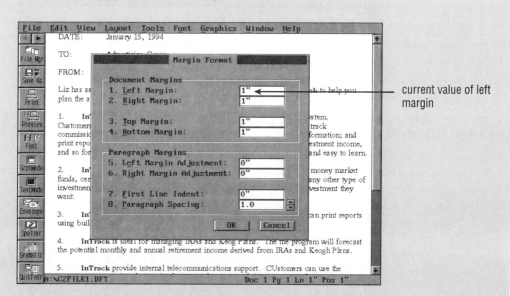

current value of left margin

Figure 2-15
Margin Format dialog box

③ Choose **1** (**L**eft Margin) or click the mouse in the box to the right of the Left Margin command. WordPerfect now highlights the current value for the left margin. See Figure 2-16.

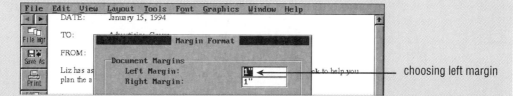

choosing left margin

Figure 2-16
Left margin box highlighted

Whenever you see a value highlighted in a dialog box, you can start typing to erase the old value and replace it with the new value. You don't have to delete the old value first, although you may do so by pressing [Backspace] or [Del].

④ Type **1.5** and press **[Enter]**.

The dialog box now displays the new value for the left margin. If you wanted to change other margin values, you could do so at this time. But in this case, you want to leave the other margins at 1 inch, because Liz didn't ask David to change those margin values.

⑤ Choose OK by clicking the OK button or by pressing **[Enter]**.

⑥ If WordPerfect returns to the Format dialog box, choose Close by clicking the Close button or by pressing **[Enter]**.

The cursor returns to the document window, and the text along the left margin moves to the right. See Figure 2-17. Your screen may not show the full effect of changing the margin until you move the cursor down through the text or tell WordPerfect to "rewrite" the screen, that is, to show you what the entire screen looks like with any changes.

1.5" margin

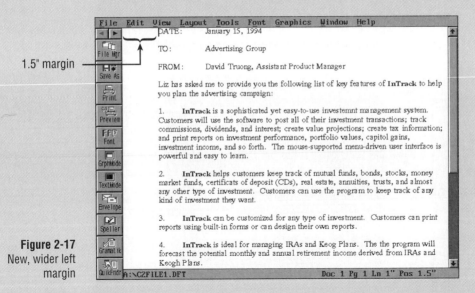

Figure 2-17
New, wider left
margin

⑦ Make sure the cursor is on the "D" in "DATE." Press **[Ctrl][F3]** (Screen) to display the Screen dialog box. See Figure 2-18.

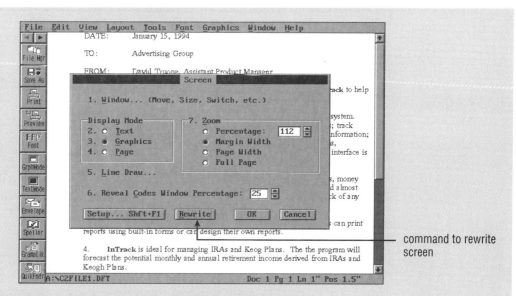

command to rewrite
screen

Figure 2-18
Screen dialog box

⑧ Choose Rewrite by pressing **R**, clicking the Rewrite button, or pressing **[Enter]**. (You
can access the Screen dialog box only by using the function-key command.)

The Rewrite command causes WordPerfect to rewrite the screen to show the effects
of any format change you make in a document. In most cases you won't have to use
the Rewrite command because WordPerfect automatically reformats the screen
when you move the cursor into the area of the screen that includes the change.

Justifying Text

Justification usually means adjusting the spacing between characters in any given line so that
text is aligned along the right margin as well as along the left. Modern word processors and
desktop publishing software, however, define justification to mean more than this. Specifically
WordPerfect supports four types of justified text: full, left, right, and center (Figure 2-19 on the
following page).

Full Justification
This paragraph is an example of *full* justification. The lines of text are aligned along the left and the right margins. This gives an ordered look to the document but is generally more difficult to read than left-justified text.

Left Justification
This paragraph is an example of *left* justification. The lines of text are aligned along the left margin but ragged along the right margin. This gives a less ordered look to the document but is generally easier to read than fully justified text. Left justification is the initial default setting in WordPerfect.

Right Justification
This paragraph is an example of *right* justification. The lines of text are aligned along the right margin but ragged along the left margin. You would never use right justification in the body of a normal document, but you might use it for special effects.

Center Justification
This paragraph is an example of *center* justification. The lines of text are centered between the left and right margins. You would never use center justification in the body of a normal document, but you would frequently use it in creating title pages.

Figure 2-19
The four type of
justification

The WordPerfect default format setting is left justification, and that is how David formatted the first draft of his product description memo, as shown in Figure 2-1. But Liz has suggested that he change the format setting to full justification to make the memo appear more formal. David does this by using the Justification command on the Layout menu.

To change justification:

1. Press **[Home]**, **[Home]**, **[↑]** to make sure the cursor is at the beginning of the document.
   Remember that since you want to change justification for the entire document, you must move the cursor to the beginning of the document before you change the format setting.

2. Choose **L**ayout, **J**ustification, **F**ull. See Figure 2-20.

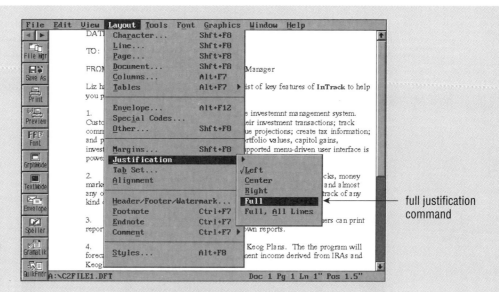

Figure 2-20
Full Justification
menu command

full justification
command

Alternatively, press **[Shift][F8]** (Format) and choose **1** (**L**ine) to display the Line Format dialog box. See Figure 2-21.

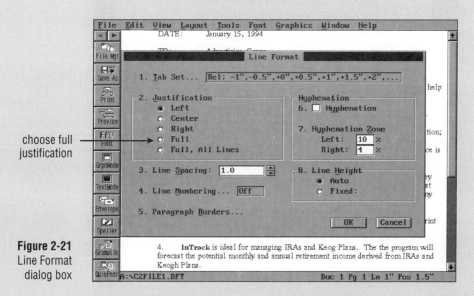

choose full
justification

Figure 2-21
Line Format
dialog box

Next choose **2** (**J**ustification) and **4** (**F**ull). Finally, choose OK in the Line Format dialog box, then choose Close in the Format dialog box.

In this instance, using the pull-down menu is simpler than using the keyboard to execute the Full Justification command. In other cases, the keyboard commands are easier to execute than the pull-down menus. As you gain experience using WordPerfect, you'll learn the easiest method of executing the commands.

From the cursor's current location — the beginning of the memo in this instance — to the end of the document, the text is now full-justified. Since the document window in text mode looks the same for full and for left justification, you can't see any change if you are in text mode. In graphics mode, however (Figure 2-22), you can clearly see the change. In text mode, you can see the full justification only by using Print Preview or by printing the document.

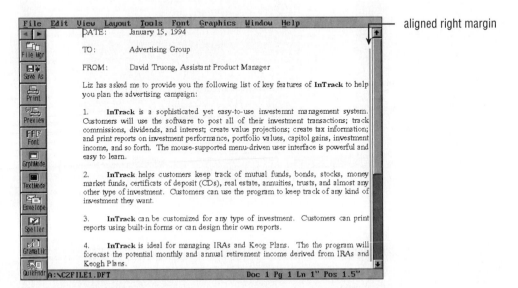

aligned right margin

Figure 2-22
Document with full
justification

Using Tabs

As Figure 2-1 shows, David's next task in revising the memo is to insert the "RE," or reference line, below the "FROM" line. In the following steps you'll use [Enter] to insert new lines, and then press [Tab] to insert space between the word "RE:" and the word "Product," as was already done between "TO:" and "Advertising" (Figure 2-23).

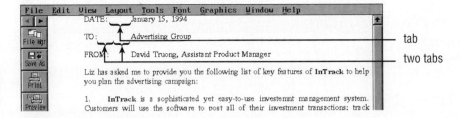

tab

two tabs

Figure 2-23
Space created
by tabs

The Tab key indents text by inserting space from the current cursor location to the next tab stop. **Tab stops** are precise locations on the text lines; WordPerfect's default tab settings are every one-half inch from the left margin. Tabs are useful in aligning text vertically in your documents. In the case of David's memo, the tab stops after "DATE:," "TO:," and "FROM:" keep the text precisely aligned (Figure 2-24). You should never use the Spacebar to align text. If you do, the text might appear aligned in the document window, but it might not be aligned when you print the document.

aligned

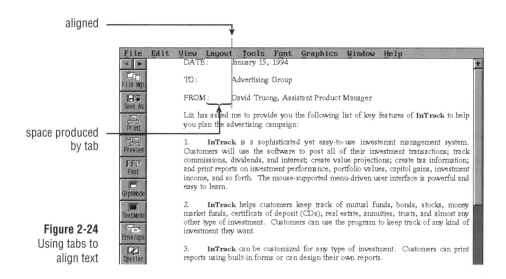

space produced by tab

Figure 2-24
Using tabs to align text

To use [Tab] to insert space:

➊ Move the cursor to the "F" in "FROM" on the third line of text in the memo.

➋ Press **[End]** to move the cursor to the end of the line, after the word "Manager."

➌ Press **[Enter]** twice to double-space after the "FROM" line.

➍ Type **RE:** and press **[Tab]** twice.

Pressing [Tab] twice inserts space between "RE:" and the tab stop at Pos 2.5". The cursor is now directly beneath the word "David."

➎ Type **Product Description of** and press **[Spacebar]**.

You're now ready to type the word **InTrack** in boldface.

Creating Boldface Text

One way to highlight a word in your document is to use boldfacing. **Boldface text** is text with thicker characters than normal text. Let's type the word "InTrack" in boldface in David's memo.

To create boldface text:

➊ Make sure the cursor is to the right of the space after the phrase "Product Description of" that you typed in the previous section.

➋ Choose **F**ont, **B**old or press **[F6]** (Bold).

Note that the position number after "Pos," on the far right side of the status bar, now appears in boldface or in a different color to represent boldface. (This is difficult to see in graphics mode.) With Bold turned on, whatever new text you type will appear in boldface on the screen and in your printed document.

❸ Type **InTrack** and choose F**o**nt, **B**old or press **[F6]** (Bold) again to turn off bold. See Figure 2-25.

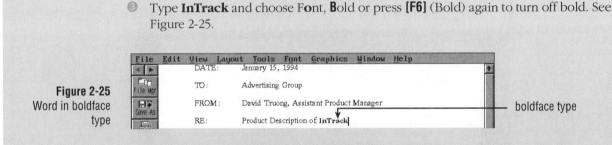

Figure 2-25
Word in boldface
type

boldface type

When you execute the Bold command the second time, bold is turned off. The "Pos" number on the status bar returns to normal text.

As you can see from these steps, the Bold command is a toggle switch. Remember that a toggle switch is any key or command that alternates between "on" and "off."

Underlining Text

David next wants to address Liz's question at the end of paragraph 5 in the memo. David decides to insert a note explaining that the brokers mentioned in the memo must also have InTrack. He wants the note to be in parentheses, with the word "Note" underlined.

To underline text:
❶ Move the cursor to the end of paragraph numbered 5, after the phrase ". . . directly from within InTrack."
❷ Press **[Spacebar]** twice to insert two spaces at the end of the sentence and type **(** (left parenthesis).
❸ Choose F**o**nt, **U**nderline or press **[F8]** (Underline).

The position number on the status bar indicates underline mode. See Figure 2-26. In graphics mode, the "Pos" number is underlined. In text mode, the "Pos" number changes colors or appears in reverse video. With underline turned on, whatever text you type will be underlined in your printed document. The Underline command, like the Bold command, is a toggle switch.

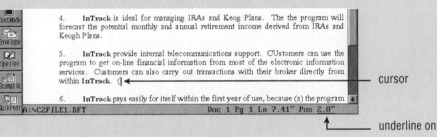

Figure 2-26
Screen after
choosing the
Underline command

cursor

underline on

❹ Type **Note** and then choose F**o**nt, **U**nderline or press **[F8]** (Underline) to toggle off underlining.

Notice that the position number no longer indicates underlining and that the word "Note" is underlined. See Figure 2-27.

Figure 2-27
Word in underlined
type

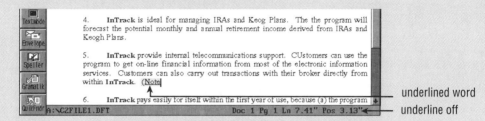

underlined word
underline off

❺ Type a colon (:), press **[Spacebar]** twice, then type **Their broker must also have** and press **[Spacebar]**.

❻ Press **[F6]** (Bold) to turn on boldfacing for the word "InTrack."

Feel free to use the F**o**nt pull-down menu and choose **B**old to execute the Bold command, but the keyboard method is easier in this case.

❼ Type **InTrack** and press **[F6]** (Bold) to toggle off boldfacing.

❽ Press **[Spacebar]** and type **to use this option.)**. See Figure 2-28.

Figure 2-28
Document window
with inserted phrase

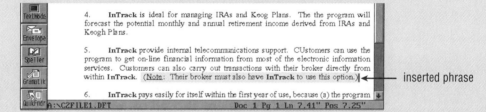

inserted phrase

Italicizing Text

Also in paragraph 5, Liz has asked David to list the names of two on-line information services, *Dow Jones* and *CompuServe*. Because these are titles, David knows he must type them in italics.

To italicize text:

❶ Move the cursor to the right of the period following the phrase "electronic informa-tion services."

❷ Press **[Backspace]** to delete the period, type a comma (,) and press **[Spacebar]**, and then type **such as** and press **[Spacebar]**.

You're now ready to type the first italicized title, *Dow Jones*.

❸ Choose F**o**nt, **I**talics or press **[Ctrl][I]** (Italics).

This turns on italics, but in this case, the "Pos" value remains unchanged.

④ Type **Dow Jones** and choose Font, **I**talics or press **[Ctrl][I]** (Italics) to turn off italics. Like Bold and Underline, the Italics command is a toggle switch.

⑤ Press **[Spacebar]** after the word *Jones*, type **and** and then press **[Spacebar]** again.

⑥ Turn on italics, type **CompuServe**, turn off italics, and type a period.

You have added the phrase with the italicized text. Your document window should now look like Figure 2-29.

italicized words →

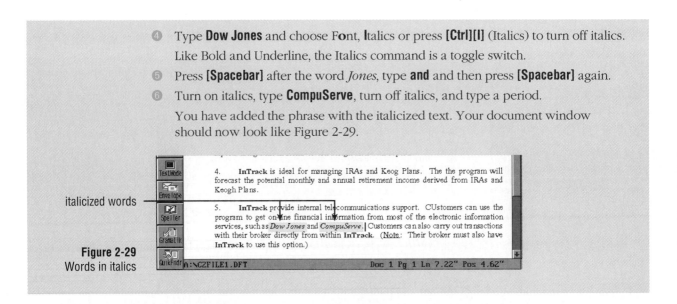

Figure 2-29
Words in italics

Saving an Intermediate Version of the Document

David has now worked on the document for over 15 minutes and feels that it's time to save his changes. Let's save the document now. For instructional purposes, we'll use a new filename.

To save the document with a new filename:

① Make sure your WordPerfect data disk is still in drive A.

② Choose **F**ile, Save **A**s, or press **[F10]** (Save As), or click the Save As button on the button bar.

WordPerfect displays the Save Document dialog box.

③ Type the new filename **a:\s2file2.dft** and choose OK.

WordPerfect saves the edited memo to your data disk using the filename S2FILE2.DFT.

Revealing Format Codes

Whenever you execute a WordPerfect format command, WordPerfect inserts invisible format codes into your document. These codes tell WordPerfect how to format the document on the screen and how to print the document.

When you're typing a document, you usually don't need to see these format codes. But every once in a while — for instance, when you've pressed the wrong key or you want to change one of the format codes — you need to reveal them.

To reveal the hidden format codes:

❶ Press **[Home]**, **[Home]**, **[↑]** to move the cursor to the beginning of the document.

❷ Choose **V**iew, Reveal **C**odes or press **[Alt][F3]** or **[F11]** (Reveal Codes).

The screen is now divided into two windows. The top is the document window and the bottom is the Reveal Codes window. See Figure 2-30.

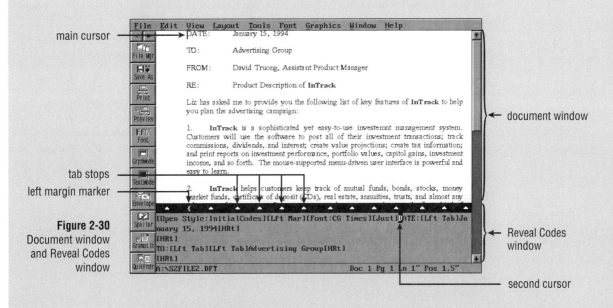

main cursor

tab stops
left margin marker

Figure 2-30
Document window
and Reveal Codes
window

document window

Reveal Codes
window

second cursor

The bar separating the document window and the Reveal Codes window contains a left brace (⌊) to mark the left margin, a right brace (⌋) to mark the right margin, and triangles (–) to mark the tab stops. (Your screen might not show the right margin code.)

You can tell the location of the cursor in the Reveal Codes window because the code or character at the cursor is highlighted. For example, in Figure 2-30 the cursor is on the "D" in "DATE," so the "D" is highlighted in the Reveal Codes window. Since both the document window and the Reveal Codes window have a cursor, the screen actually shows two cursors. Let's move the cursor to demonstrate how they move together.

To move the cursor with Reveal Codes on:

❶ Move the cursor down to the "3" at the beginning of paragraph 3 in the memo.

As you press [↓], the text in the document window and the information in the Reveal Codes windows scroll up.

❷ Press and hold down [→] for two or three seconds to watch how the two cursors move across the screen. As you can see, the two cursors always move together through the document.

❸ Press **[Home]**, **[Home]**, **[↑]** to move the cursor back to the beginning of the document.

In the Reveal Codes window, the words in square brackets are the format codes. Notice that the first code is [Open Style:Initial Codes]. Every document begins with this code to set the default format codes for your documents. The next code, [Lft Mar] (the left margin code), was inserted into the document when you changed the margin settings earlier in this tutorial. [Font] was inserted when you changed the font. And [Just] was inserted when you changed the justification.

You can see the settings of these format codes by moving the cursor to the codes. Let's move the cursor to the [Lft Mar] code to see what the left margin setting actually is.

To view the left margin setting associated with the format code:

❶ Press [←] until the cursor in the Reveal Codes window is on the left margin code, or click on the left margin code. See Figure 2-31.

Figure 2-31
Left margin code
showing value of
left margin

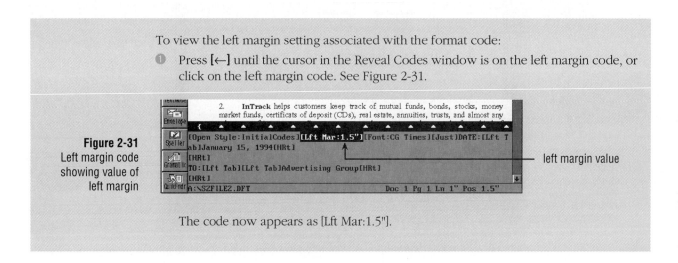

left margin value

The code now appears as [Lft Mar:1.5"].

Other format codes in the document include [Lft Tab] to mark where you pressed [Tab] (because the tab code marks the left edge of the text that follows it), [HRt] for hard return, [SRt] for soft return, and the paired codes [Bold On] to mark the beginning of boldfaced text and [Bold Off] to mark the end of boldfaced text. You can view these various codes by moving the cursor down through the document.

Figure 2-32 is a list of common WordPerfect format codes. Some of these codes won't make sense to you now, but their meanings will become clear as you work through this and later tutorials.

WORDPERFECT FORMAT CODES	
Code	**Meaning**
[HSpace]	Hard space
[-]	Hyphen
-	Hard hyphen
[Dec Tab]	Decimal align in Tab
[Bold On][Bold Off]	Bold begin and end
[Block]	Block begin
[Cntr on Mar]	Center line between margins
[Flsh Rgt]	Flush right
[Italc On][Italc Off]	Italic begin and end
[HPg]	Hard page break
[HRt]	Hard return
[Hyph On/Off]	Hyphenation on or off
[Lft Indent]	Indent
[Lft/Rgt Indent]	Left/Right indent
[Just]	Justification
[Lft Mar][Rgt Mar]	Left and right margin values
[Ln Spacing]	Line spacing
[SPg]	Soft page break
[SRt]	Soft return
[Subscpt On][Subscpt Off]	Subscript begin and end
[Suprscpt On] [Suprscpt Off]	Superscript begin and end
[Lft Tab]	Tab (move to next tab stop)
[Top Mar][Bot Mar]	Top and bottom margin values
[Und On][Und Off]	Underline begin and end
[Wid/Orph]	Widow/Orphan protection

Figure 2-32
Common
WordPerfect
format codes

Keep Reveal Codes on, because in the next section you'll use the Reveal Codes window to help you edit the document.

Indenting a Paragraph

The Reveal Codes window will help David perform his next task. One of Liz's suggestions for the product description memo is to indent the numbered paragraphs, aligning all the text under the first letter following the number. David realizes that he can't use tabs to do this because a tab inserts space only on one line at a time. Instead, he must use the Indent command, which indents not just the first line of the paragraph, but all subsequent lines until the end of the paragraph, which is marked by a hard return. David's task, therefore, is to change the [Lft Tab] format code to the [Lft Indent] format code at the beginning of each numbered paragraph.

To change [Lft Tab] codes to [Lft Indent] codes:

1. Make sure the Reveal Codes window appears on the screen.

   If necessary, choose **V**iew, Reveal **C**odes or press **[Alt][F3]** or **[F11]** (Reveal Codes).

2. Move the cursor to the "1" of the first numbered paragraph. You can now see a [Lft Tab] code to the right of the 1 in the Reveal Codes window.

3. Press **[→]** twice to put the cursor on the [Lft Tab] code. See Figure 2-33.

left tab code

Figure 2-33
Cursor on the
left tab code

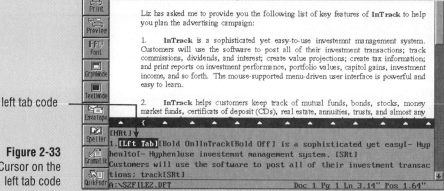

4. Press **[Del]** to delete the [Lft Tab] code. (If you use the [Del] key on the numeric keypad, Num Lock must be off.)

   The [Lft Tab] code disappears and the text beginning with "InTrack is a . . ." moves next to the "1."

5. Choose **L**ayout, **A**lignment, **I**ndent →, or press **[F4]** (Indent). The [Lft Indent] code is inserted into the document. See Figure 2-34.

paragraph indented

left indent code

Figure 2-34
Document after
deleting Left Tab
code and inserting
Left Indent code

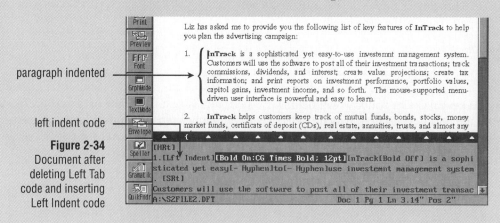

As you can see, when [Lft Indent] appears in the Reveal Codes window, the paragraph in the document window is indented. If the entire paragraph isn't indented on your screen, press [Ctrl][F3] (Screen) and choose Rewrite to have WordPerfect reformat the screen.

The amount of space that the text is indented depends on the location of the tab stops. Since WordPerfect's default format settings have a tab stop every 0.5 inch, executing the Indent command once would normally indent a paragraph 0.5 inch from the left margin. Therefore, in this case, where the left margin is 1.5 inches, the paragraph is indented 2.0 inches from the left edge of the page.

⑥ Move the cursor to the [Lft Tab] code at the beginning of the next numbered paragraph, delete the code, and choose **L**ayout, **A**lignment, **I**ndent →, or press **[F4]** (Indent) to insert the [Lft Indent] code at that location. Repeat this step until you have indented all seven paragraphs.

⑦ Choose **V**iew, Reveal **C**odes or press **[Alt][F3]** or **[F11]** (Reveal Codes) to close the Reveal Codes window and display a full-screen document window.

The document window should now look similar to Figure 2-35. As you can see, Reveal Codes is a toggle command: Choosing it once opens the Reveal Codes window, and choosing it again closes it.

soft page break

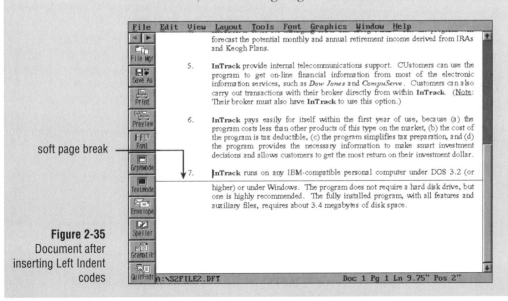

Figure 2-35
Document after inserting Left Indent codes

As you made these changes, WordPerfect may have automatically inserted a **soft page break** — a code that indicates where one page ends and another begins. If the font you are using is narrow, the text may all fit on one page. If your font is wider, some text may have spilled onto page 2. A soft page break is shown as a horizontal line across the document window (Figure 2-35). It is called a *soft* page break because if you add or delete text before the break, the page break may change.

In this section, you've learned how to reveal the format codes, delete the codes, and insert other codes. You can use these same methods to change any format code. For example, if you decide that you want to change some boldface text back to regular type, you could turn on Reveal Codes, move the cursor to the code that marks the beginning or the end of the boldface text, and delete the code. When you delete one of a pair of codes, WordPerfect automatically deletes the other.

Deleting Words and Lines of Text

You are already familiar with using [Backspace] to delete a character or a code to the left of the cursor and with using [Del] to delete a character or a code at the cursor. WordPerfect also provides ways for you to delete larger chunks of text.

For example, in the first line of paragraph 2 in the product description memo, Liz suggests that the phrase "keep track of" be simplified to "track." David will use [Ctrl][Backspace] (Delete Word) to delete the words "keep" and "of." Let's make the change in your document.

To delete a word from the text:

1. Move the cursor to the first letter of the word "keep" in the first line of paragraph 2.

   To use the [Ctrl][Backspace] (Delete Word) command, you can move the cursor anywhere within the word or immediately to the right of the word that you want to delete.

2. Press **[Ctrl][Backspace]** (Delete Word). The word and the space after it disappear from the document.

3. Press **[Ctrl][→]** (Word Right) to move the cursor past "track" and to the word "of."

4. Press **[Ctrl][Backspace]** (Delete Word). The word and the space after it disappear from the document. See Figure 2-36.

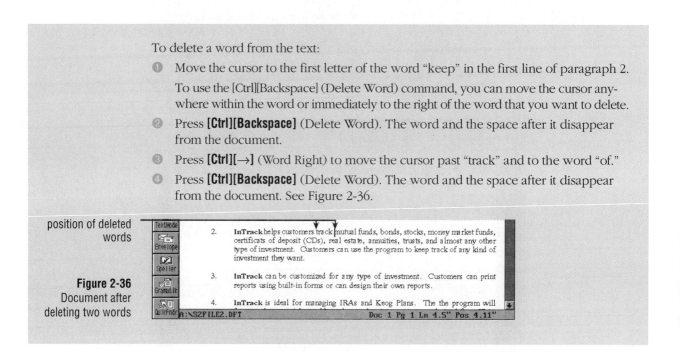

position of deleted words

Figure 2-36
Document after deleting two words

Another valuable deletion command is [Ctrl][End] (Del to EOL), which instructs WordPerfect to "delete all characters from the cursor to the end of the current line." You can use this command to delete a complete or partial line of text. In the product description memo, Liz wants David to delete the last sentence of paragraph 2 because the sentence is redundant. Let's use [Ctrl][End] (Del to EOL) to delete this sentence.

To delete from the cursor to the end of a line:

1. Move the cursor to the end of the first sentence in paragraph 2. See Figure 2-37.

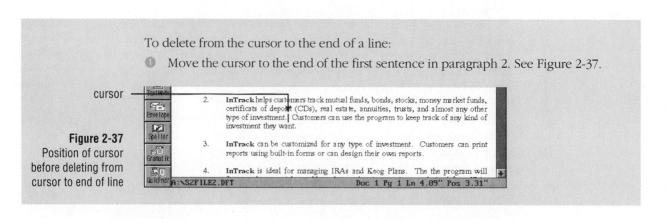

cursor

Figure 2-37
Position of cursor before deleting from cursor to end of line

② Press **[Ctrl][End]** (Del to EOL).

WordPerfect deletes the text from the cursor to the end of the line, and the remaining text in the sentence moves into the place of the deleted text. See Figure 2-38.

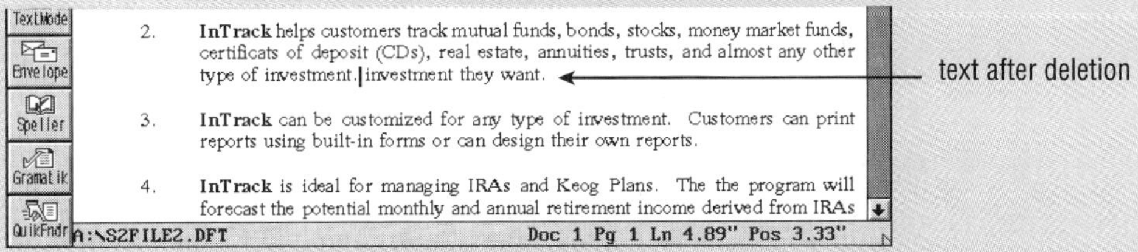

Figure 2-38
Document after
deleting from cursor
to end of line

text after deletion

③ Press **[Ctrl][End]** (Del to EOL) once or twice until you have deleted the entire sentence.

In addition to [Ctrl][Backspace] (Delete Word) and [Ctrl][End] (Del to EOL), you can use the other keystrokes shown in Figure 2-39 to delete text. As you become more familiar with WordPerfect, you'll be able to use these other delete commands in your own documents.

Figure 2-39
Common
WordPerfect
deletion keystrokes

WORDPERFECT DELETION KEYSTROKES	
Key(s)	**Deletion**
[Del]	Character at the cursor
[Backspace]	Character to the left of the cursor
[Ctrl][Backspace]	Word at the cursor
[Ctrl][End]	From the cursor to the end of the line
[Ctrl][PgDn]	From the cursor to the end of the page
[Home], [Backspace]	From the cursor to the beginning of the word
[Home], [Del]	From the cursor to the end of the word

Undeleting Text

Whenever you delete text from a document, WordPerfect temporarily saves the deleted text, just in case you want to **undelete** (restore) it later. WordPerfect doesn't store all your deletions, *only the last three.* Let's use WordPerfect's Undelete capability to delete and then restore the word "investment."

To undelete text:
① Make sure the cursor is still at the end of paragraph 2 in the product description memo.
② Press **[Ctrl][←]** (Word Left) to move the cursor to the beginning of the word "investment."
③ Press **[Ctrl][Backspace]** (Delete Word) to delete the word "investment" and the period.

Let's suppose that now you want the word and the period back in your document.

④ Choose **E**dit, **Un**delete or press **[Esc]** (Cancel).

WordPerfect immediately restores the most recent deletion to the screen, highlights it, and displays the Undelete dialog box. See Figure 2-40. To see the next-to-the-last deletion, you would select 2 (Previous Deletion); to see the deletion before that, you would select 2 (Previous Deletion) again.

command to restore deletion

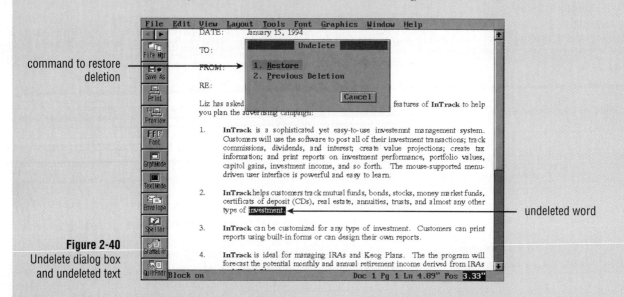

Figure 2-40
Undelete dialog box
and undeleted text

undeleted word

⑤ Select **1** (**R**estore). The deleted word "investment" and the accompanying period are restored to the document.

After deleting text, you can type new text, move the cursor, or execute other commands before you undelete the deleted text. For example, if you pressed [Esc] (Cancel) and chose 1 (Restore), WordPerfect would restore the deleted text at the current location of the cursor, not where the deleted text originally appeared. David can, therefore, use Undelete to move a word or a phrase from one location to another. Let's try this by deleting the word "pays" in paragraph 6 and restoring it after the word "easily" to switch the order of the words, as Liz suggests.

To use Undelete to move a word:

① Move the cursor to the word "pays" in the first line in paragraph 6.

② Press **[Ctrl][Backspace]** (Delete Word) to delete the word.

③ Press **[Ctrl][→]** (Word Right) to move the cursor past "easily" to the "f" in the word "for."

④ Choose **E**dit, **Un**delete, and choose **1** (**R**estore) or press **[Esc]** (Cancel), and choose **1** (**R**estore). See Figure 2-41.

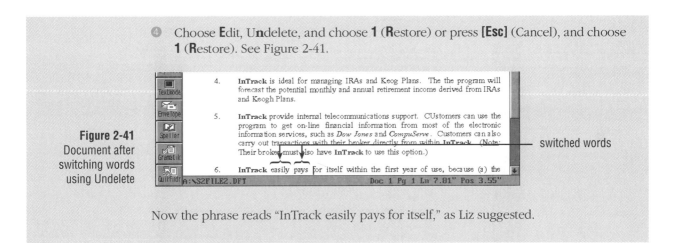

Figure 2-41
Document after switching words using Undelete

Now the phrase reads "InTrack easily pays for itself," as Liz suggested.

Using the Undo Command

WordPerfect's Undo command lets you undo (reverse) your last editing action. It works similarly to Undelete, except (1) Undo doesn't display a prompt, but immediately reverses the action; (2) Undo reverses *any* kind of action, not just deletions; and (3) Undo can only undo the most recent editing action.

Let's use Undo in an example. Suppose David decides to add the phrase "several times over" following the phrase "easily pays for itself." Then, after adding the new phrase, he realizes it's an overstatement and wants to "undo" it, that is, reverse the operation of adding the phrase.

To use the Undo command:

① Move the cursor to the "w" in "within" after the phrase "easily pays for itself" in paragraph 6.

As you type the phrase given in step 2, resist the temptation to correct any typographical errors. Because the Undo command reverses the most recent editing action, it will undo the entire phrase only if you have *not* taken any other editing action, such as [Backspace] or [Del].

② Type **several times over** and press **[Spacebar]** so that the line appears as shown in Figure 2-42 on the following page.

added text

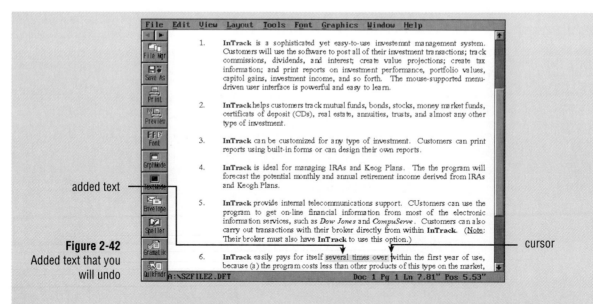

cursor

Now you decide that you really don't like the phrase. Rather than executing several commands (like [Backspace] or [Ctrl][Backspace]) to delete the phrase, you can execute one command to undo it.

❸ Choose **E**dit, **U**ndo or press **[Ctrl][Z]** (Undo).

The most recently typed text disappears from the document window.

❹ If the entire phrase does not disappear from the screen, delete it now using familiar deletion keys, like [Backspace] and [Del].

The important point to understand about Undo is that it has the ability to undo only the most recent editing action. If you make a mistake while editing a document, and you catch the mistake immediately, you can undo the action. Furthermore, if you undo an action but decide that you shouldn't have, you can undo the undo!

Using Typeover Mode

When you start WordPerfect, the document window starts out in **insert mode**, which means that the characters you type are inserted into the document at the cursor and existing characters (if any) move to the right. If you press [Ins] (Insert), the document window toggles from insert mode to **typeover mode**, which means that the characters you type *replace* existing text at the cursor. When typeover mode is on, the word "Typeover" appears on the left side of the status bar at the bottom of the screen. The filename of the document no longer appears on the status bar.

As shown in Figure 2-1, Liz wants David to add "3.1 (or higher)" to the second line of paragraph 7. Let's use insert mode to insert this text and then use typeover mode to change "3.4" to "2.5" later in that same paragraph.

To use insert mode:

❶ Move the cursor to the period (.) after the word "Windows" at the end of the first sentence in paragraph 7.

❷ Make sure "Typeover" does *not* appear on the status bar. If it does, press **[Ins]** to return to insert mode.

❸ Press **[Spacebar]** and type **3.1 (or higher)**.

When you type this phrase, watch as the sentence "The program does not require . . ." is pushed to the right and then wrapped to the next line.

Next let's use typeover mode to change "3.4" to "2.5."

To use typeover mode:

❶ Move the cursor to the "3" in "about 3.4 megabytes" in the last line of paragraph 7.

❷ Press **[Ins]**. The word "Typeover" appears on the left side of the status bar at the bottom of the screen, replacing the document name.

❸ Type **2.5**. With typeover mode on, the new characters replace, or type over, the original characters at the cursor. See Figure 2-43.

typeover mode

Figure 2-43
Typeover mode after
new text replaced
old text

new text

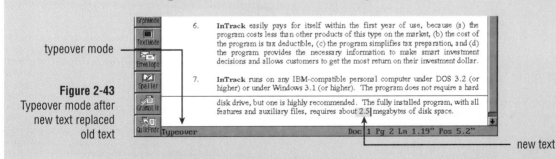

❹ Press **[Ins]** to turn off typeover mode and return to insert mode.

Inserting a Hard Page Break

Look at Liz's question at the bottom of Figure 2-1: "Dave, what about other hardware options?" In response to this question, David decides to add a paragraph at the end of the product description.

To add a paragraph to the memo:

❶ Press **[Home]**, **[Home]**, **[↓]** to move the cursor to the end of the document.

❷ Press **[Enter]** twice to double-space between paragraph 7 and the new paragraph you're about to type.

● Type paragraph number 8, as shown in Figure 2-44. Don't forget to indent after the paragraph number and to make the word "InTrack" boldface. When you're finished, your screen should look like Figure 2-44.

Figure 2-44
Document after
adding new
paragraph

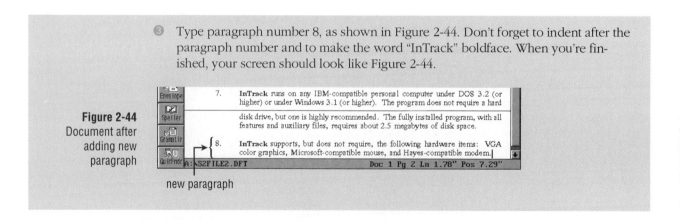

new paragraph

This last paragraph completes the text of the memo. But notice that some or all of paragraph 7 is split between page 1 and page 2. (On your screen, paragraph 7 might not be split between the two pages because of differences in font sizes. Even if it is not split, continue reading and follow the next set of steps.) David doesn't want a page break within a numbered paragraph, so he decides to use what is called a hard page break just before paragraph 7. A **hard page break** is a format code that forces the text following it onto the next page. Even if a page had only one line of text in it before a hard page break, the text on the page will end at that point, and the text that follows will go onto the next page. WordPerfect marks the location of a hard page break with a double horizontal line that extends across the width of the screen.

Let's insert a hard page break to force paragraph 7 and the text that follows it onto the next page.

To insert a hard page break:

● Move the cursor to the "7" at the beginning of paragraph 7.

● Choose **L**ayout, **A**lignment, Hard **P**age or press **[Ctrl][Enter]** (Hard Page) to force paragraph 7 onto the next page. The hard page break appears on the screen. See Figure 2-45.

cursor on page 2 ——

Figure 2-45
Document after
inserting hard page
break

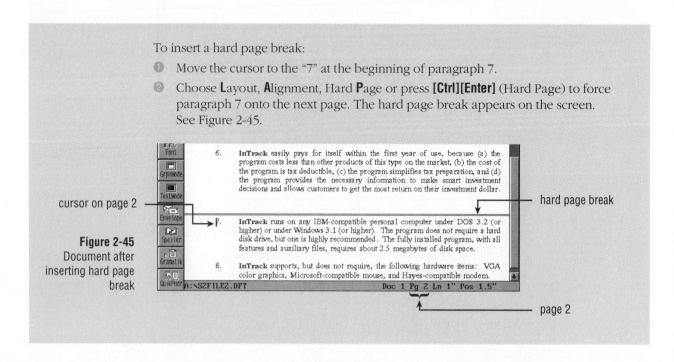

—— hard page break

—— page 2

The format code for a hard page break is [HPg]. You can treat this code as you have the other codes you've already learned about. For example, to delete a hard page break, you would move the cursor to the location of the page break, turn on Reveal Codes, move the cursor to the [HPg] code, and press [Del] to delete it.

Checking the Spelling in a Document

David's memo still contains misspelled words and other typographical errors, commonly called "typos." You can catch most misspellings and typos by running the **speller** — a WordPerfect feature that checks the spelling within a document — as Liz suggested to David in the first paragraph of the memo. When you run the speller, WordPerfect checks each word in your document against the WordPerfect **dictionary**, which is a file on your hard disk.

Running the Speller

Let's correct the spelling errors in David's memo by using the speller.

To run the speller:

❶ Choose **T**ools, **W**riting Tools, and **1** (**S**peller), or press **[Ctrl][F2]** (Speller), or click the Speller button on the button bar. WordPerfect displays the Speller dialog box. See Figure 2-46.

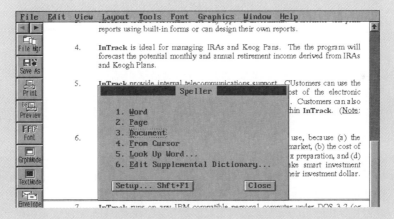

Figure 2-46
Speller dialog box

❷ Choose **3** (**D**ocument) to check the spelling in the entire document. WordPerfect automatically starts checking from the beginning of the document, no matter where the cursor is. Other options in the Speller dialog box allow you to check the spelling for different-sized chunks of text.

Skipping a Word Not Found in the Dictionary

The first "misspelled" word detected by WordPerfect is "Truong" (Figure 2-47). Although "Truong" is spelled correctly, it is not in WordPerfect's dictionary. WordPerfect highlights the word to flag it as a potential error and divides the screen in two, with the document window on top and the Speller window on the bottom. The current "misspelled" word and a list of suggested spellings appear in the Word Not Found dialog box within the Speller window. Because we don't want to change "Truong" to any of the suggested spellings, let's tell WordPerfect to skip this word from now on.

"misspelled" word ——

Speller window ——

Figure 2-47
Speller window with
"misspelled" word

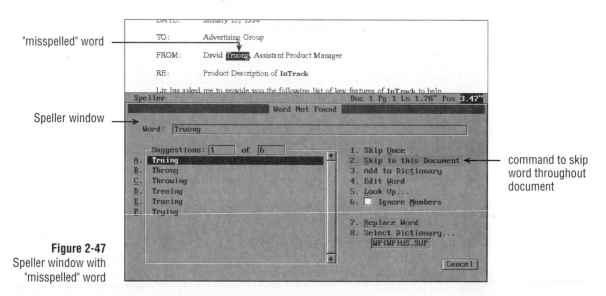

command to skip
word throughout
document

To skip a word not found in WordPerfect's dictionary:

❶ Choose **2** (**S**kip in this Document). This option tells WordPerfect to skip all occurrences of the word "Truong" in the remainder of the document. WordPerfect next stops at "InTrack." This is another example of a correctly spelled word that isn't in WordPerfect's dictionary.

❷ Choose **2** (**S**kip in this Document) to skip this and all future occurrences of "InTrack" in this document.

WordPerfect continues checking words in the document against words in the dictionary until it comes to the next word not found in the dictionary.

Selecting a Suggested Spelling

The first word that David actually misspelled is "investemnt." WordPerfect highlights the word, gives a suggested spelling ("investment"), and displays the Word Not Found dialog box within the Speller window (Figure 2-48).

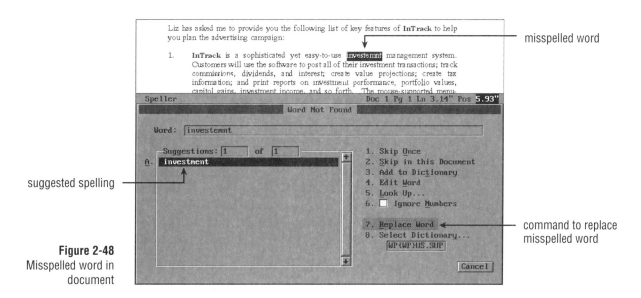

Figure 2-48
Misspelled word in
document

suggested spelling

misspelled word

command to replace
misspelled word

In the following steps, you'll select a replacement word from the Speller window. WordPerfect will then replace the misspelled word in the document with the word you selected.

To select a suggested spelling from the dictionary window:

● Press the letter key that corresponds to the letter next to the correct word in the Speller window. In this example, press **A** or **a**. WordPerfect immediately replaces the misspelled word with "investment" and continues the spell checking.

Note that WordPerfect provides other ways of replacing the misspelled word with a suggested word. For example, with the desired suggested word highlighted, you can choose 7 (Replace Word).

The next misspelled word is "certificats." WordPerfect displays two suggested words in the Speller window, as shown in Figure 2-49.

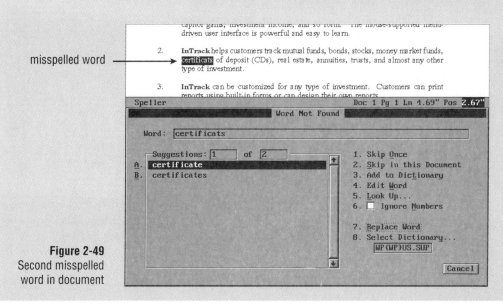

misspelled word

Figure 2-49
Second misspelled
word in document

② Choose "certificates" from the Speller window to replace the misspelled word. You can choose "certificates" by pressing **B**, by using the arrow keys or the mouse to highlight the word and then choosing **7** (**R**eplace Word) or pressing **[Enter]** because Replace Word is the default option, or by double-clicking the mouse pointer on the word.

Skipping a Word Once

WordPerfect next stops at the word "CDs," an abbreviation for "certificates of deposit," and presents a list of possible words in the Speller window (Figure 2-50). Since none of these words is correct, let's tell WordPerfect to skip this word once but flag any later occurrence of "CDs" or "cds" in the document.

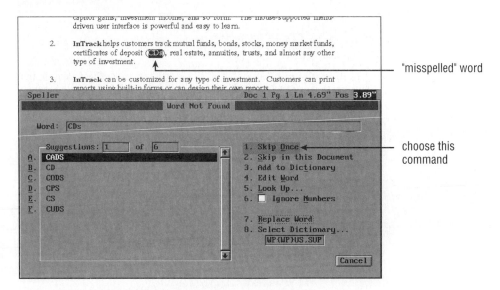

"misspelled" word

choose this command

Figure 2-50
Using the Skip Once command in speller

To skip a word once:

① Choose **1** (Skip **O**nce). This option tells WordPerfect that you want to skip the word this time, but stop at any future occurrences.

The next "misspelled" word is "IRAs."

② Choose **2** (**S**kip in this Document) to skip this and all future occurrences of "IRAs" in the document.

As a general rule, you should choose 1 (Skip Once) if there's a chance that the flagged word may actually be a misspelling later in the document. Choose 2 (Skip in this Document) if you know that the word will appear again later in the document but you don't want the speller to flag it.

Editing a Misspelled Word

WordPerfect next stops at the word "Keog" and displays several suggested words in the Speller window (Figure 2-51). The correct word is "Keogh," which is the name of a retirement investment plan. In this case, "Keog" is not a correct spelling, nor is the correct spelling found in the WordPerfect dictionary. Thus, you need to edit the word so that it is spelled correctly.

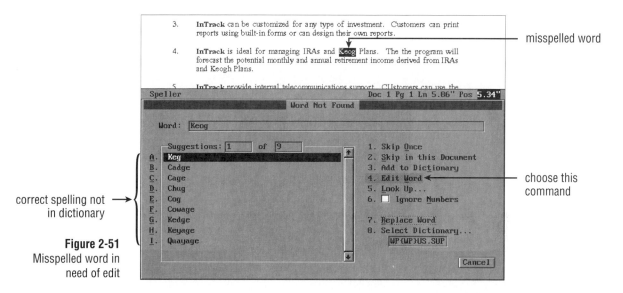

misspelled word

choose this
command

correct spelling not
in dictionary

Figure 2-51
Misspelled word in
need of edit

To edit a misspelled word:

① Choose **4** (Edit **W**ord). The cursor moves into the document window at the beginning of the misspelled word, and the Speller dialog box prompts you to press [F7] or [Enter] when you have corrected the word.

② Move the cursor to the right of "Keog," type **h** to make the word "Keogh," and press **[F7]** (Exit) or **[Enter]** to exit the document window and return to the speller.

The word is now spelled correctly. However, it's still not in the WordPerfect dictionary, so it remains highlighted.

③ Choose **2** (**S**kip in this Document) to skip this and all future occurrences of the word "Keogh" in the document.

Correcting Duplicate Words

WordPerfect next stops at the duplicate words "The the" and displays the Duplicate Word Found dialog box (Figure 2-52).

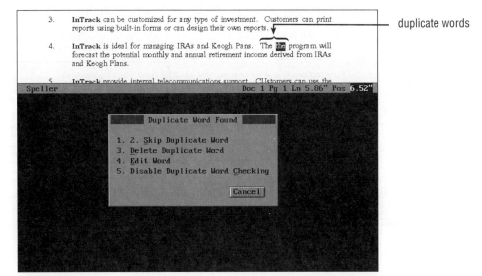

duplicate words

Figure 2-52
Duplicate Word
Found dialog box

To correct duplicate words:

🔵 Press **3** (**D**elete Duplicate Word) to delete the second occurrence of the word "the."

You would choose option 1 or 2 if you wanted to skip the duplicate words and leave both words in your document. You would choose one of the other options if you wanted to edit the duplicate word or if you wanted WordPerfect to stop checking for duplicate words.

Your document now has only "The" instead of "The the" in Paragraph 4 of the document.

Correcting Irregular Case

The next typo that WordPerfect encounters is an irregular case error. An **irregular case** error is a word that has some lowercase letters and one or more uppercase letters after the initial letter. When David typed the rough draft of the memo, he accidentally held the Shift key down too long and typed "CUstomer" instead of "Customer." When such an error occurs, WordPerfect highlights the affected word and displays the Irregular Case dialog box (Figure 2-53).

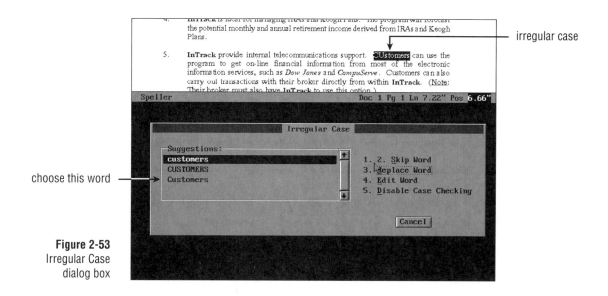

Figure 2-53
Irregular Case
dialog box

To correct irregular case:

❶ Choose "Customers" from the list of suggestions by highlighting it and then choosing **3** (**R**eplace Word) or pressing **[Enter]**, or by double-clicking that word.

❷ Continue through the spell check. When the speller stops at any other word not found in the dictionary (such as "CompuServe," "VGA," or "Microsoft"), choose **1** (Skip **O**nce) or **2** (**S**kip in this Document). Repeat this step until the speller reaches the end of the document.

❸ After spell checking is complete, choose OK to close the Speller window and return to full document window.

You have now completed spell checking the document.

Checking for Misused Words

Keep in mind that the WordPerfect speller checks only spelling, not meaning or usage. For example, in paragraph 1 of his memo, David used the word "capitol," which means a building in which a legislature convenes, instead of "capital," which means assets or wealth. WordPerfect doesn't have a program to help you catch this type of error, so you must carefully proofread your document for correct usage. Let's correct the error now.

To correct a misused word:

① Move the cursor to the "o" in "capitol" in paragraph 1 of the memo.

② Press **[Ins]** to turn on typeover mode.

③ Type **a** to change "capitol" to "capital."

④ Press **[Ins]** to toggle back to insert mode.

Using the Thesaurus

David is now ready to address Liz's last suggestion. In paragraph 1, David used the verb "create" twice in the same series of items. Liz thinks this is repetitious and suggests he choose better words. He agrees but isn't sure what words to use instead, so he decides to use WordPerfect's thesaurus to help him. The **thesaurus** is a WordPerfect program that contains a list of words and their synonyms and antonyms.

To use the thesaurus:

① Move the cursor to the first occurrence of "create" on the third or fourth line of the first numbered paragraph.

The cursor can be anywhere in the word or at the space just after the word.

② Choose Tools, Writing Tools, **2** (Thesaurus) or press **[Alt][F1]** (Writing Tools) and then choose **2** (Thesaurus). WordPerfect displays the Thesaurus dialog box, which contains a list of the synonyms and antonyms of "create." See Figure 2-54. You will see only a partial list; you must scroll the list to see all the synonyms and antonyms.

selected word

synonyms

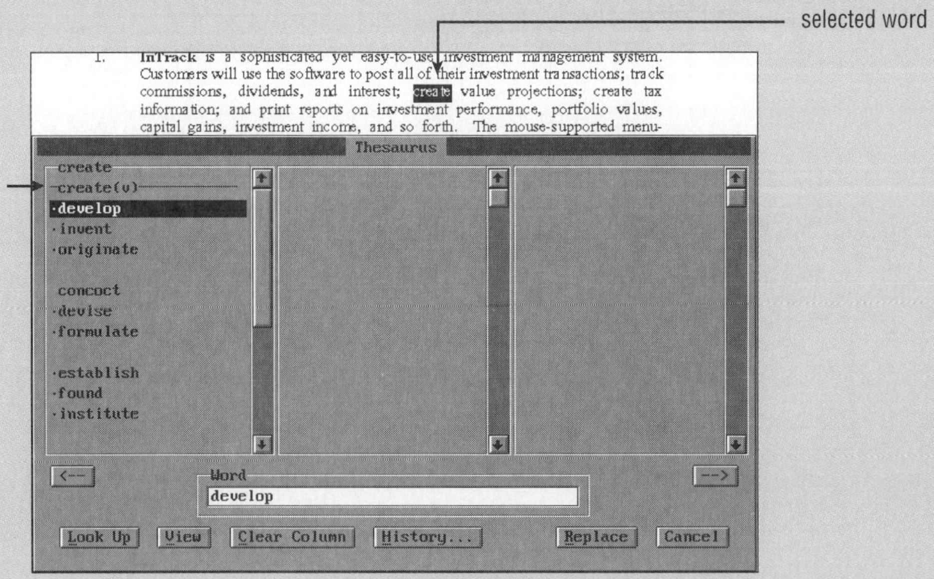

Figure 2-54
Thesaurus dialog
box for "create"

3️⃣ Scroll through the list of words until the antonym "destroy" appears at the bottom of the list. See Figure 2-55.

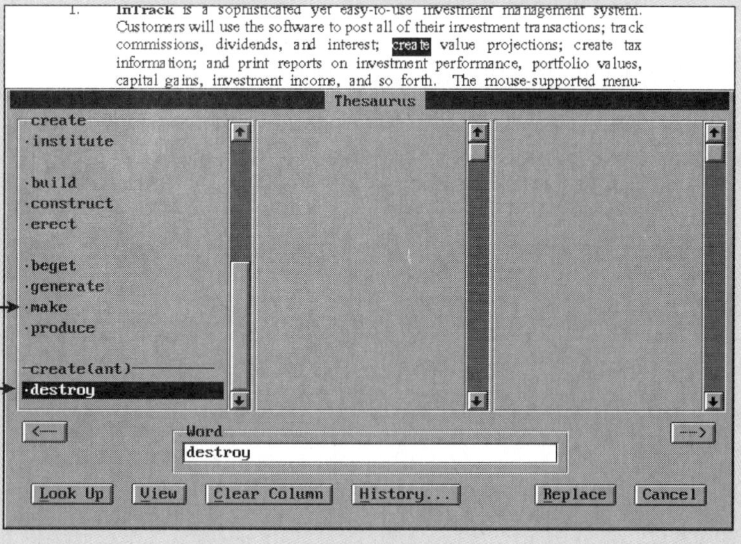

choose this word →

antonym →

Figure 2-55
List of synonyms
and antonyms after
scrolling to bottom

David looks over the synonyms and decides that the word "make" is the best choice to replace "create."

4️⃣ Highlight the word "make" in the list of words and then choose **R**eplace.

WordPerfect makes the replacement and closes the Thesaurus window. David decides to replace the second occurrence of "create" as well. Because WordPerfect closes the Thesaurus window after an option is chosen from the Thesaurus dialog box, David has to reissue the Thesaurus command.

5️⃣ Move the cursor to the second occurrence of "create" in the same paragraph and execute the Thesaurus command.

David looks at the list again and decides to use "generate" this time.

6️⃣ From the list of words in the Thesaurus dialog box, highlight "generate" and choose **R**eplace.

As you can see, the thesaurus is a powerful tool to help you increase your word power as you write.

Using the Grammar Checker

Just to make sure his document is as polished as possible, David decides to run Grammatik, WordPerfect's grammar checker and style analysis program. Grammatik is an aid, but by no means a cure-all, for grammatical and stylistic problems. In fact, Grammatik works best for those writers who are already familiar with the basic rules of grammar and style. As you'll see, Grammatik makes many suggestions that may or may not be appropriate for your document.

Let's execute Grammatik now to analyze David's memo.

To execute Grammatik:

● Choose **T**ools, **W**riting Tools, **3** (**G**rammatik), or press **[Alt][F1]** (Writing Tools) and choose **3** (**G**rammatik), or click the Grammatik button on the button bar.

The Grammatik program appears on the screen in text mode. See Figure 2-56. The menu bar at the top of the screen provides various options, such as opening a document file from the disk (File), choosing the items that you want Grammatik to check (Checking), setting preferences for the writing style (Preferences), and generating statistics about your document (Statistics). The bar at the bottom of the screen provides a menu of function-key options.

Figure 2-56
Grammatik
grammar checker
screen

default writing style ──→

← menu bar

← list of options

The Preferences item on the menu bar allows you to select the writing style that is appropriate to the type of document you are writing. These styles include General (standard formality), Business Letter, Memo, Report, Technical, Documentation, Proposal, Journalism, Advertising, and Fiction. The main difference in how Grammatik checks your document in these writing styles is in the level of formality. For example, in the formal writing style of a business letter or a report, Grammatik flags any contractions ("can't," "won't"), jargon, and colloquial language. In the informal writing style of advertising, on the other hand, Grammatik doesn't flag these constructions. For most documents, you can accept the default writing style, General, as shown in Figure 2-56.

Because David doesn't want to change any of the default settings in Grammatik, he proceeds to checking his document.

To start checking a document with Grammatik:

● Choose **C**hecking, Interactive from the menu bar or choose **I**nteractive Check by pressing the letter **I** or by clicking anywhere within the phrase "Interactive Check" at the bottom of the screen. This command checks potential grammar and style problems one at a time and allows you to interactively modify your text based on Grammatik's suggestions. It works similarly to WordPerfect's speller. The first flagged problem is the "misspelling" of "Truong." See Figure 2-57.

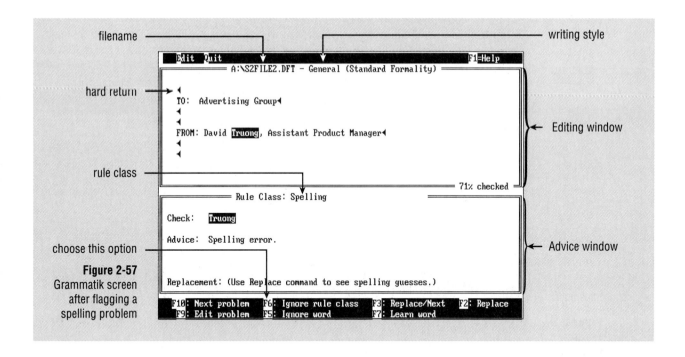

Figure 2-57
Grammatik screen
after flagging a
spelling problem

Whenever Grammatik finds a potential problem in your document, a screen similar to the one shown in Figure 2-57 appears. The list of function-key commands at the bottom of the screen provides various options for handling the problem. You can also execute these commands using the Edit pull-down menu at the top of the screen.

In Figure 2-57, the top window, called the Editing window, displays a portion of your document and highlights the word or phrase in which Grammatik has detected a potential problem. In the Editing window, hard returns are marked by the left arrow head (◀). At the top of the Editing window, Grammatik displays the filename of your document (if it has a filename) and lists the writing style used in checking the document. The bottom window, called the Advice window, displays an explanation of the problem and a suggestion for correcting it.

Grammatik uses 58 rule classes to detect potential grammatical and stylistic problems in your documents. A **rule class** is a general rule relating to correct usage in instances such as subject/verb agreement, possessive form, split infinitive, capitalization, spelling, punctuation, passive voice, wordiness, and cliches. The Advice window lists the rule class for the current problem Grammatik has detected.

As you can see in Figure 2-57, the current rule class is Spelling. Because you have already checked the spelling in this memo, you can disable this rule class so Grammatik doesn't flag potential spelling errors.

To continue checking the document:

◐ Choose **[F6]** (Ignore Rule Class). You can choose this option by pressing [F6] or by clicking on the phrase.

Grammatik now scans for the next problem and stops at a potential subject-verb dis-agreement. See Figure 2-58. The program has incorrectly interpreted "easy-to-use" as the verb "use." Grammatik proposes that the phrase "InTrack use" should be "InTrack uses," but of course that's not what David wants in the memo. Since this is a false error, you can ignore it by skipping the problem. To skip a false error, choose [F10].

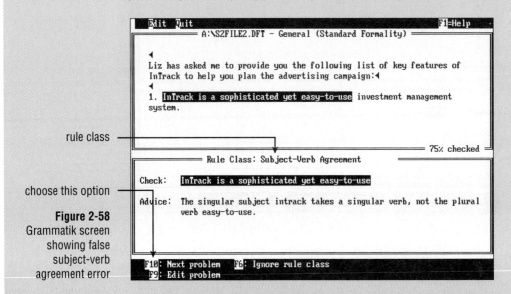

rule class ⎯

choose this option ⎯

Figure 2-58
Grammatik screen
showing false
subject-verb
agreement error

②   Choose **[F10]** (Next Problem).

Now Grammatik marks "a sophisticated" as a potential problem. In reality, the sentence has no problems, so you can again skip this suggestion.

③   Choose **[F10]** (Next Problem) to ignore the false error.

④   Choose **[F10]** (Next Problem) for the next two suggestions (regarding the use of a semicolon to join independent clauses and the problem about "and") because both are false errors.

Now Grammatik finds the problem of a paragraph with only one sentence (paragraph 2). This is normally not a good practice, but in this case, because each paragraph is an item in a numbered list, we want to ignore this occurrence here and throughout the document. Let's instruct Grammatik to ignore this rule class.

⑤   Choose **[F6]** (Ignore rule class).

Next, Grammatik finds a serious grammatical error — the disagreement between subject and verb in "InTrack provide." See Figure 2-59.

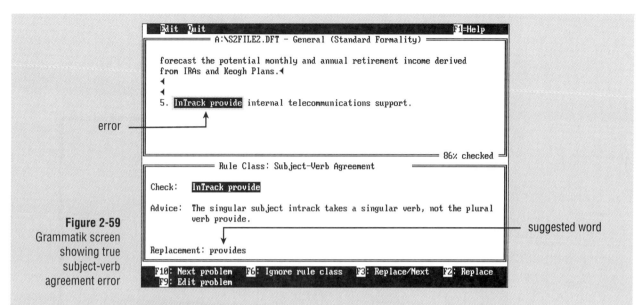

Figure 2-59
Grammatik screen
showing true
subject-verb
agreement error

error ⟶

suggested word ⟶

Screen text:

Edit Quit   F1=Help
══ A:\S2FILE2.DFT – General (Standard Formality) ══

forecast the potential monthly and annual retirement income derived
from IRAs and Keogh Plans.◀
◀
◀
5. InTrack provide internal telecommunications support.

══ 86% checked ══

══ Rule Class: Subject-Verb Agreement ══

Check: InTrack provide

Advice: The singular subject intrack takes a singular verb, not the plural
          verb provide.

Replacement: provides

F10: Next problem   F6: Ignore rule class   F3: Replace/Next   F2: Replace
F9: Edit problem

⑥ Choose **[F3]** (Replace/Next) to replace "provide" with "provides" and go to the next problem.

Continue choosing **[F10]** (Next Problem) for all the remaining problems that Grammatik flags.

After checking the entire document, Grammatik displays the message "You have turned off some rule classes," and allows you to save these changes.

⑧ Choose **N**o. The grammar checking screen is displayed.

⑨ Choose **Q**uit Grammatik.

This ends your Grammatik session and returns you to WordPerfect. You should now read paragraph 5 to verify that Grammatik changed the word "provide" to "provides."

Saving the Final Version of the Document

David has now completed all the changes that Liz suggested. Your sample memo should look like Figure 2-60.

DATE: January 15, 1994

TO: Advertising Group

FROM: David Truong, Assistant Product Manager

RE: Product Description of **InTrack**

Liz has asked me to provide you the following list of key features of **InTrack** to help you plan the advertising campaign:

1.   **InTrack** is a sophisticated yet easy-to-use investment management system. Customers will use the software to post all of their investment transactions; track commissions, dividends, and interest; make value projections; generate tax information; and print reports on investment performance, portfolio values, capital gains, investment income, and so forth. The mouse-supported menu-driven user interface is powerful and easy to learn.

2.   **InTrack** helps customers track mutual funds, bonds, stocks, money market funds, certificates of deposit (CDs), real estate, annuities, trusts, and almost any other type of investment.

3.   **InTrack** can be customized for any type of investment. Customers can print reports using built-in forms or can design their own reports.

4.   **InTrack** is ideal for managing IRAs and Keogh Plans. The program will forecast the potential monthly and annual retirement income derived from IRAs and Keogh Plans.

5.   **InTrack** provides internal telecommunications support. Customers can use the program to get on-line financial information from most of the electronic information services, such as *Dow Jones* and *CompuServe*. Customers can also carry out transactions with their broker directly from within **InTrack**. (<u>Note</u>: Their broker must also have **InTrack** to use this option.)

6.   **InTrack** easily pays for itself within the first year of use, because (a) the program costs less than other products of this type on the market, (b) the cost of the program is tax deductible, (c) the program simplifies tax preparation, and (d) the program provides the necessary information to make smart investment decisions and allows customers to get the most return on their investment dollar.

Figure 2-60
Final printout of
David's memo
(continued on next
page)

7. **InTrack** runs on any IBM-compatible personal computer under DOS 3.2 (or higher) or under Windows 3.1 (or higher). The program does not require a hard disk drive, but one is highly recommended. The fully installed program, with all features and auxiliary files, requires about 2.5 megabytes of disk space.

8. **InTrack** supports, but does not require, the following hardware items: VGA color graphics, Microsoft-compatible mouse, and Hayes-compatible modem.

Figure 2-60
Final printout of David's memo (continued from previous page)

After editing any document, you should save it to your disk; otherwise, the disk copy of the document will still be the previous version, without any of the corrections you made since your last save. In this case, let's assume David wants to keep a record of his original rough draft (C2FILE1.DFT) and the most recently saved version (S2FILE2.DFT). He saves the *final* version of the memo as S2FILE3.MEM.

To save the final version of the document:

① Make sure your WordPerfect data disk is still in drive A.

② Choose **F**ile, Save **A**s, or press **[F10]** (Save As), or click the Save As button on the button bar.

WordPerfect displays the Save Document 1 dialog box.

③ Type the new filename **a:\s2file3.mem** and press **[Enter]**.

WordPerfect saves the final version of the memo to your disk using the filename S2FILE3.MEM. See Figure 2-61.

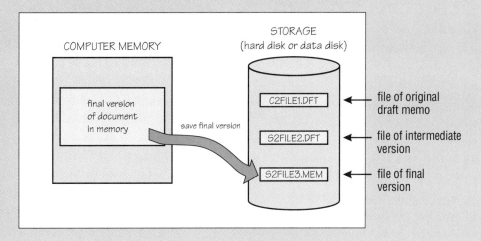

Figure 2-61
Saving the third version of the document disk

Printing Multiple Copies of a Document

David's final task is to print three copies of the memo. He could simply execute the Print command three times, but there is an easier way. Let's use WordPerfect's Number of Copies feature to print three copies of the memo.

To print multiple copies of a document:

❶ Choose **F**ile, **P**rint/Fax, or press **[Shift][F7]** (Print/Fax), or click the Print button on the button bar.

WordPerfect displays the Print/Fax menu. See Figure 2-62.

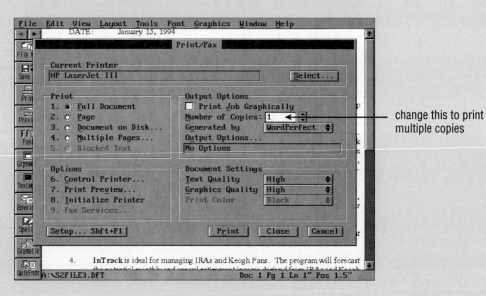

Figure 2-62
Print/Fax dialog box

❷ Choose N (**N**umber of Copies), type **3**, and press **[Enter]** to set the number of copies to 3. Alternatively, you can use the small up arrow located to the right of the number of copies. Click this up arrow twice to change the number of copies from 1 to 3.

❸ Make sure **1** (**F**ull Document) is selected (the circle after the 1 is darkened) and choose P**r**int. WordPerfect prints three copies of the memo.

This completes Tutorial 2. If you want to exit WordPerfect, choose File, Exit WP or press [Home], [F7] (Exit). The Exit WordPerfect dialog box appears on the screen. Because you've already saved the final version of the memo, choose Exit to leave WordPerfect.

■   ■   ■

Exercises

1. Which key(s) do you press to move the cursor in the following directions?
   a. To the beginning of the document
   b. To the end of the document
   c. One word to the left
   d. One word to the right
   e. To the left side of the screen
   f. To the right side of the screen

2. Describe what you would do to change the right margin of a document to 1.5 inches.

3. Write a list of steps required to do the following:
   a. Turn on underlining
   b. Turn off underlining
   c. Turn on italics
   d. Turn off italics
   e. Turn on boldfacing
   f. Turn off boldfacing
   g. Change the font

4. What would you do to see the format code that marks the location where you changed the margins within a document?

5. What is the WordPerfect code for each of the following?
   a. Soft return
   b. Hard return
   c. Soft page break
   d. Hard page break
   e. Tab (normal left tab)
   f. Change in the Left Margin

6. Explain the meaning of the following WordPerfect terms:
   a. Full justification
   b. Left justification
   c. Center justification
   d. Right justification

7. Explain the difference between [Tab] and [F4] (Indent).

8. What is the difference between a soft return and a hard return?

9. Explain the difference between insert mode and typeover mode. What key do you press to change from one mode to the other?

10. What key(s) do you press to force a page break? Why would you want to do this?

11. What key(s) do you press to delete the following portions of a document? *Hint:* See Figure 2-39.
    a. The word at the cursor
    b. From the cursor to the end of the line
    c. From the cursor to the beginning of a word
    d. From the cursor to the end of a word

12. After you've carried out an editing action in WordPerfect, how to you undo it?

13. After you've deleted a word or a phrase, how do you undelete, or restore, the word or phrase?

14. How many instances of deleted text does WordPerfect save for future undelete operations?

15 Name at least three types of errors that WordPerfect's speller can find.

16. If you type the sentence "That is just to bad!" and then run the speller, why won't the speller detect the incorrect usage of the word "to?"

17. What WordPerfect feature can you use to detect errors of the type given in the previous question?

18. Besides synonyms, what does the WordPerfect thesaurus list?

19. What procedure would you follow to print five copies of a memo?

20. Define the word "toggle" as it applies to WordPerfect commands.

Tutorial Assignments

In the following Tutorial Assignments, make sure you clear the document window before opening each file. Open the file T2FILE1.DFT and do the following:

1. Change the justification from left to full for the entire document.

2. Change the spaces after "MEMO TO:," "FROM:," and "SUBJECT:," to tabs, so that the text opposite these words is vertically aligned.

3. In the numbered paragraphs, change the tabs to indents.

4. Use the WordPerfect speller to correct misspelled words, duplicate words, and irregular case words.

5. Use Grammatik to check the grammar and style of the document. Make changes to the document in response to grammatical errors, but ignore the suggested problems with style.

6. Carefully read the document and make a list of the words that are "misspelled" or incorrectly used but that the speller and Grammatik failed to flag. Edit the document to correct these words.

7. Save the document as S2FILE4.MEM.

8. Print the document.

Open the file T2FILE2.DFT and do the following:

9. Use the thesaurus to substitute another word for the word "obtuse." Use a more common word that has approximately the same meaning.

10. Use the thesaurus to list the antonym(s) of the word "truculent," then reword the sentence using an antonym.

11. Save the document as S2FILE5.MEM.

12. Print three copies of the document by changing the Number of Copies option in the Print/Fax dialog box.

Open the file T2FILE3.DOC and do the following:

13. Change the font for the document to a Times Roman-type font.

14. Insert a hard page break after the date (March 1994), so that the first several lines, down to the date, become a title page and the rest of the document is on a separate page.

15. At the beginning of the second page, just after the page break, change the justification to full.

16. Center justify the title page.

17. Save the document as S2FILE6.DOC.

18. Print one copy of the document.

Open the file T2FILE4.DFT and do the following:

19. After the first paragraph to the right of the colon, type "I'm impressed! InTrack helped me dramatically improve the earnings on my investments." Make "InTrack" boldface.

20. Use typeover mode to change the number "6,438.15" to "5,892.46."

21. Run the speller to correct the typos in the document.

22. Save the document as S2FILE7.MEM.

23. Print one copy of the document.

Open the file T2FILE5.DOC and do the following *in the order given*:

24. Turn on Reveal Codes and make a handwritten list of all the format codes you can see in the document.

25. Clear the document window, then type the list of format codes you found. Type only one code per line.

26. Number each code in the list and indent ([F4]) after each number.

27. After each format code, type a colon (:), then type the meaning of the code.

28. Save the document as S2CODES.DOC.

29. Print the document.

Case Problems

1. Intelligent Inventions, Inc.

Roger Plunkett has always wanted to market one of his inventions. He sees an advertisement in the newspaper from Intelligent Inventions, Inc. offering help in marketing new inventions. He decides to write a letter to find out more about the company and about marketing new products.

Open the file P2INVENT.DFT and do the following:

1. Set the entire document to full justification.

2. Change the font to Times Roman or a similar font.

3. Change the left margin to 1.5 inches.

4. Change the date in the document to the current date.

5. Number the three paragraphs that ask a question. Indent all the lines of the paragraph *after* the paragraph number.

6. After the third numbered question, add a fourth numbered paragraph with the following question: "Does the inventor retain the patent (if any) for the new invention?"

7. In the second question, use the thesaurus to pick a better word for "promulgate."

8. Run the speller to correct any typos and spelling errors.

9. Run Grammatik to correct any grammatical errors.

10. Proofread the document for errors that the speller and Grammatik might have missed.

11. Save the document as S2INVENT.LET.

12. Use WordPerfect's number of copies feature to print two copies of the letter.

2. LawnTools, Inc.

Sujat Jahmiel works as a product manager for LawnTools, Inc. He would like to begin marketing a line of low-cost, environmentally safe push-mowers. He feels that the product has significant market potential, but he must get approval from the members of the Corporate Products group. He decides to send them each a memo extolling the virtues of his proposed push-mower.

Open the file P2LAWN.DFT and do the following:

1. Set the font to Times Roman or one of its variations.

2. Change the left margin to 1.5 inches.

3. Change the justification to full.

4. Change the date of the document to the current date.

5. Insert tabs between "FROM:" and "Sujat Jahmiel" so his name is aligned above the SUBJECT information.

6. After the SUBJECT information (following the comma at the end of the line), insert the name of the product in boldface type: "SwiftBlade."

7. In the numbered paragraphs, change the [Lft Tab] codes to [Lft Indent] codes.

8. At the beginning of numbered paragraph 2, insert the phrase "According to *Consumer Report.*" Type the name of the magazine in italics. Type a comma after the name of the magazine and change the "T" in "Today" to a lowercase "t."

9. Using typeover mode, change the value in paragraph 2 from $139 to $150.

10. To ensure that the final paragraph of the document is not split between two pages, insert a hard page break before the paragraph.

11. Run the speller to correct any typographical and spelling errors.

12. Save the memo as S2LAWN.MEM.

13. Use WordPerfect's Number of Copies feature to print two copies of the memo.

3. Buñuelos

Luz Reyes is the chief executive officer for Buñuelos, a successful Puerto-Rican restaurant chain of eight stores. She has arranged a meeting with the members of the board of directors to discuss company growth and set goals for the future. She prepares a short report describing company performance over the past fiscal year.

Open the file P2BUNUEL.REP and do the following:

1. Change the justification to center, so that the title and the author's name at the beginning of the report will be centered.

2. After the author's name, change the justification back to left, so that the remainder of the report will be left-justified.

3. Below the title, set the left and right margins to 2.0 inches.

4. Change the font in your report to any other font of your choosing.

5. Save the report as S2BUNUEL.REP.

6. Use WordPerfect's Number of Copies feature to print three copies of the report.

Tutorial 3

Using Additional Editing Features

Writing an Inventory Observation Memo

Case: Sorority Designs, Inc.

Melissa Walborsky graduated last June with a degree in accounting and has earned her C.P.A. certificate. She recently began work on the auditing staff at McDermott & Eston, an accounting firm in Syracuse, New York. One of Melissa's first assignments is an audit of Sorority Designs, Inc. (SDI), a clothing company that markets stylish apparel designed for college-age women. As a member of the audit team, she observed the inventory at SDI's warehouse in Syracuse. Susan Guttmann, Melissa's manager, has asked her to write the inventory observation memo for the audit working papers (documents that verify the nature of an audit and the results). Melissa will write a first draft of the memo. Then, based upon her own proofreading, she will revise the memo. Finally, she will submit her draft to Susan for approval, in accordance with the established policy for all McDermott & Eston documents.

OBJECTIVES

In this tutorial you will learn to:

- Align text flush right

- Center a line of text between the left and right margins

- Search and replace text

- Use block operations to change the appearance of existing text

- Use block operations to move, delete, and copy text

- Drag and drop text to move or copy it

Planning the Document

Before writing the memo, Melissa looks at her own notes, the audit working papers, and several other inventory observation memos to help her determine the content, organization, style, and format of her document.

Content

Melissa decides to base the content of her memo primarily on her notes (Figure 3-1) and her personal recollection of the inventory.

Organization

Melissa's document will follow the standard organizational structure of an inventory observation memo, with the headings **Observation of Inventory Taking, Slow-Moving and Damaged Merchandise, Test Counts, Cutoff Controls,** and **Conclusions.** She determines that the memo needs only one or two paragraphs under each heading.

Style

Melissa decides to use a straightforward writing style. She will also use auditing terminology because her audience will be other accountants at McDermott & Eston.

Figure 3-1
Melissa's handwritten notes from the inventory observation

Inventory Observation, Syracuse warehouse, September 15, 1994

- Arrived 7:20 a.m.
- No merchandise shipped that day.
- Slow moving and damaged merchandise: shipped to Ithaca outlet.
- Periodic test counts on 31% of inventory.
- Cutoff controls: noted apparel received on September 13 and noted no merchandise shipped on September 14.

Format

Melissa decides not to change any of WordPerfect's default format settings. She leaves the margins at one inch on the left, right, top, and bottom and keeps the (default) left justification. Melissa will modify the format of the heading, however, so that the document follows the standard McDermott & Eston format for inventory observation memos.

Opening the Document Using the File Manager

Let's begin by opening Melissa's rough draft of her inventory observation memo. Instead of using the Open command (under File in the main menu bar), let's use WordPerfect's File Manager. The File Manager allows you to display a list of the files on a disk or in a directory and to open, look at (without opening), delete, rename, copy, or print the document files. The advantage of using the File Manager to open a document is that you don't have to remember the exact name of the document file — you can look over the list of filenames and select the one you want. In addition, the File Manager saves you time because you don't have to type the name of the document file — you simply select it and choose Open.

To open the document using the File Manager:

①   Insert your WordPerfect data disk into drive A and make sure the document window is blank.

②   Choose **F**ile, **F**ile Manager, or press **[F5]** (File Manager), or click the File Manager button on the button bar. WordPerfect displays the Specify File Manager List dialog box. See Figure 3-2.

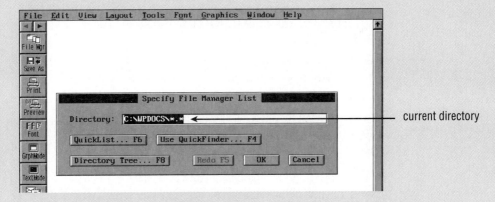

Figure 3-2
Specify File
Manager List
dialog box

current directory

You can now accept the default directory path or type a new directory path to get a directory listing.

③ Type **a:** and press **[Enter]**. WordPerfect displays a File Manager dialog box, similar to the one in Figure 3-3. Your dialog box may show a different list of files.

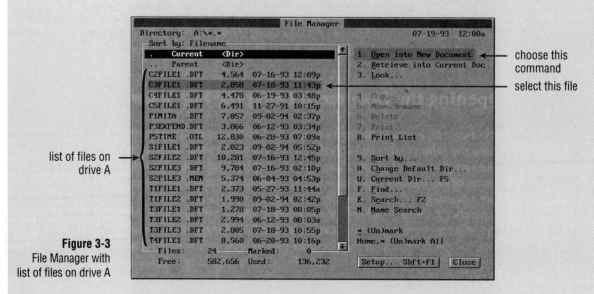

Figure 3-3
File Manager with
list of files on drive A

list of files on
drive A

choose this
command

select this file

④ Highlight the filename C3FILE1.DFT.

You can use the mouse pointer to click on the filename or use the keyboard cursor-movement keys to move the highlight bar to it.

⑤ Choose **1** (**O**pen into New Document).

The rough draft of the inventory observation memo appears in the WordPerfect document window. Your screen will look similar to Figure 3-4.

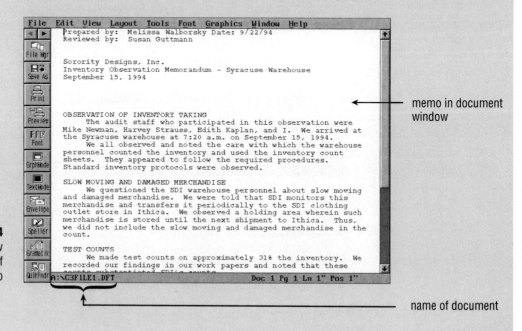

Figure 3-4
Document window
with the first draft of
Melissa's memo

memo in document
window

name of document

Remember that this is Melissa's *rough draft*, which she has not yet revised. It contains formatting, spelling, and other errors. In the following section, Melissa will revise the memo before she submits it to Susan. Take time now to read through the entire document and familiarize yourself with its content and some of its problems (Figure 3-5). Don't make any revisions at this time.

```
Prepared by:  Melissa Walborsky  Date:  9/22/94
Reviewed by:  Susan Guttmann

Sorority Designs, Inc.
Inventory Observation Memorandum - Syracuse Warehouse
September 15, 1994


OBSERVATION OF INVENTORY TAKING
     The audit staff who participated in this observation were
Mike Newman, Harvey Strauss, Edith Kaplan, and I.  We arrived at
the Syracuse warehouse at 7:20 a.m. on September 15, 1994.
     We all observed and noted the care with which the warehouse
personnel counted the inventory and used the inventory count
sheets.  They appeared to follow the required procedures.
Standard inventory protocols were observed.

SLOW MOVING AND DAMAGED MERCHANDISE
     We questioned the SDI warehouse personnel about slow moving
and damaged merchandise.  We were told that SDI monitors this
merchandise and transfers it periodically to the SDI clothing
outlet store in Ithica.  We observed a holding area wherein such
merchandise is stored until the next shipment to Ithica.  Thus,
we did not include the slow moving and damaged merchandise in the
count.

TEST COUNTS
     We made test counts on approximately 31% the inventory.  We
recorded our findings in our work papers and noted that these
counts substantiated SDI's counts.

CUTOFF CONTROLS
     We took time to gain access to and examine the Receipt Log
and the Shipping Log for this warehouse.  We noted the
merchandise received on September 13, 1994; we also noted that no
merchandise was shipped on September 14, 1994. We used the
September 13 numbers for our subsequent purchases and sales
cutoff tests.

Conclusions
     I believe we made an accurate count of all saleable
merchandise in the Syracuse warehouse on September 15, 1994,
because the SDI personnel followed all required procedures and
because the merchandise held for delivery to the Ithica outlet
store was not counted.
```

Figure 3-5
Printed copy of Melissa's memo

Using Flush Right

Melissa begins by observing that in most of the other company memos, the date on the top line of the document appears flush against the right margin. She decides, therefore, to use WordPerfect's Flush Right feature to move the date in her memo. Let's use Flush Right to position the date at the right margin.

To move existing text flush right:

1 Move the cursor to the "D" in "Date" on the first line of the document.

Whenever you use Flush Right, you must position the cursor on the first letter of the word or group of words you want to move.

2 Choose **L**ayout, **A**lignment, **F**lush Right or press **[Alt][F6]** (Flush Right).

The date text moves to the right margin. See Figure 3-6.

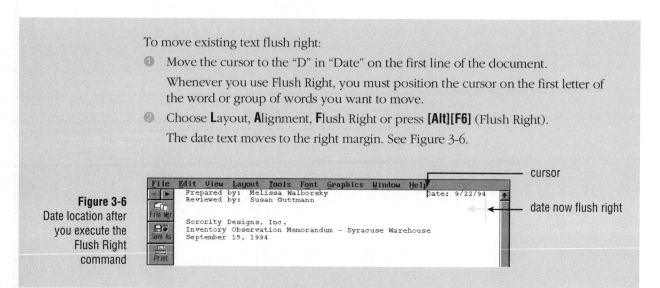

Figure 3-6
Date location after
you execute the
Flush Right
command

cursor

date now flush right

Melissa then decides to add the date that she thinks Susan Guttmann will review the memo, opposite Susan's name.

To type flush-right text:

1 Move the cursor to the end of the second line, after "Susan Guttmann."

2 Choose **L**ayout, **A**lignment, **F**lush Right or press **[Alt][F6]** (Flush Right). The cursor is now at the right margin of the document.

3 Type **Date: 9/26/94**.

Notice that as you type, the cursor stays in the same place rather than moving from left to right. The characters move from right to left, away from the right margin. See Figure 3-7.

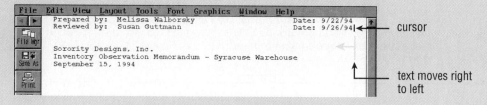

Figure 3-7
Typing the second
date with
Flush Right

cursor

text moves right
to left

Centering Text

Melissa realizes that the three title lines in the inventory observation memo — starting with "Sorority Designs, Inc." and ending with the date of the audit, "September 15, 1994" — should be centered between the left and right margins. Let's use WordPerfect's Center command to format these three lines of text.

To center text:

❶ Move the cursor to the "S" in "Sorority," at the beginning of the third line of the document.

To center any line of existing text, you first place the cursor at the beginning of that line.

❷ Choose **L**ayout, **A**lignment, **C**enter or press **[Shift][F6]** (Center). As soon as you choose the Center command, WordPerfect centers the line of text between the margins. See Figure 3-8.

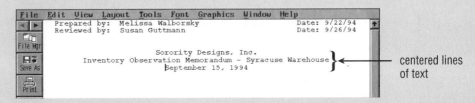

cursor

Figure 3-8
Centered first line of the memo title

line of text centered between left and right margins

❸ Move the cursor to the beginning of the next line.

❹ Choose **L**ayout, **A**lignment, **C**enter or press **[Shift][F6]** (Center).

❺ Use the same procedure to center the last line of the title. See Figure 3-9.

Figure 3-9
Complete memo title centered between the left and right margins

centered lines of text

❻ Turn on Reveal Codes to see the [Flsh Rgt] and [Cnt on Mar] format codes that WordPerfect inserted into the document in this and the previous set of steps. (You will have to move the cursor to the beginning of the document to see the [Flsh Rgt] codes.) After you have viewed the codes, turn off Reveal Codes.

As a general rule, when you want to center many lines of text, such as all the lines on a title page of a report, use the Justification Center command on the Layout menu or press

[Shift][F8], 1 (Line), 2 (Justification), and 2 (Center), which you learned in Tutorial 2. When you want to center only a few lines of text, use the Alignment Center command on the Layout menu or press [Shift][F6] (Center).

Searching for Text

When you're working with a short document — a half page in length, for example — you can find a specific word or phrase or move the cursor to a specific location just by using the cursor-movement keys. But when you're working with a longer document, the best way to find a specific word or phrase or move to a specific location is usually with the Search command. A search is an operation you use to position the cursor at a specified sequence of characters or codes, called the search string. The search string may include a single character, such as "T" or "4"; a format code, such as [Lft Indent] or [HRt]; a word or group of words, such as "inventory" or "shipping log"; or any combination of characters, codes, or words.

Let's look at an example of how you would use the Search command. Melissa notices that in her memo she left out the word "of" after "31%" in the first line under "TEST COUNTS." She decides to use WordPerfect's Search command to move the cursor quickly to that location in the memo.

To search for text:

① Move the cursor to the beginning of the document.

Since you will tell WordPerfect to search *forward* from the cursor to the end of the document, you want to make sure that you find the specified search string, no matter where it is in your document.

② Choose **E**dit, Sear**ch** or press **[F2]** (Search).

WordPerfect displays the Search dialog box (Figure 3-10) and waits for you to enter the search string. If the cursor is not at the beginning of the document, and you want to find text that precedes the location of the cursor, you can perform a Backward Search (also called a Left Search) by pressing [Shift][F2] (Left Search). WordPerfect displays the same dialog box (Figure 3-10), but with Backward Search checked.

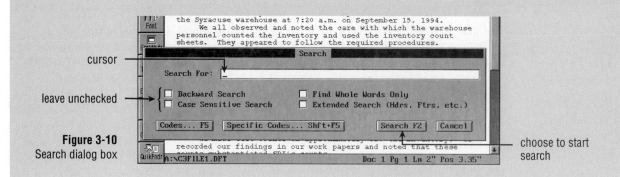

cursor

leave unchecked

Figure 3-10
Search dialog box

choose to start
search

③ Make sure none of the boxes below the Search For text box is checked. You want to search forward, not backward, through the document. You don't need the search to be case-sensitive, because you're going to search for a number. You don't need to find whole words only, and you don't need to carry out an extended search because your search string is in the body of the document, not in a header or footer.

④ Type **31%** into the Search For text box and press **[Enter]**.

⑤ Choose S**e**arch or press **[F2]** (Search).

You can choose Search by pressing [Enter] again (because the dotted box is on the Search button), by pressing the mnemonic "E," by pressing [F2], or by clicking the Search button with the mouse pointer.

WordPerfect searches through the document until it finds the search string — "31%" — and then positions the cursor immediately after it.

⑥ Press **[Spacebar]** and type **of** to add the missing word. See Figure 3-11.

Figure 3-11
Document window after you search for "31%" and insert new text

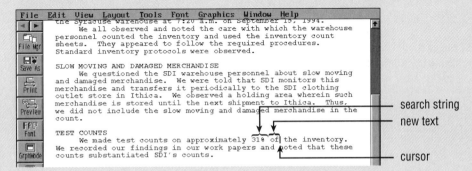

After you have had some practice, you'll find that using the Search command to move the cursor to specific locations within your document is usually much faster than using the cursor-movement keys or the scroll bar.

Searching and Replacing Text

Search and replace, sometimes simply called **replace**, is an operation that searches through a document for a search string and then replaces one or more occurrences of that search string with another specified string, called the **replacement string**. The replacement string, like the search string, can be any combination of characters, codes, or words. You can use search and replace to change one word to another word, one phrase to another phrase, one set of format codes to another set of format codes, and so forth, throughout your document.

Let's use search and replace to change an incorrect word in the inventory observation memo to the correct word. For example, Melissa notices that she misspelled "Ithaca" throughout the document. She can't use WordPerfect's speller to make the correction, because "Ithaca" is not in the speller dictionary. She decides, therefore, to use WordPerfect's Replace feature to search for all occurrences of "Ithica" and replace them with "Ithaca."

To search and replace a string of text:

① Move the cursor to the beginning of the document.

The Replace feature works from the position of the cursor to the end of the document for a forward search. Thus, to perform the operation for an entire document, you need to move the cursor to the beginning of the document.

② Choose **E**dit, Rep**l**ace or press **[Alt][F2]** (Replace). WordPerfect displays the Search and Replace dialog box. See Figure 3-12.

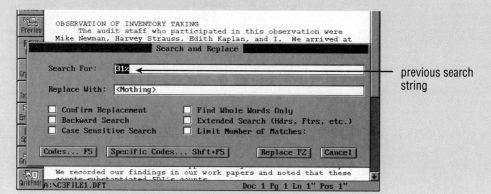

previous search string

Figure 3-12
Search and Replace
dialog box

The contents of the Search For text box is highlighted. The next thing you type will automatically replace the highlighted text.

③ In the Search For text box, type **Ithica** and press **[Enter]** or **[Tab]** to move the cursor to the Replace With text box.

④ Type **Ithaca** and press **[Enter]**. See Figure 3-13.

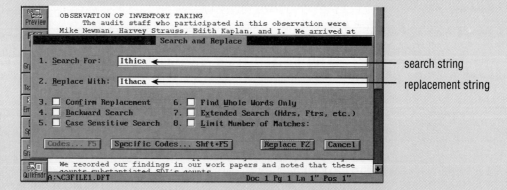

search string

replacement string

Figure 3-13
Search string and
replacement string
in the Search and
Replace dialog box

"Ithica" becomes the new search string and "Ithaca," the correct spelling of the name, becomes the replacement string.

⑤ Make sure the Confirm Replacement check box is not checked. With Confirm Replacement turned off, WordPerfect carries out the search and replace throughout the document. If Confirm Replacement were selected, WordPerfect would stop at each occurrence of "Ithica" and ask for confirmation before replacing it with "Ithaca."

⑥ Choose R**e**place or press **[F2]** (Replace) to initiate the search and replace.

WordPerfect changes all occurrences of "Ithica" to "Ithaca."

A dialog box appears, advising you that the search and replace is completed and telling you the number of replacements.

⑦ Choose OK to close the dialog box and return to the main document window. Your screen should now look like Figure 3-14.

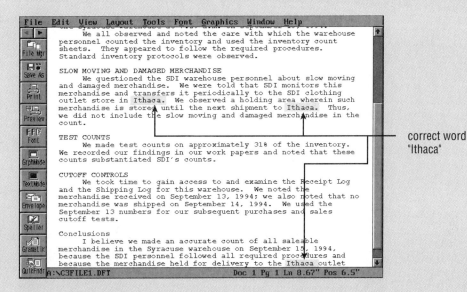

Figure 3-14
Modified words after you perform a search and replace

As Melissa reads through her draft of the memo, she realizes that she has used the word "merchandise" excessively. She decides that in some places she could use the word "apparel" instead, since apparel is the only type of merchandise that SDI sells. To avoid the repetitive use of "merchandise," she performs a search and replace with Confirm Replacement selected. This means that at each occurrence of "merchandise" in the document, WordPerfect will stop and ask her if she wants to replace "merchandise" with "apparel."

In this example, we'll use the search string "merchandise" in all lowercase letters and leave the Case Sensitive Search unselected. This instructs WordPerfect to stop at *all* occurrences of "merchandise," regardless of case. In other words, "Merchandise" and "MERCHANDISE" will both be flagged. If you wanted to search only for "merchandise" (all lowercase) you would select the Case Sensitive Search option.

Let's use search and replace with Confirm Replacement selected to change some of the occurrences of "merchandise" to "apparel." In the following steps, the choice of when to change a word and when to leave it unchanged is based on whatever seems better to Melissa, not on any rules.

To search and replace with confirmation:

① Move the cursor to the beginning of the document and choose **E**dit, Rep**l**ace or press **[Alt][F2]** (Replace).

② Type **merchandise** in the Search For text box and press **[Enter]** or **[Tab]**. The word "merchandise" becomes the search string.

③ Type **apparel** in the Replace With text box and press **[Enter]**.

The word "apparel" becomes the replacement string.

④ Choose **3** (Confirm Replacement) by pressing **3** or **F** or by clicking the check box next to the Confirm Replacement command.

⑤ Choose **R**eplace or press **[F2]** (Replace) to initiate the search and replace.

The cursor now stops at the first occurrence of "merchandise," located in the second heading, and WordPerfect displays the Confirm Replacement dialog box, prompting you to accept or decline the replacement. See Figure 3-15.

Figure 3-15
Highlighted search string when you perform a search and replace with Confirm Replacement

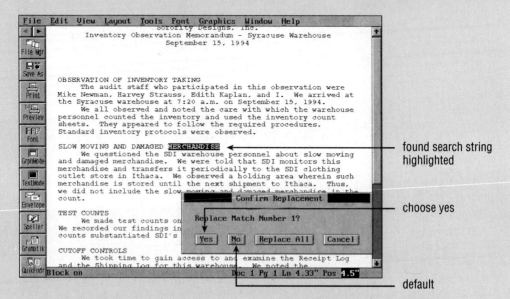

found search string highlighted

choose yes

default

⑥ Choose **Y**es to replace "merchandise" with "apparel" in the second heading.

The default response is **N**o, so you can't press [Enter] to choose **Y**es. Instead, click the Yes button or press **Y**.

The cursor then continues to move to each occurrence of "merchandise," stopping each time for you to accept or decline the replacement. The word "merchandise" occurs four times in the paragraph following the second heading.

⑦ Choose **Y**es to accept the replacement in the first sentence of the paragraph, choose **N**o to decline in the second sentence, choose **N**o again in the third sentence, and choose **Y**es in the last sentence.

⑧ Choose **N**o twice to decline replacement of both occurrences of "merchandise" in the paragraph under "CUTOFF CONTROLS." Choose **Y**es for the first occurrence in the final paragraph, then choose **N**o for the last occurrence.

The search and replace operation is now complete. WordPerfect displays the Search and Replace Complete dialog box, providing you with information on the number of occurrences of the search string and the number of replacements performed. In this example, the search string occurred nine times and was replaced four times.

⑨ Choose **OK** to close the Search and Replace Complete dialog box.

Your document will now look similar to Figure 3-16. The word "Apparel" in the second heading isn't in all uppercase letters as it should be, but you'll fix that problem later. The first letter of "Apparel" is uppercase because, in a search and replace, WordPerfect automatically capitalizes the first letter of the *replacement* word when the first letter of the *replaced* word is uppercase.

```
Prepared by:  Melissa Walborsky          Date: 9/22/94
Reviewed by:  Susan Guttmann             Date: 9/26/94


                  Sorority Designs, Inc.
     Inventory Observation Memorandum - Syracuse Warehouse
                   September 15, 1994


OBSERVATION OF INVENTORY TAKING
     The audit staff who participated in this observation were
Mike Newman, Harvey Strauss, Edith Kaplan, and I.  We arrived at
the Syracuse warehouse at 7:20 a.m. on September 15, 1994.
     We all observed and noted the care with which the warehouse
personnel counted the inventory and used the inventory count
sheets.  They appeared to follow the required procedures.
Standard inventory protocols were observed.

SLOW MOVING AND DAMAGED Apparel
     We questioned the SDI warehouse personnel about slow moving
and damaged apparel.  We were told that SDI monitors this
merchandise and transfers it periodically to the SDI clothing
outlet store in Ithaca.  We observed a holding area wherein such
merchandise is stored until the next shipment to Ithaca.  Thus,
we did not include the slow moving and damaged apparel in the
count.

TEST COUNTS
     We made test counts on approximately 31% of the inventory.
We recorded our findings in our work papers and noted that these
counts substantiated SDI's counts.

CUTOFF CONTROLS
     We took time to gain access to and examine the Receipt Log
and the Shipping Log for this warehouse.  We noted the
merchandise received on September 13, 1994; we also noted that no
merchandise was shipped on September 14, 1994.  We used the
September 13 numbers for our subsequent purchases and sales
cutoff tests.

Conclusions
     I believe we made an accurate count of all saleable apparel
in the Syracuse warehouse on September 15, 1994, because the SDI
personnel followed all required procedures and because the
merchandise held for delivery to the Ithaca outlet store was not
counted.
```

Figure 3-16
Print memo after first round of editing

Saving and Printing the Document

Melissa feels that the inventory observation memo is now ready to save to the disk and to print for review by her manager, Susan. The document is still in draft form, but Melissa needs Susan's feedback before she saves and prints the final version.

To save and print the document:

1. Make sure your data disk is in drive A.
2. Save the document using the path and filename A:\S3FILE1.DFT.

   Melissa uses the filename extension .DFT to signify that this is still a draft of the memo.
3. Make sure your printer is turned on and ready to print, then print the document.

After she prints the document, Melissa gives it to Susan, who notes errors and makes other changes. Susan returns the edited document to Melissa and asks her to make the changes before printing a copy for the file (Figure 3-17). Because Susan did, in fact, review the memo on 9/26/94, that date can remain.

Block Operations

One of the most powerful editing features in WordPerfect is the Block command, which allows you to execute block operations. A **block operation** is a set of commands that allows you to modify or otherwise act on an existing unit of text. The unit of text may be any portion of your document — a single character, a phrase, a sentence, a paragraph, a page, or a group of pages.

Block operations are powerful and efficient because they allow you to move, copy, or modify a block of text *as a unit* instead of changing each character or each word individually. For example, you could change all the text in a paragraph from regular type to boldface, from left-justified to centered, or from uppercase and lowercase to all uppercase. You can also use block operations to delete a block of text, save a block of text to a disk, or move a block of text from one location to another within your document.

Figure 3-18 shows the many Block commands that are available in WordPerfect. Some of these commands (such as Bold, Delete, and Flush Right) are familiar to you, but many of them may be unfamiliar — Append, Comment, and Convert Case. You'll learn many of these commands as you complete this and future tutorials.

```
Prepared by:  Melissa Walborsky          Date: 9/22/94
Reviewed by:  Susan Guttmann              Date: 9/26/94
```

Sororty Designs, Inc. *(bf)*   *(underline)*
Inventory Observation Memorandum - Syracuse Warehouse
September 15, 1994

OBSERVATION OF INVENTORY TAKING
   The audit staff who participated in this observation were
Mike Newman, Harvey Strauss, Edith Kaplan, and I. We arrived at
the Syracuse warehouse at 7:20 a.m. on September 15, 1994.
   We all observed and noted the care with which the warehouse
personnel counted the inventory and used the inventory count
sheets. They appeared to follow the required procedures.
~~Standard inventory protocols were observed.~~

SLOW MOVING AND DAMAGED Apparel *(all uppercase)*
   We questioned the SDI warehouse personnel about slow moving
and damaged apparel. We were told that SDI monitors this
merchandise and transfers it periodically to the SDI clothing
outlet store in Ithaca. We observed a holding area wherein such
merchandise is stored until the next shipment to Ithaca. Thus,
we did not include the slow moving and damaged apparel in the
count.

TEST COUNTS
   We made test counts on approximately 31% of the inventory.
We recorded our findings in our work papers and noted that these
counts substantiated SDI's counts.

CUTOFF CONTROLS
   We ~~took time to gain access to and~~ examined the Receipt Log
and the Shipping Log for this warehouse. We noted the
merchandise received on September 13, 1994; we also noted that no
merchandise was shipped on September 14, 1994. We used the
September 13 numbers for our subsequent purchases and sales
cutoff tests.

Conclusions *(all uppercase)*
   I believe we made an accurate count of all saleable apparel
in the Syracuse warehouse on September 15, 1994, because the SDI
personnel followed all required procedures and because the
merchandise held for delivery to the Ithaca outlet store was not
counted.

Figure 3-17
Memo with Susan's corrections

BLOCK OPERATIONS	
Command	**Description**
Append	Add block to the end of an existing file
Bold	Boldface blocked text
Comment	Convert block to a document comment
Convert Case (Switch)	Switch all characters in block to uppercase, lowercase, or first letter uppercase and others lowercase
Center	Center block horizontally
Copy	Make copy of block at another location in the document or to another document
Cut/Paste	Remove block and paste it into another location in the document
Delete	Erase block
Flush Right	Align block against the right margin
Font	Change the type size, style, or appearance of blocked text
Macro	Macro acts upon block
Mark Text	Mark block for lists, index, table of contents
Move	Move the block of text
Print/Fax	Send block of text to the printer
Protect	Keep block of text together on same page (protect against page break)
Replace	Search and replace words, phrase, or codes within block
Save	Save block of text to disk
Search	Search for text or codes within block
Sort	Sort lines or records within block
Speller	Check the spelling within block
Style	Insert style formatting codes within block
Table	Convert block of text to a table
Underline	Underline block

Figure 3-18
List of common
WordPerfect Block
commands

Block operations involve first selecting, or highlighting, the block of text that you want to modify and then executing the appropriate WordPerfect command to act on that block of text. Let's illustrate this procedure by changing an existing phrase in Melissa's inventory observation memo from regular type to boldface.

Changing Existing Text to Boldface

Look at Figure 3-17 and notice that Susan's first suggested change is to make the client's name boldface in the document title. This is a common practice at McDermott & Eston.

Melissa already knows how to use the Font menu or [F6] (Bold) to create *new* boldface text, but to change *existing* text to boldface, she has to first use the Block command. Let's use WordPerfect's Block command to change the client's name to boldface.

To change a block of existing text to boldface:

① Move the cursor to the "S" in "Sorority" in the document title.

In most block operations, you first move the cursor to the beginning of the block of text you want to modify. You are now ready to turn on Block, that is, mark a block of text.

② Choose **E**dit, **B**lock or press **[Alt][F4]** or **[F12]** (Block).

WordPerfect displays the message **Block on** on the left side of the status bar and highlights the cursor's position number on the right side of the status bar. See Figure 3-19.

cursor at beginning of block

Block on

Figure 3-19
Cursor at beginning of block with Block on

indicates block on

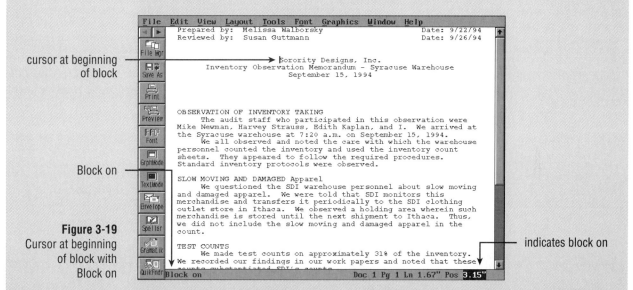

③ Use the keyboard (for example, press **[End]**), not the mouse, to move the cursor to the end of the phrase "Sorority Designs, Inc."

In most block operations, you define the block of text by moving the cursor to the beginning of it, turning Block on, and using the keyboard to move the cursor to the end of it. WordPerfect then highlights the block of text you have defined. See Figure 3-20.

Figure 3-20
Highlighted text with Block on

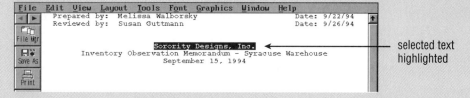

selected text highlighted

You can also use the mouse to highlight a block of text. Move the mouse pointer to the beginning of the block of text you want to modify, press and hold down the left mouse button, drag the mouse pointer to the end of the block of text, and release the mouse button. If you use the mouse to select a block of text, don't choose Edit, Block or press the function keys to turn Block on. The "Block on" message will automatically appear on the status bar as you drag the mouse.

④ Choose **F**ont, **B**old or press **[F6]** (Bold).

WordPerfect makes the selected phrase boldface and turns off Block. The "Block on" phrase disappears from the status bar. See Figure 3-21.

Figure 3-21
Document window after you apply boldface to a block of text

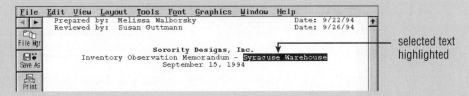

bold text

If you accidentally apply boldface to a block of text that you want in regular type, turn on Reveal Codes, move the cursor to the [Bold On] or [Bold Off] code, and delete the code. When you delete either [Bold On] or [Bold Off], WordPerfect automatically removes both codes from the document.

Underlining a Block of Text

Look again at Figure 3-17. Susan's next suggestion is to underline "Syracuse Warehouse" in the second line of the memo title. Let's use a block operation to underline this text.

To underline a block of existing text:

➊ Move the cursor to the "S" in "Syracuse," which is the beginning of the block of text you want to highlight.

➋ Choose **E**dit, **B**lock or press **[Alt][F4]** or **[F12]** (Block).

WordPerfect displays the message "Block on" and highlights the position number on the status bar.

➌ Move the cursor to the end of "Syracuse Warehouse."

The selected block of text becomes highlighted. See Figure 3-22.

Figure 3-22
Selected text with block on

selected text highlighted

As an alternative to steps 1 through 3, you could drag the mouse pointer over the text you want to modify.

➍ Choose F**o**nt, **U**nderline or press **[F8]** (Underline).

WordPerfect underlines the block of text (Figure 3-23), and Block is automatically turned off.

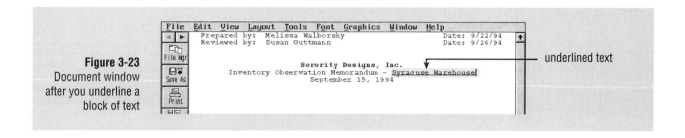

Figure 3-23
Document window
after you underline a
block of text

Deleting a Block of Text

Another time-saving Block command is deleting a block of text. If you want to delete more than two or three words, you can save time by using Block. For example, in Figure 3-17, in the paragraph headed "CUTOFF CONTROLS," Susan suggests that Melissa delete the unnecessary and wordy phrase "took time to gain access to and." Let's use a block operation to delete this phrase.

To delete a block of text:

1. Highlight the phrase "took time to gain access to and" by moving the cursor to the "t" in "took," just below the heading "CUTOFF CONTROLS," turning on Block, then moving the cursor to the right of the "d" in "and." Alternatively, you can highlight the phrase by dragging the mouse pointer over it.

2. Press **[Backspace]** or **[Del]**.

   WordPerfect deletes the text without prompting you for confirmation.

3. Delete the extra space between "We" and "examine," then edit "examine" to become "examined." See Figure 3-24.

Figure 3-24
Document window
after you delete a
phrase and edit a
word

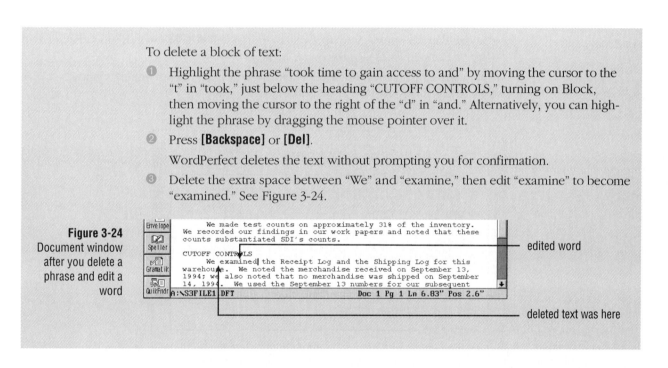

The more text you have to delete, the more keystrokes you will save by using the Block feature.

If you accidentally delete the wrong block of text, you can restore it by choosing Undelete from the Edit menu or by pressing [Esc] (Cancel) and then choosing 1 (Restore). WordPerfect doesn't allow you to use Undo to restore a deleted block of text.

Converting a Block of Text to All Uppercase

Turn once again to Figure 3-17. In the second heading, Susan has marked the word "Apparel" to be all uppercase. When Melissa used search and replace to change "merchandise" to "apparel," she forgot to change "Apparel" to all uppercase in the heading. Susan also noted that the last heading, "Conclusions," should be in all uppercase letters as well. Melissa knows that she can use a Block command to convert the case.

To convert the case of a block of text:

➊ Using the keyboard or the mouse, select (block) the word "Apparel" in the second heading as the block of text to be converted.

➋ Choose **E**dit, Con**v**ert Case, **U**ppercase or press **[Shift][F3]** (Switch) and choose **1** (**U**ppercase).

WordPerfect converts the word "Apparel" to "APPAREL," and Block is turned off.

➌ Using the same technique as in step 1, select the word "Conclusions" just above the last paragraph of the memo.

➍ Choose **E**dit, Con**v**ert Case, **U**ppercase or press **[Shift][F3]** (Switch) and choose **1** (**U**ppercase).

The word "Conclusions" becomes "CONCLUSIONS." Your document window should now be similar to Figure 3-25.

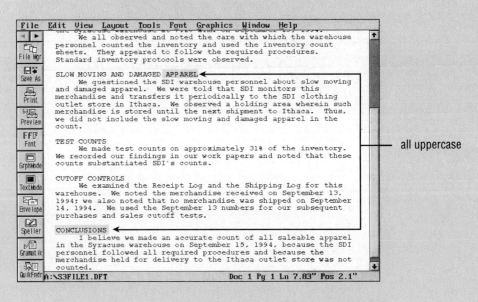

Figure 3-25
Document window
after you convert
words to all
uppercase

You can also use the Convert Case command to convert a block of text to all lowercase characters or make the first letter of each word uppercase and the other letters lowercase.

Cutting and Pasting a Block of Text

One of the most important uses of the Block command is for moving text. Suppose, for example, you have typed a paragraph into a document but then realize the paragraph is in the wrong place. You could solve the problem by deleting the paragraph and then retyping it at the new location. But a much more efficient approach would be to use a block operation to move the paragraph. This is sometimes called "cut and paste," because after highlighting the block of text you want to move, you cut (delete) it from the text and then paste (restore) it back again in the appropriate place (Figure 3-26).

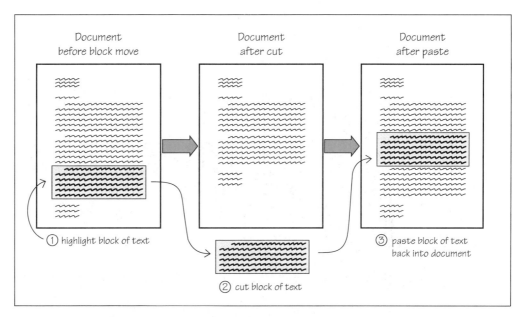

Figure 3-26
Cut and Paste
Operation

In Figure 3-17, Susan suggests that Melissa move the "TEST COUNTS" section so that it is the second section in the memo instead of the third. Melissa knows that instead of deleting and retyping the paragraph, she can use Block with the Move command to move the entire section. Let's do this now.

To move a block of text:

1 Move the cursor to the first "T" in "TEST COUNTS," turn on Block, then move the cursor to the "C" in "CUTOFF" to highlight the entire block you want to move. See Figure 3-27. (You can also drag the mouse pointer over the block of text you want to move.)

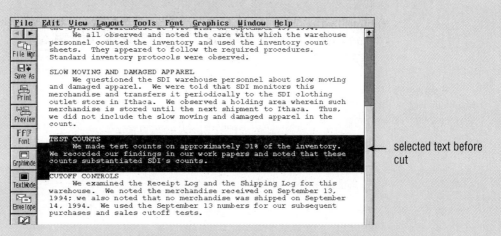

Figure 3-27
Selected text that
you want to cut

Because you want to move the entire section of text, you should block from the beginning of one heading to the beginning of the next to include the blank line after the paragraph.

② Choose **E**dit, Cu**t** or press **[Ctrl][X]**. See Figure 3-28.

Cut command →

Paste command →

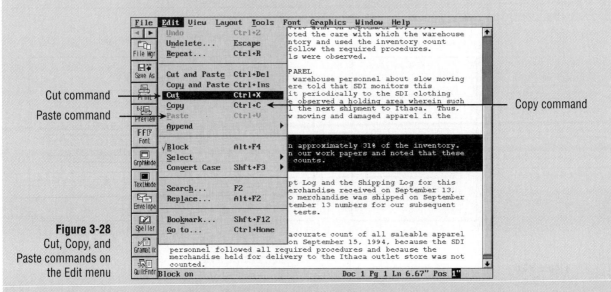

← Copy command

Figure 3-28
Cut, Copy, and
Paste commands on
the Edit menu

This cuts, or deletes, the selected block of text from the document. See Figure 3-29. The deleted block of text is stored temporarily in a special memory location called the **clipboard.** Whatever text is in the clipboard can be "pasted" into the document. (If you choose Cut and Paste, as shown in Figure 3-28, instead of just Cut, WordPerfect also cuts the text and saves it in the clipboard, but then prompts you to move the cursor and press Enter to paste the block of text back into the document. Sometimes choosing Cut and Paste saves you a step in moving a block of text.)

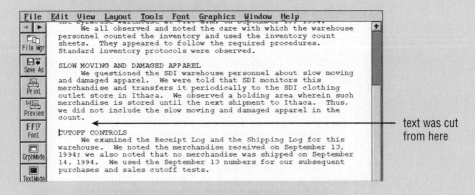

← text was cut
from here

Figure 3-29
Document window
with text removed

3. Move the cursor up to the "S" in "SLOW," the first word of the second heading. This is the position to which you want to move the block of text.
4. Choose **E**dit, **P**aste or press **[Ctrl][V]**. The "TEST COUNTS" section now appears before the "SLOW-MOVING AND DAMAGED APPAREL" section of the memo. See Figure 3-30.

text pasted into document here

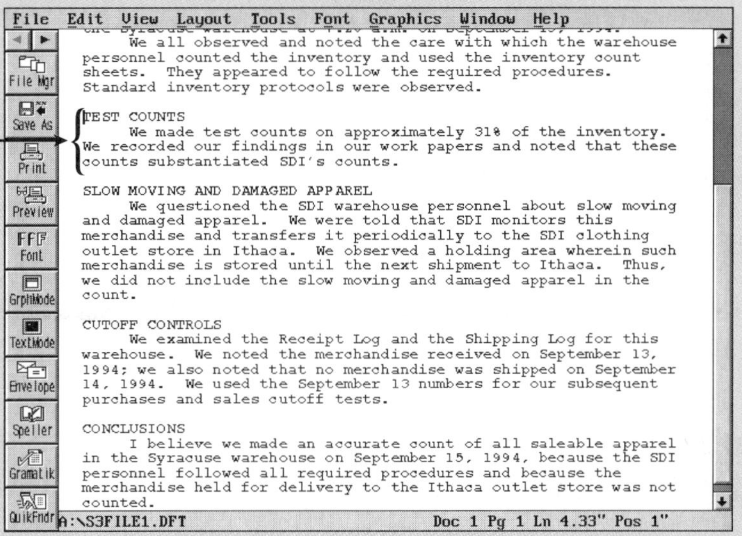
File Edit View Layout Tools Font Graphics Window Help
File Mgr
Save As
Print
Preview
Font
GrphMode
TextMode
Envelope
Speller
Gramatik
QuikFndr
We all observed and noted the care with which the warehouse personnel counted the inventory and used the inventory count sheets. They appeared to follow the required procedures. Standard inventory protocols were observed.
TEST COUNTS
We made test counts on approximately 31% of the inventory. We recorded our findings in our work papers and noted that these counts substantiated SDI's counts.
SLOW MOVING AND DAMAGED APPAREL
We questioned the SDI warehouse personnel about slow moving and damaged apparel. We were told that SDI monitors this merchandise and transfers it periodically to the SDI clothing outlet store in Ithaca. We observed a holding area wherein such merchandise is stored until the next shipment to Ithaca. Thus, we did not include the slow moving and damaged apparel in the count.
CUTOFF CONTROLS
We examined the Receipt Log and the Shipping Log for this warehouse. We noted the merchandise received on September 13, 1994; we also noted that no merchandise was shipped on September 14, 1994. We used the September 13 numbers for our subsequent purchases and sales cutoff tests.
CONCLUSIONS
I believe we made an accurate count of all saleable apparel in the Syracuse warehouse on September 15, 1994, because the SDI personnel followed all required procedures and because the merchandise held for delivery to the Ithaca outlet store was not counted.
A:\S3FILE1.DFT
Doc 1 Pg 1 Ln 4.33" Pos 1"

Figure 3-30
Document window after you paste block back into document

Selecting Units of Text

The **Select** command allows you to highlight sentences, paragraphs, and pages usually in less time than it takes to highlight text using the Block command. To use Select, you move the cursor to any location within a sentence, paragraph, or page, execute the Select command to highlight the text, and then perform the desired operation, such as Move or Delete.

Deleting a Sentence Using Select

Melissa wants to use the Select command to delete the unnecessary sentence at the end of the first section of her memo, as Susan suggests. (Refer to Figure 3-17.)

To delete a sentence using the Select command:

1. Move the cursor anywhere within the sentence that begins "Standard inventory protocols . . ."

With the Select command, you can position the cursor anywhere in the sentence or on the punctuation mark at the end of the sentence.

② Choose **E**dit, **S**elect, **S**entence. Alternatively, you can triple-click the mouse pointer anywhere in the sentence.

WordPerfect highlights the entire sentence just as if you had used the Block command. See Figure 3-31.

Figure 3-31
Highlighted
sentence after you
execute the Select
Sentence command

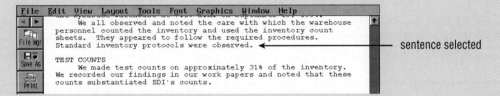

sentence selected

③ Press **[Backspace]** or **[Del]** to delete the sentence.

Note that this *deletes* the text, which is different from *cutting* the text. Cutting allows you to paste the text back into the document. Deleting doesn't save the text to the clipboard, so you can't paste it back into the document. (You can, however, restore the deleted block of text using Undelete.)

④ Press **[Backspace]** twice to delete the extra spaces. Your screen should now look like Figure 3-32.

Figure 3-32
Document window
after you delete the
selected sentence

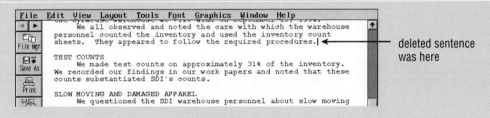

deleted sentence
was here

Copying a Paragraph Using Select

You can also use the Select command to copy a sentence, a paragraph, or a page. Although Melissa has no reason to copy text in her memo, let's copy the second paragraph to the end of the memo, for illustration purposes only, and then use Select to delete it.

To copy a paragraph using the Select command:

① Leave the cursor to the right of the period following "required procedures," or move the cursor anywhere within that paragraph.

② Choose **E**dit, **S**elect, **P**aragraph. The entire paragraph is highlighted. See Figure 3-33.

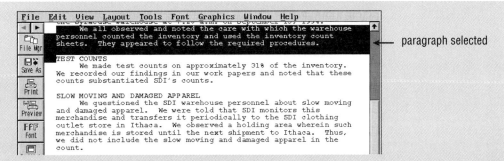

Figure 3-33
Highlighted paragraph after you execute the Select Paragraph command

paragraph selected

③ Choose **E**dit, **C**opy or press **[Ctrl][C]** (Copy).

WordPerfect leaves the selected paragraph intact, turns off the highlight, and copies the paragraph onto the clipboard. (The clipboard contains only the most recently cut or copied text. If you were to execute a second Cut or Copy command at this point, the paragraph you just copied would be deleted from the clipboard.)

Now you need to move the cursor to the place in the document where you want the copied paragraph to go.

④ Move the cursor to the end of the document.

⑤ Choose **E**dit, **P**aste or press **[Ctrl][V]** (Paste).

A copy of the selected paragraph appears at this new location in the text.

⑥ Press **[Enter]** twice to insert hard returns so that the copy of the paragraph appears two lines below the preceding paragraph. See Figure 3-34.

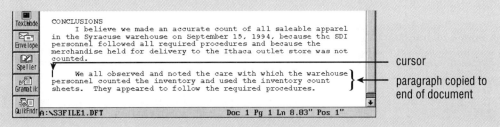

Figure 3-34
Document window after paragraph is copied to end of the document

cursor

paragraph copied to end of document

Deleting a Paragraph Using Select

Just as you can delete a sentence using Select, you can also delete a paragraph. To demonstrate this feature, let's delete the paragraph we just copied to the end of the memo.

To delete a paragraph using Select:

① Make sure the cursor is somewhere in the paragraph beginning "We all observed and noted" at end of the document.

② Choose **E**dit, **S**elect, **P**aragraph. The entire paragraph you want to delete is highlighted.

③ Press **[Backspace]** or **[Del]** to delete the paragraph.

Using Drag and Drop to Move Text

If you have a mouse, you can use the **drag and drop** method to move text. Let's use drag and drop to move the word "periodically" as Susan suggested in Figure 3-17. If you don't have a mouse, follow the alternative instructions.

To move text using drag and drop:

① Select the word "periodically" and the space after it, located in the paragraph under "SLOW MOVING AND DAMAGED APPAREL," by dragging the mouse over the word and the space or by double-clicking the word. See Figure 3-35.

Figure 3-35
Text selected by
dragging mouse
pointer

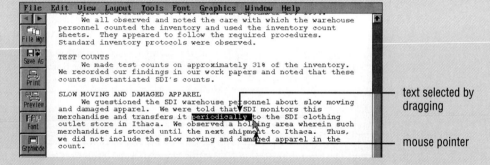

text selected by
dragging

mouse pointer

(Double-clicking anywhere in a word selects the word. Triple-clicking anywhere in a sentence selects the sentence.)

Alternatively, move the cursor to the "p" in "periodically," turn Block on, then move the cursor to the "t" in "to."

② Move the mouse pointer anywhere within the highlighted area, press and hold down the left mouse button, and (while still holding down the button) move the cursor to the letter "t" in "transfers," and release the mouse button.

As you move the mouse pointer, it displays a little box (called a **move box)** representing the text it's "dragging." See Figure 3-36. Be sure, as you move the mouse pointer to the location where you want to drop the text, that you focus on the location of the *cursor* rather than on the location of the mouse pointer or the move box. The cursor marks the precise location of the drop.

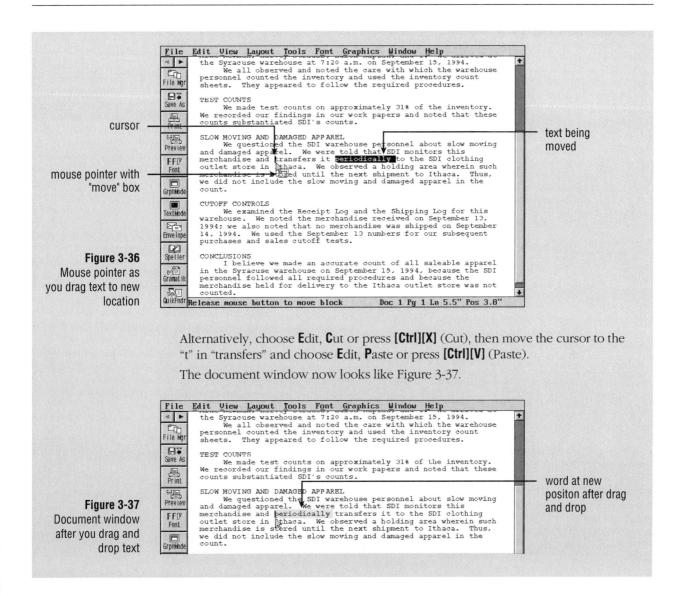

Figure 3-36
Mouse pointer as
you drag text to new
location

cursor

mouse pointer with
"move" box

text being
moved

Alternatively, choose **E**dit, **C**ut or press **[Ctrl][X]** (Cut), then move the cursor to the "t" in "transfers" and choose **E**dit, **P**aste or press **[Ctrl][V]** (Paste).

The document window now looks like Figure 3-37.

Figure 3-37
Document window
after you drag and
drop text

word at new
positon after drag
and drop

With a little practice, you will see that using the drag and drop method to move words, sentences, paragraphs, or any unit of text smaller than the screen itself is the most efficient method. For blocks of text that cover more than one screen, Block usually works better.

The final version of your document should now look similar to Figure 3-38.

Prepared by: Melissa Walborsky   Date: 9/22/94
Reviewed by: Susan Guttmann   Date: 9/26/94

Sorority Designs, Inc.
Inventory Observation Memorandum - <u>Syracuse Warehouse</u>
September 15, 1994

OBSERVATION OF INVENTORY TAKING
     The audit staff who participated in this observation were
Mike Newman, Harvey Strauss, Edith Kaplan, and I. We arrived at
the Syracuse warehouse at 7:20 a.m. on September 15, 1994.
     We all observed and noted the care with which the warehouse
personnel counted the inventory and used the inventory count
sheets. They appeared to follow the required procedures.

TEST COUNTS
     We made test counts on approximately 31% of the inventory.
We recorded our findings in our work papers and noted that these
counts substantiated SDI's counts.

SLOW MOVING AND DAMAGED APPAREL
     We questioned the SDI warehouse personnel about slow moving
and damaged apparel. We were told that SDI monitors this
merchandise and periodically transfers it to the SDI clothing
outlet store in Ithaca. We observed a holding area wherein such
merchandise is stored until the next shipment to Ithaca. Thus,
we did not include the slow moving and damaged apparel in the
count.

CUTOFF CONTROLS
     We examined the Receipt Log and the Shipping Log for this
warehouse. We noted the merchandise received on September 13,
1994; we also noted that no merchandise was shipped on September
14, 1994. We used the September 13 numbers for our subsequent
purchases and sales cutoff tests.

CONCLUSIONS
     I believe we made an accurate count of all saleable apparel
in the Syracuse warehouse on September 15, 1994, because the SDI
personnel followed all required procedures and because the
merchandise held for delivery to the Ithaca outlet store was not
counted.

Figure 3-38
Final version of the inventory observation memo

Saving and Printing the Memo

Melissa has completed all the corrections that Susan suggested and can now save and print the finished memo. Before she prints it, Melissa should run the speller and possibly Grammatik to check the final version for errors. She might also want to use View Document to see how the memo will look on the printed page. We'll assume that she's already done these things, and is ready to print the memo.

To save and print the memo:

1. Make sure your data disk is still in drive A.
2. Save the document as A:\S3FILE2.MEM.

   In this example, the .MEM filename extension signifies that this is the final version of the memo. WordPerfect saves the final version of the memo to the disk.
3. Make sure your printer is on and ready to print, then print the document.

Exercises

1. Describe an instance in which you would use each of the following function-key commands:
   a. [Shift][F6] (Center)
   b. [Alt][F6] (Flush Right)
   c. [Alt][F4] or [F12] (Block)
   d. [F2] (Search)
   e. [Alt][F2] (Replace)

2. List the pull-down menu commands and function-key commands that would perform the following operations:
   a. Center a line of text between the left and right margins
   b. Move a phrase flush against the right margin
   c. Search for a previous occurrence (that is, earlier in the document than the current position of the cursor) of the word "audit" in a document
   d. Search for the first occurrence of the word "payment" in a document

3. What happens when you choose the following pull-down menu commands with Block on? *Hint:* Look at Figure 3-18.
   a. **E**dit, Cu**t**
   b. **F**ile, **P**rint/Fax
   c. **L**ayout, **J**ustification, **C**enter
   d. F**o**nt, **I**talics

4. What happens when you press the following key(s) with Block on? *Hint:* Look at Figure 3-18.
   a. [Ctrl][F2] (Speller)
   b. [Del]

    c. [Shift][F3] (Switch), 2 (Lowercase)
    d. [F10] (Save As)

5. List five common commands you can execute with Block on.

6. Describe how you would create boldface text as you type it, then describe how you would change existing text to boldface.

7. Describe the "drag and drop" operation.

8. How would you copy a sentence in your document
    a. without using a function-key command or a pull-down menu?
    b. without using the mouse?

9. For which of the following operations can you use the Select command to highlight the desired unit of text?
    a. Deleting three adjacent paragraphs of text
    b. Deleting an entire page of text
    c. Deleting a sentence
    d. Copying a paragraph
    e. Copying a page
    f. Copying a phrase

10. Under what conditions could you safely carry out a search and replace operation with Confirm Replacement *off?* Under what conditions would you need to carry out search and replace with Confirm Replacement *on?*

Tutorial Assignments

For the following Tutorial Assignments, make sure the document window is blank before you open a document.

Open the file T3FILE1.DFT and do the following:

1. Without retyping the title (the first line of the document), change it to all uppercase letters.

2. Center the first three lines of text. Do not use the center-justification feature.

3. Italicize the title using a Block command.

4. Do a search and replace operation to change all occurrences of "SDI" to "Sorority Designs, Inc."

5. Save the document as S3FILE3.DOC.

6. Print the document.

Open the file T3FILE2.DFT and do the following:

7. Use Flush Right to right-justify the date in the top line of the memo.

8. Center the title lines (the two lines under Melissa Walborsky's name).

9. Make the title "Solving the Problem of Employee Turnover" uppercase and underlined.

10. Move numbered paragraph 2 above numbered paragraph 1, then renumber the paragraphs.

11. Without retyping them, underline the first sentence in each of the three numbered paragraphs.

12. Without retyping it, italicize the phrase "ad hoc" in the last paragraph.

13. Copy the second (unnumbered) paragraph, which begins with "The major cause of turnover . . .," to the end of the document.

14. Use the Select command to delete the last sentence of the (new) last paragraph.

15. Edit the beginning and end of the last sentence to say "If the major cause . . . at Ithaca College, should we hire fewer students?"

16. Save the document as S3FILE4.MEM.

17. Print the document.

Open the file T3FILE3.DFT and do the following:

18. Use the Replace command to replace all occurrences of the invisible [Lft Indent] code with the code [Lft Tab]. *Hint:* In the Search and Replace dialog box, choose [F5] (Codes), and then choose Lft Indent as the Search For string and Lft Tab (*not* LFT TAB) as the Replacement string. You may want to turn on Reveal Codes here, but you can execute the command with Reveal Codes off.

19. Use search and replace with confirmation to change all occurrences of "ICOS" to "Ithaca Clothing Outlet Store" in the body of the letter, but not in the **Re:** statement.

20. Move numbered paragraph 3 above numbered paragraph 1, and then renumber the paragraphs.

21. Without retyping it, italicize the phrase "esprit de corps" in numbered paragraph 4.

22. Use the Select command to delete the second sentence of the last (unnumbered) paragraph, which begins "Your suggestion will . . .."

23. Save the document as S3FILE5.LET.

24. Print the document.

Case Problems

1. Supplies Expenditures Memo

Flora Martinez, the office manager for the public accounting firm of Black, Doman, & Zapata (BDZ), sends a report each month to the senior partners to summarize expenditures for office supplies. The report on expenditures, which provides comparisons with previous periods and with industry averages, includes a spreadsheet file printout summarizing expenditure data. The main purpose of this month's report is to summarize and explain a higher-than-normal expenditure rate for office supplies.

Do the following:

1. Open the file P3EXPEND.DFT.

2. In the first line, make the date (including the word "Date" flush against the right margin.

3. Center the two title lines of the memo.

4. Convert the first title line "Increase in Expenditures for Office Supplies" to all uppercase letters and boldface type.

5. Change the three headings (which start "Expenditures During," "Reasons for," and "Items to") to all uppercase.

6. Move the numbered paragraph 3 above numbered paragraph 2. Revise the paragraph numbers so they are consecutive.

7. Move the last sentence of the last paragraph to become the second sentence in that same paragraph.

8. Use Block or Select to delete the second sentence, which begins "With the increased cost of wood," in the newly numbered paragraph 3.

9. Where such changes wouldn't cause an error in the meaning of the text, carry out a search and replace operation to change all occurrences of "the company" to "BDZ."

10. Carry out a search and replace with confirmation to change the tabs ([Lft Tab] codes) after the numbers in the numbered paragraphs to indents ([Lft Indent] codes).

11. Save the memo as S3EXPEND.MEM.

12. Print the memo.

2. Review of a Fast-Growing, Small, Public Company

Grant Seymour is a freelance writer for *Investor's Review*, a financial magazine that reviews stocks and other investments. His editor has asked him to write an article on Innovo Group, a fast-growing business that manufactures and markets aprons. Figure 3-39 shows the first paragraphs of Grant's rough draft of the article.

Do the following:

1. Open a new document and type the header lines, as shown in Figure 3-39, at the beginning of the document. This header is a standard format used by freelance writers.
   a. On the left, type the author's name, address, and phone number.
   b. Flush right on the first line, type the word count for the article.
   c. Flush right on the second line, type the rights that the author is offering: "First [World] Serial Rights."
   d. Flush right on the third line, insert today's date (not the date in Figure 3-39).

2. Type the title in boldface type and center it between the left and right margins.

3. Make the first line of the title all uppercase.

4. Type the author's byline centered between the left and right margins.

5. Type the remainder of the article, as shown in Figure 3-39.

6. Save the article as S3INNOVO.DOC.

7. Print the document.

```
Grant Seymour                    Word Count (approx):  1200
811 West Heather Road              First World Serial Rights
White Plains, NY 10602                  November 10, 1994
(914) 384-4400
```

LETTING GO OF THE APRON STRINGS
The Innovo Group Success Story

by Grant Seymour

Don't be fooled by its name or its product. Innovo Group--which
sounds like a company that ought to make cellular phones or
computer software--actually manufactures and markets aprons.

You heard me right: <u>aprons</u>. You know, those cloth things that you
wear when you cook a meal in the kitchen or serve hamburgers in
the back yard. Sounds like an unlikely product for a new,
thriving company.

But the Innovo Group has elevated aprons to new heights. They
don't just make aprons--they make **APRONS!** Colorful, artistic,
bizarre, humorous, personal, philosophical, and political aprons.

Want to make a political statement, create a mood, or just look
wild? Innovo has an apron to fit the bill.

Want to make a wild investment? Innovo can probably help you out
there, too.

Figure 3-39

3. Collins Consulting, Inc.

Allison Sanders is director of Collins Consulting, Inc., a small financial consulting business.
The company presents seminars on developing and managing small startup businesses.
Allison is planning the program for a seminar to be held August 27, 1994, in Atlanta, Georgia.
A copy of her tentative schedule is shown in Figure 3-40.

Do the following:

1. Open a new document window and type the four title lines of the program.

2. Center all four title lines. Make the first title line Boldface.

3. Type the first four items in the program. Make the text on the right side flush right
    with dot leaders. *Hint:* Press [Alt][F6] *twice* to move the text flush right with dot lead-
    ers. Center the titles of the speeches and of the videos.

4. To create the fifth item in the program (the second video), use a copy and paste operation to copy the fourth item (the first video), and then edit the video title rather than retype the entire text.

5. Save the document as S3FINANC.DOC.

6. Print the document.

```
                    MANAGING YOUR STARTUP BUSINESS
                       Collins Consulting, Inc.
                 Peachtree Center Auditorium, Atlanta, Georgia
                           August 27, 1994



     Welcome . . . . . . . . . . . . . . . . . . . . Allison Sanders
                            Director, Collins Consulting, Inc.

     Comments . . . . . . . . . . . . . . . . . . . . . Paul Johnson
                            Atlanta Area Chamber of Commerce

     Speaker . . . . . . . . . . . . . . . . . . Gabriella Trujillo
                       Professor of Marketing, Emory University
                 "The Entrepreneurial Climate in the Southeast"

     Video. . . . . . . . . . . . . . . Introduced by Allison Sanders
                       "Managing your Startup Business"

     Video . . . . . . . . . . . . . . Introduced by Allison Sanders
                   "Profits vs. Cash Flow in Small Businesses"
```

Figure 3-40

Tutorial 4

Formatting Multiple-Page Documents

Writing a Sales Report

Case: Camino Office Equipment Corporation

Steven Tanaka is a sales representative for the Camino Office Equipment Corporation (COEC), which sells photocopy machines, fax machines, dictaphones, telephone answering equipment, and other high-technology office equipment. Steven's sales territory is Arizona and New Mexico. He is the only COEC representative covering that area.

At the end of every year, Steven writes a report that summarizes his sales results, compares these results with his previous years' sales, and presents strategies for future sales. Steven is currently working on his 1994 annual sales report.

OBJECTIVES

In this tutorial you will learn to:

- Change the line spacing in a document

- Center a page between the top and bottom margins

- Change the tab settings

- Number the pages in a document

- Create headers and footers

- Create and use styles

- Create and format tables

- Use bookmarks

- Set Conditional End of Page

- Set Widow/Orphan Protection

Planning the Document

Steven wrote his first annual sales report in 1989. At that time, he was trained by company personnel on how to write reports, and he studied several reports by successful COEC sales representatives. He now prepares for his annual report throughout the year by filing notes and data on his sales activities and results. At the end of the year, he organizes and analyzes this information and follows company guidelines for the content, organization, style, and format of his report.

Content

The main contents of Steven's annual report, besides his own notes and observations, are his quarterly sales figures for the current year and the previous two years. He obtains prior-year sales figures from his previous annual reports and current-year sales figures from COEC's main office.

Just as important as the sales data are his interpretations of it. Steven knows that a good sales report includes analysis and recommendations.

Organization

Steven organizes his report according to company policy, with a title page, an introduction, a presentation and interpretation of the gross sales for the current and the previous two years, an analysis and summary of the year's sales effort, and recommendations for improved sales in the future.

Style

The report follows established standards of business-writing style, emphasizing clarity, simplicity, and directness.

Format

In accordance with COEC policy, Steven's report will include a title page, with each line of text centered between the left and the right margins and the entire text centered between the top and the bottom margins. The text in the body of the report will be double-spaced. Every page, except the title page, will include a header and a page number. Tabs at the beginning of each paragraph will be 0.3 inch. The sales data will be presented in a table.

Changing the Line Spacing

Steven has already written and edited the body of his report, but he has yet to type the title page and format the report as COEC requires. He marks a copy of his report with the changes he needs to make (Figure 4-1). As he looks over his copy, Steven decides that first he should double-space the text. Let's change the line spacing in Steven's report.

include a title page

decrease
indent to 0.3"

center & bold
heading

full-justify

INTRODUCTION

This report summarizes my sales results in territory 703 (Arizona and New Mexico) from 1 January 1994 to 31 December 1994. In this report, I will:

double-space
entire document

1. Summarize gross sales in territory 703.
2. Compare my 1994 gross sales with gross sales for 1993 and 1992.
3. Document my success in obtaining major corporate accounts.
4. Suggest a 1995 marketing strategy for my territory and for other U.S. sales territories.

GROSS SALES   center & bold

The following table summarizes the total sales in my region during the years 1992 to 1994:

This table shows a 6.7% increase in sales from 1992 to 1993, and then a 53% increase from 1993 to 1994. Since COEC spent almost the same amount of money to advertise product during this three-year period, I attribute the dramatic increase in income to improved targeting of our advertising and marketing and to improved customer relations. I especially credit COEC's new customer 800 number. This "hot line" allows us to handle customer orders and complaints more quickly and effectively. Most of my major corporate accounts reported improved satisfaction with our service and cited this as a major reason why they bought COEC products.

CORPORATE ACCOUNTS   center & bold

COEC's strategy to focus on large corporate accounts has paid big dividends for me. During 1994, I visited 82 potential large-corporation customers in my territory. I was able to promise them better terms under our large-accounts discount program and our new customer hot line. To date, twenty-seven of these companies have begun buying their office equipment from COEC. I attribute this new business to the success of COEC's strategy.

The large corporations in my territory that seem to respond best to COEC are more service intensive than manufacturing intensive. This is probably because the service industries require more of the type of office equipment that we sell.

RECOMMENDATIONS   center & bold

Based upon my 1994 sales success, I recommend the following:

1. We should focus our sales calls and advertising on service-oriented industries, where we will get the most benefit from our marketing dollars.
2. We should continue our 800 "hot line." The additional and retained sales that are generated more than pay for this service.
3. We should continue to add new lines of office equipment. Our customers want a wider choice of new technology, in particular, fax machines, color copiers, and telephone-answering equipment.
4. We should consider adding office computers to our line of products. Many of the large corporations want to buy their computers from the same company that sells them their laser printers and fax machines.

Figure 4-1
Rough draft of Steven's report with his editing marks

To change the line spacing in a document:

① Open the document C4FILE1.DFT from your data disk into a new document window.

② Make sure the cursor is at the beginning of the document.

Remember that WordPerfect's formatting features take effect from the current position of the cursor to the end of the document. If you want to set new line spacing for the entire document, you must move the cursor to the beginning of the document before you make the change.

③ Choose **L**ayout, **L**ine or press **[Shift][F8]** (Format) and select **1** (**L**ine).

WordPerfect displays the Line Format dialog box shown in Figure 4-2.

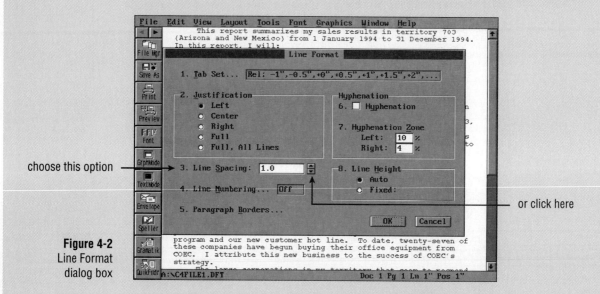

choose this option →

or click here →

Figure 4-2
Line Format
dialog box

Notice that option 3 is Line Spacing and that to the right of the option is the value of current line spacing. If you want to make the document double-spaced, you have to change this value from 1.0 (single spacing) to 2.0 (double spacing).

④ Choose **3** (Line **S**pacing). The cursor moves to the current value in the Line Spacing text box.

⑤ Type **2** and press **[Enter]** to set the spacing to 2.0. Alternatively, instead of step 4, you could click the mouse pointer on the up-arrowhead to the right of the Line Spacing value and hold it down until the value becomes 2.0.

⑥ Choose OK to close the Line Format dialog box, and, if necessary, choose Close to close the Format dialog box.

The text of the report is double-spaced. See Figure 4-3.

cursor

double spacing

Figure 4-3
Document window
after you set double
spacing

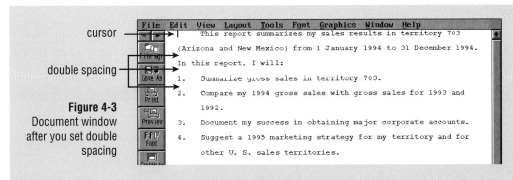

⑦ Turn on Reveal Codes to view WordPerfect's format code for double spacing, then turn off Reveal Codes.

The code for a line-spacing change is [Ln Spacing]. If you highlight the code, you'll see that it appears as [Ln Spacing:2.0]. This code is a signal to WordPerfect to double-space the text from that point until the end of the document or until the next [Ln Spacing] code.

You can set the line spacing to any value you want. The most common line spacings, however, are 1.0 for single spacing, 1.5 for one and one-half spacing, 2.0 for double spacing, and 3.0 for triple spacing.

Centering a Page Top to Bottom

Steven next decides to create the title page. To do this, he must insert a hard page break at the beginning of the document, instruct WordPerfect to center the lines between the left and the right margins, and then type the title page.

To create the title page:

① Make sure the cursor is at the beginning of the document, just to the right of the [Ln Spacing] code.

If necessary, turn on Reveal Codes to make sure the cursor is in the right place, and then turn off Reveal Codes.

② Press **[Ctrl][Enter]** (Hard Page) to force a hard page break.

The hard-page-break mark appears as a double line across the document window, and the status bar indicates that the cursor is now on page 2. See Figure 4-4. You have now created a separate page (page 1) where you'll type the title of the report.

hard page break

cursor

Figure 4-4
Document window
after you insert a
hard page break

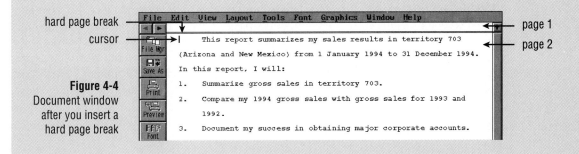

page 1

page 2

③ Choose **L**ayout, **J**ustification, **F**ull to set the body of the document — that is, everything except the title page — to full justification. Alternatively, press **[Shift][F8]** (Format), select **1** (**L**ine), **2** (**J**ustification), and **4** (**F**ull), then choose OK and Close.

Setting full justification here accomplishes two things. First, it sets the body of the report to full justification, which Steven wants. Second, it avoids the problem of having WordPerfect center-justify the entire report when you move to the beginning of the document and center-justify the title page.

④ Move the cursor to the first page.

⑤ Execute the Center Justification command, using the menus or keystrokes similar to those for setting full justification. This will cause all the text on the title page to be center-justified. The cursor is now centered in the middle of the document window.

⑥ Type the text of the title page, as shown in Figure 4-5. After you type the title ("1994 ANNUAL SALES REPORT") in boldface characters, turn off Bold and press **[Enter]** four times to insert four double-spaced blank lines. Then type the next block of text (name, title, territory) and press **[Enter]** five times to insert five more double-spaced blank lines. Finally, insert today's date using WordPerfect's Date Text command. Your screen should look similar to Figure 4-5.

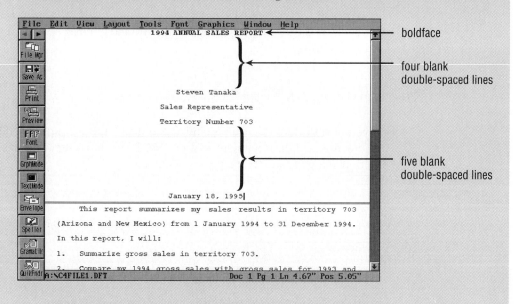

Figure 4-5
Document window
after you type
title page

COEC requires that the text of the title page be centered between the top and bottom margins. As you can see from the Print Preview window (Figure 4-6), the text of the title page is too high up on the page. You could insert hard returns at the beginning of the page until the text is centered, but WordPerfect provides an easier, more accurate method to center text on a page — a feature called Center Page Top to Bottom. Once Steven sets this feature at the beginning of a page, the text will stay centered between the top and the bottom margins, regardless of how much or how little text is on the page. This format command affects only the page you indicate. It doesn't affect the entire document. Let's center the title page now.

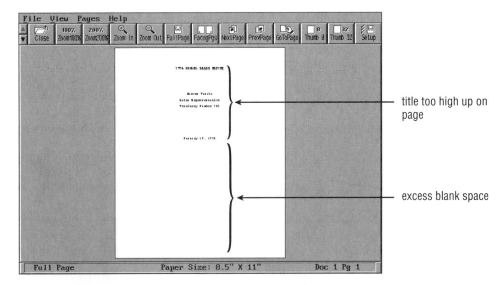

title too high up on
page

excess blank space

Figure 4-6
Print Preview
window of title page

To center the page top to bottom:

● Press **[Home]**, **[Home]**, **[Home]**, **[↑]** to move the cursor to the very beginning of the document, before any format codes.

For the Center Page Top to Bottom feature to work, the cursor must be located before any text on the page and before any format code that affects the appearance of the first line of text on the page, such as [HRt], [Lft Tab], or [Bold On]. Pressing [Home] three times prior to pressing [↑] moves the cursor before all text and all codes in the document. (If you press [Home] only twice, the cursor moves to the beginning of the text of the document, but after any initial formatting codes.)

● Choose **L**ayout, **P**age or press **[Shift][F8]** (Format) and select **3** (**P**age). The Page Format dialog box appears on the screen. See Figure 4-7.

choose this
command

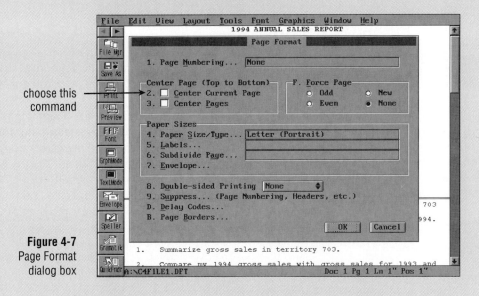

Figure 4-7
Page Format
dialog box

③ Choose **2** (**C**enter Current Page), or click the Center Current Page checkbox. Then choose OK. If necessary, choose Close from the Format dialog box. WordPerfect inserts the [Cntr Cur Pg] code into your document at the location of the cursor, as you can see if you turn on Reveal Codes. Turn off Reveal Codes before going to step 4.

④ Choose **F**ile, Print Pre**v**iew, or press **[Shift][F7]** (Print/Fax) and choose **7** (Print Pre**v**iew), or click the Preview button on the button bar. If necessary, choose **V**iew, **F**ull Page or click the Full Page button to see the entire page.

The Print Preview window appears on the screen. See Figure 4-8.

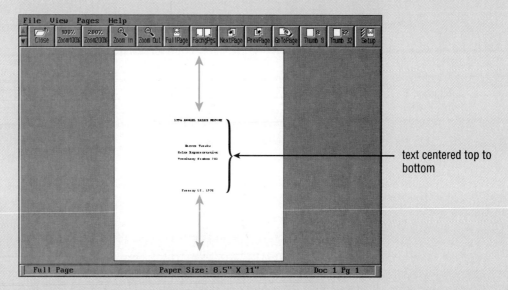

text centered top to bottom

Figure 4-8
Print Preview
window after you
center title page top
to bottom

⑤ After you have viewed the document, choose **F**ile, **C**lose, or press **[F7]** (Exit), or click the Close button to return to the document.

Changing the Tab Stops

Steven looks over his edited report (Figure 4-1) and decides to change the amount of indented space at the beginning of each paragraph from 0.5 inch to 0.3 inch, according to COEC requirements.

When Steven wrote the draft of his report, he pressed [Tab] at the beginning of each paragraph. This created a 0.5-inch space at the beginning of each paragraph, because the first tab stop was at 0.5 inch. A **tab stop** is a location (usually specified in inches) along each text line to which the cursor will move when you press [Tab] or [Indent] (Figure 4-9). In WordPerfect, the default setting for tab stops is every 0.5 inch from the left margin. With a 1-inch left margin and the cursor located at the left margin (Pos 1", as indicated on the status bar), pressing [Tab] moves the cursor and all text to the right of the cursor to the tab stop at Pos 1.5".

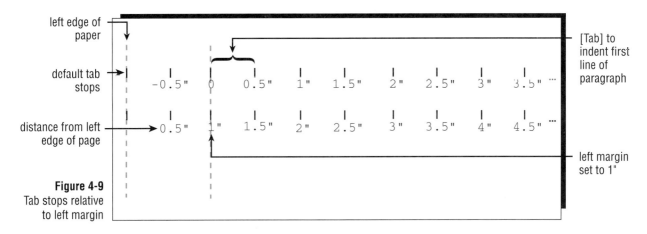

Figure 4-9
Tab stops relative to left margin

To create the numbered paragraphs in his report, Steven typed a number and a period, which positioned the cursor at about Pos 1.2", and then he pressed [F4] (Indent). This caused the entire paragraph to be indented to the next tab stop at Pos 1.5", which is 0.5" from the left margin (Figure 4-10). The cursor returns to the left margin (Pos 1") after you press [Enter] at the end of the paragraph.

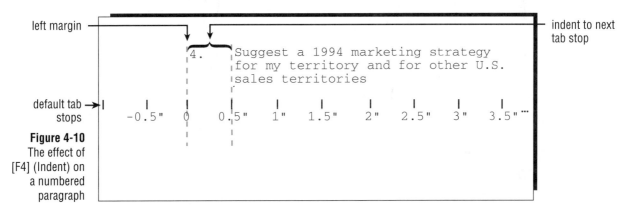

Figure 4-10
The effect of [F4] (Indent) on a numbered paragraph

Because the COEC format calls for the first line of each paragraph to be indented 0.3 inch, Steven has to change the tab stops. Let's first instruct WordPerfect to display the Tab Set dialog box, which shows the location of the current tab stops.

To display the Tab Set dialog box:

1. Move the cursor to the beginning of page 2 (the first page of the body of the text). This will cause the change in location of tab stops to affect the entire body of the report.

❷ Choose **L**ayout, Ta**b** Set or press **[Shift][F8]** (Format), choose **1** (Line), and then **1** (**T**ab Set). WordPerfect displays the Tab Set dialog box, as shown in Figure 4-11.

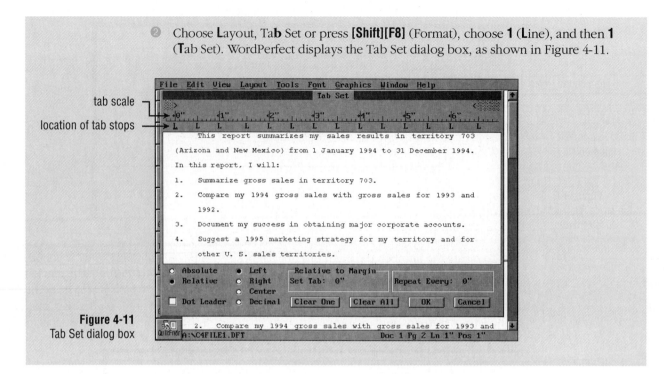

tab scale

location of tab stops

Figure 4-11
Tab Set dialog box

The dialog box consists of a tab scale, usually labeled in inches, that indicates the location of each tab stop. Each tab stop is marked with the letter L, which stands for left tab stop. A left tab stop allows you to align words and phrases along their left edges, as shown in Figure 4-12, which also demonstrates center and right tabs.

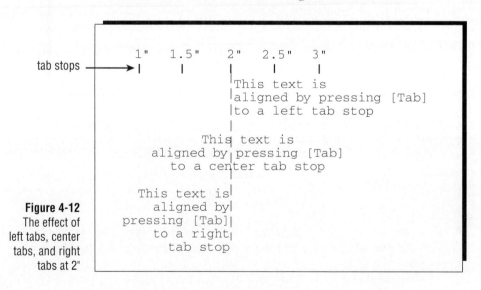

tab stops

Figure 4-12
The effect of left tabs, center tabs, and right tabs at 2"

Next let's clear the current tab stops so we can set new ones.

To clear the tab stops:

1 Make sure the cursor is located at 0" on the tab scale, underneath the first L at position 0".

You can use [→] and [←] or the mouse pointer to move the cursor, or you can type the value (in this case, 0 or zero) and press **[Enter]** to position the cursor on the tab scale. The 0" means that the cursor is zero inches from the left *margin* of the page, not from the *left* edge of the page.

2 Choose Clear **A**ll or press **[Ctrl][End]** (Del to EOL) to delete the tab stops from the cursor to the end of the line. See Figure 4-13.

clear tab stops —→

cursor —

Figure 4-13
Tab Set dialog box
after you clear the
tab stops

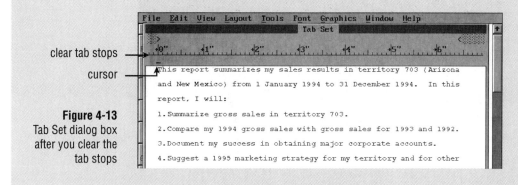

With all the old tab stops cleared, you are ready to set the new tab stops. You can set tab stops one at a time by moving the cursor to the desired location and pressing [L] (for Left Tab), or you can set several evenly spaced tabs in one operation. Let's set evenly spaced tabs, starting at 0.3" and continuing every 0.5" after that. To set evenly spaced tabs, you first type the position number for the first (leftmost) tab, type a comma, and then, without typing a space after the comma, type the amount of space you want between the remaining tabs.

To set the tab stops:

1 Choose Set Tab in the Relative to Margin box.

The cursor moves into the Set Tab Relative to Margin box and highlights the value of the current location of the cursor on the tab scale.

2 Type **0.3,0.5** and press **[Enter]**.

The leading zeros in these decimal numbers are optional. The command **0.3,0.5** tells WordPerfect to set a tab stop at 0.3 inch from the left margin and subsequent tabs every 0.5 inch from the first one. The new tab settings appear on the tab scale. See Figure 4-14 on the following page.

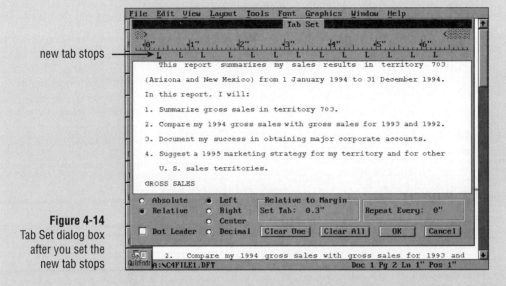

new tab stops

Figure 4-14
Tab Set dialog box
after you set the
new tab stops

③ Choose OK or press **[F7]** (Exit) to exit the Tab Set dialog box. If necessary, choose OK or press **[F7]** from the Line Format dialog box and then choose Close from the Format dialog box to return to the document window.

Now scroll down through the body of the document. Notice that the first line of each paragraph is indented 0.3 inch from the left margin, rather than 0.5 inch.

Numbering Pages

Because the report is now longer than one page, Steven wants to number the pages. He can do this automatically with the Page Numbering command. The COEC standard format requires that reports have page numbers centered at the bottom of each page.

To set page numbering:

① Make sure the cursor is at the beginning of the document — before any text and before any code that affects the first line of text. This ensures that Page Numbering is turned on for the entire document. You may need to turn on Reveal Codes and move the cursor to the right of [Ln Spacing] and on [Just].

② Choose **L**ayout, **P**age or press **[Shift][F8]** (Format) and select **3** (**P**age). The Page Format dialog box appears on the screen.

③ Choose **1** (Page **N**umbering). The Page Numbering dialog box appears on the screen. See Figure 4-15.

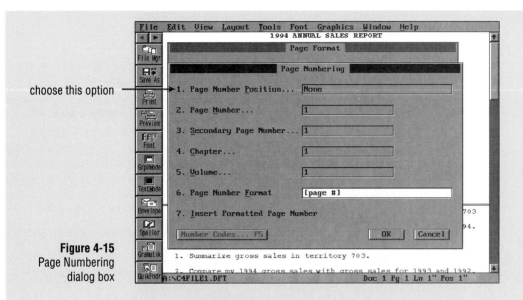

choose this option →

Figure 4-15
Page Numbering
dialog box

⓸ Choose **1** (Page Number **P**osition). The Page Number Position dialog box appears on the screen. See Figure 4-16. The numbers on the page diagrams at the right indicate where the page numbers will print.

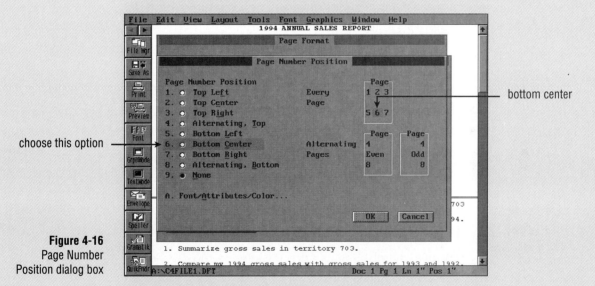

choose this option →

bottom center

Figure 4-16
Page Number
Position dialog box

Remember that Steven wants his page numbers centered at the bottom of each page, so you want option 6.

⓹ Choose **6** and then choose OK. Continue to choose OK or Close to exit all the dialog boxes until you return to the document window.

This Page Number command instructs WordPerfect to print a page number at the bottom center of every page, below the last line of text and just above the bottom margin. Page numbers do not appear in the document window in either text or graphics mode, but they do appear in Print Preview.

Creating Headers and Footers

Next, Steven wants to instruct WordPerfect to print the title of his report and his name at the top of every page. Text printed at the top of each page is called a **header**. Most books have headers on each page to guide the reader. Headers may contain, for example, the page number and the name of the book or the chapter name or number. Similarly, a **footer** is one or more lines of text, intended to guide the reader, printed at the bottom of each page.

When you create a header, WordPerfect prints it just below the top margin and then inserts a blank line between the header and the first line of text on the page. Similarly, WordPerfect prints a footer just above the bottom margin and inserts a blank line between the footer and the last line of text on the page.

Let's create a header that includes the name of the report and Steven's full name.

To create a header:

❶ Make sure the cursor is still at the beginning of the document, before any text or code that affects the first line of text.

❷ Choose **L**ayout, **H**eader/Footer/Watermark or press **[Shift][F8]** (Format) and choose **5** (**H**eader/Footer/Watermark). WordPerfect displays the Header/Footer/Watermark dialog box. See Figure 4-17.

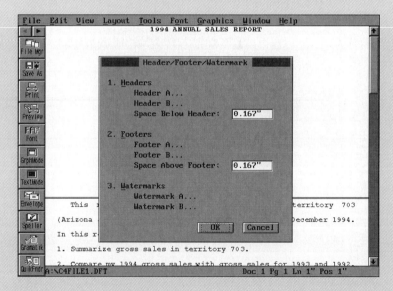

Figure 4-17
Header/Footer/
Watermark dialog box

❸ Choose **1** (**H**eaders).

WordPerfect lets you define up to two different headers at a time, Header A and Header B. In this report you'll use only one header. In other documents, you might want two headings — one heading, such as the title, on odd-numbered pages, and another heading, such as the author's name, on even-numbered pages.

❹ Choose **1** (Header **A**). The Header A dialog box appears on the screen. See Figure 4-18. You'll use this dialog box to select the pages on which headers will appear. This dialog box also allows you to turn off any current header or to edit an existing header.

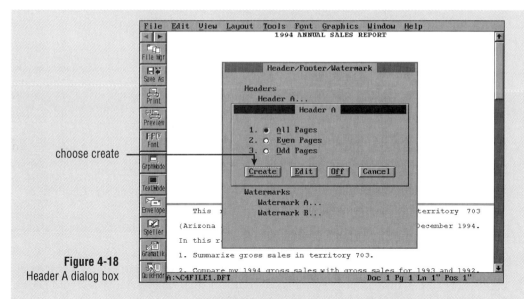

choose create

Figure 4-18
Header A dialog box

⑤ Make sure **1** (**A**ll Pages) is selected, as indicated by the darkened circle to the right of the number. If it isn't selected, choose **1** (**A**ll Pages). Then choose **C**reate. WordPerfect fills the document window with the Header A window, as shown in Figure 4-19.

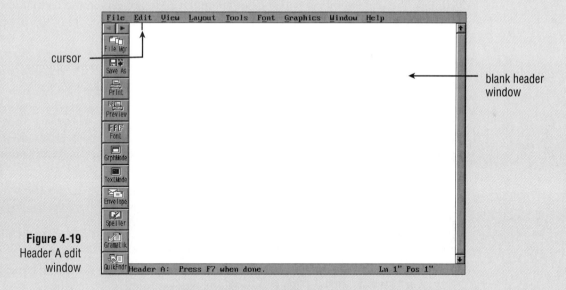

cursor

blank header window

Figure 4-19
Header A edit window

⑥ Type **1994 ANNUAL SALES REPORT**, choose **L**ayout, **A**lignment, **F**lush Right or press **[Alt][F6]** (Flush Right), type **Steven Tanaka**, and press **[Enter]**. See Figure 4-20 on the following page. Because WordPerfect automatically inserts one blank line between the header and the body of the text, pressing [Enter] inserts an additional blank line after the header.

text of header

cursor

Figure 4-20
Header edit window
after you type
header

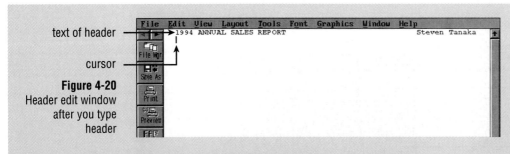

⑦   Choose **F**ile, **E**xit or press **[F7]** (Exit) to return to the document window.

You can't see the header in the document window, but you can see it in the Print Preview window.

To create a footer you would use the same procedure, except that in step 3 you would choose 2 (Footers) instead of 1 (Headers). To edit a header or a footer, you would choose Edit from the Header or Footer dialog box in step 5.

If you want page numbers to be part of headers or footers, do *not* set Page Numbering. Instead, include the page number in the definition of the headers or footers by choosing **L**ayout, **P**age, **1** (Page **N**umbering), **7** (**I**nsert Formatted Page Number) or by pressing [Ctrl][P] to insert the [Formatted Pg Num] code into the header or footer. Then when you print the document, the page numbers will appear where the code appears in the definition of the header or footer. In his report, Steven put page numbering at the bottom of the page, so it won't interfere with the headers.

Suppressing Page Numbering, Headers, and Footers

Steven has inserted the codes for page numbering and a header, but he doesn't want these elements to appear on the title page. To eliminate headers, footers, and page numbering on any particular page, you can use the Page Suppress feature. Let's use this feature now.

To suppress the page numbering and the header on a specific page:

①   Make sure the cursor is at the beginning of the title page, just after the format code for Header A. If necessary, use Reveal Codes to position the cursor properly.

②   Display the Page Format dialog box, and then choose **9** (**Su**ppress). WordPerfect displays the Suppress (This Page Only) dialog box. See Figure 4-21.

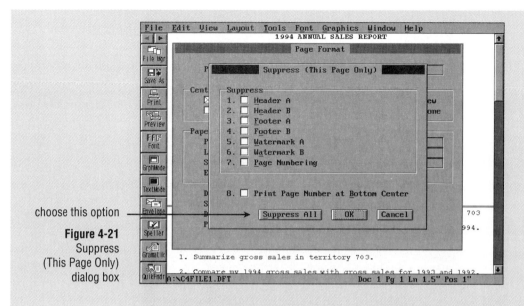

choose this option

Figure 4-21
Suppress
(This Page Only)
dialog box

③ Choose **S**uppress All. Notice how options 1 through 7 become checked, so that no page numbering, header, or footer will be printed on the current page.

④ Choose OK or Close from the dialog boxes until you return to the document window.

Now when Steven prints his annual report, no page number or header will appear on the title page.

Setting a New Page Number

Even though a page number won't appear on the title page when Steven prints the report, the title page is still page 1 of the document, and the body of the report begins on page 2. But Steven wants the body of the report to begin on page 1. This requires that he change the page numbering for the document, beginning on the page after the title page. Let's use WordPerfect's Page Numbering command to set a new page number.

To set a new page number:

① Move the cursor to the beginning of page 2, so that the cursor is below the [HPg] code and on the [Just:Full] code. You may have to turn on Reveal Codes to position the cursor properly, and then turn off Reveal Codes.

② Display the Page Format dialog box, and choose **1** (Page **N**umbering). As before, WordPerfect displays the Page Numbering dialog box.

③ Choose **2** (Page **N**umber). The Set Page Number dialog box appears on the screen. See Figure 4-22.

choose this option —→

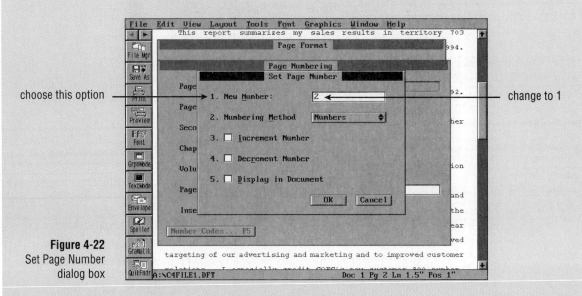

←— change to 1

Figure 4-22
Set Page Number
dialog box

④ Choose **1** (New **N**umber), type **1**, and press **[Enter]**.

⑤ Choose OK or Close as many times as necessary to return to the document window. WordPerfect inserts the [Pg Num Set] code into the document.

Now when Steven prints the document, the body of the report will begin on page 1, with pages numbered consecutively after that.

Viewing and Saving the Document

You can't see headers, footers, or page numbers in the document window, but you can see these features in the Print Preview window. Let's see how Steven's document looks now.

To view the document:

1 Make sure the cursor is still on the first page of the body of the report.

2 Choose **F**ile, Print Pre**v**iew, or press **[Shift][F7]**, **7** (Print Preview), or click the Preview button on the button bar.

3 If necessary, choose **V**iew, **F**ull Page or click the Full Page button on the button bar so you can see the entire page at once. See Figure 4-23.

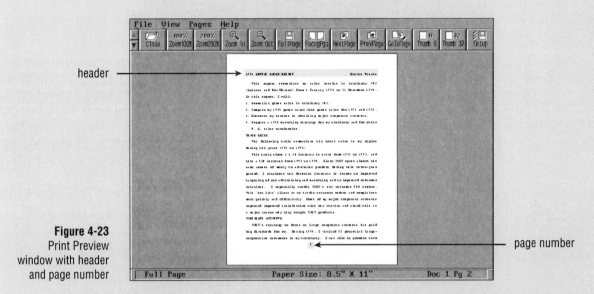

header

page number

Figure 4-23
Print Preview
window with header
and page number

Even though the words are too small to read, you can see the position of the header at the top of the page and the page number at the bottom of the page.

4 Choose **V**iew, **1**00% View, or press **1**, or click the Zoom 100% button so you can read the header at the top of the page. Then scroll down the screen so you can read the page number at the bottom of the page.

5 Click the Next Page button or press **[PgDn]** to view a subsequent page of the document, or click the Prev Page button or press **[PgUp]** to view a previous page of the document.

6 Choose **F**ile, **C**lose, or press **[F7]** (Exit), or click the Close button when you're ready to return to the document window.

Having worked on this version of his report for about 15 minutes, Steven decides to save the document with the changes he's made so far.

To save the document:

1. Choose **F**ile, Save **A**s or click the Save As button on the button bar. Alternatively, press **[F10]** (Save As).

2. Type **a:s4file2.dft** and press **[Enter]** to save this draft of the report.

Using WordPerfect Styles

One of the most powerful features of WordPerfect is the ability to apply styles. A WordPerfect **style** is a set of format codes or other codes and text that you can apply to words, phrases, paragraphs, or even entire documents to change their appearance or format. Once you define the format codes of a particular style, WordPerfect saves the style as part of the document, allowing you to use the style over and over again without having to go through the formatting keystrokes each time. For example, Steven wants to specify the format for section headings within his report. He can create a style that tells WordPerfect to insert an extra blank line just before each heading and to center the text and make it boldface each time.

The advantages of using styles to format titles, headings, and other elements of your document include the following:

- **Efficiency.** Once you specify the format codes within a style, you can apply that style to every like element of the document. When Steven creates the style for the headings in his annual report, he has to set Center and Bold only once; he can then use that style with all the headings in his document.

- **Flexibility.** If you later decide to change the style, you have to change it only once, and the format of all the affected parts of the document will automatically change. If Steven decided that he wanted all headings to be underlined instead of boldface, he could go through the entire document and change each heading individually. Using a style, he would have to make the change only once, in the style itself.

- **Consistency.** Without styles you can sometimes forget exactly how you formatted a particular element in your document. With styles, the same format codes apply to every instance of the element. Steven can be confident that his report will follow the required COEC style and that all headings will have the same format.

Once you understand how to create and use styles, you'll want to create styles for document titles, headings, numbered lists, and other features within your document that require special formatting.

Creating a Style

The headings in Steven's report don't follow the required COEC format. He decides to create a style to format all the headings efficiently and consistently. Let's create the heading style now.

To create a style:

➊ With the cursor anywhere in the document window, choose **L**ayout, **S**tyles or press **[Alt][F8]** (Style). WordPerfect displays the Style List dialog box. See Figure 4-24. The styles listed are WordPerfect's built-in styles. Your style list may include other styles also.

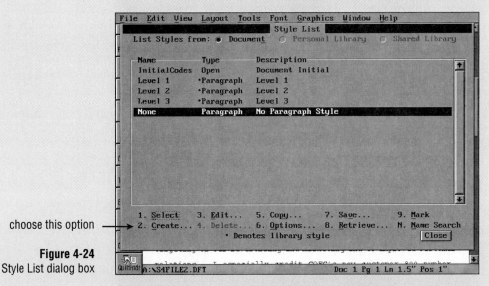

choose this option →

Figure 4-24
Style List dialog box

Creating a style doesn't insert a code into the document, so the cursor can be anywhere in the document when you define the style.

➋ Choose **2** (**C**reate). The Create Style dialog box appears on the screen. See Figure 4-25.

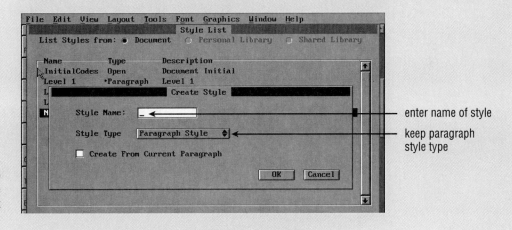

enter name of style

keep paragraph
style type

Figure 4-25
Create Style
dialog box

Next, you want to name the style you're going to create. Let's call the style "Heading."

③ Type **Heading** into the text box opposite Style Name, and press **[Enter]**.

Notice the option called Style Type in the Create Style dialog box. WordPerfect allows three types of styles: paragraph, character, and open. "Paragraph" means that when you turn the style on, the new formatting features apply to the current paragraph (the one in which the cursor is located). "Character" means that when you turn the style on, WordPerfect also automatically inserts the style off code; thus the style applies to a block of text or to the text you are about to type. "Open" means that when you turn the style on, the new formatting features begin and affect all of the text until the end of the document or until the formatting features are changed.

Steven wants to treat the Heading style as a paragraph, so you don't need to change the default setting. In general, "paragraph" is a good style type for headings and titles. This completes the necessary information for the Create Style dialog box.

④ Choose OK from the Create Style dialog box. WordPerfect displays the Edit Style dialog box. See Figure 4-26. In this dialog box, you'll give the style a description so you can remember its purpose and later define the style contents.

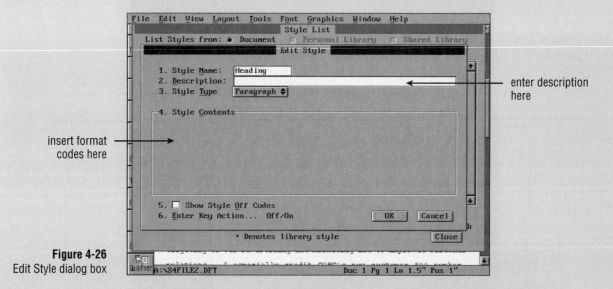

insert format codes here

enter description here

Figure 4-26
Edit Style dialog box

⑤ Choose **2** (**D**escription), type **Heading of a section of text**, and press **[Enter]**.

Next you'll next enter the format codes for the Heading style.

⑥ Choose **4** (Style **C**ontents).

The Edit Style dialog box now looks like Figure 4-27, with the cursor in the Style Contents box. Above the box, you see a list of key combinations for common formatting commands.

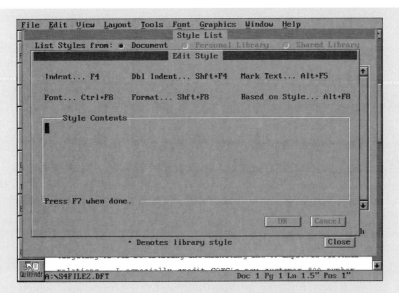

Figure 4-27
Edit Style dialog box
after you choose
Style Contents

Now you're ready to add format codes to the Style Contents box within the Edit Style dialog box.

To add format codes to the Styles Contents box:

1. Press **[Enter]** to tell WordPerfect that you want a hard return above the paragraph to which you apply the Heading style.
2. Choose **L**ayout, **A**lignment, **C**enter or press **[Shift][F6]** (Center) to have the style center the heading.
3. Choose **F**ont, **B**old, or press **[F6]** (Bold) to make the heading boldface.

These keystrokes insert the codes [HRt], [Cntr on Mar], and [Bold On] into the Style Contents box, as shown in Figure 4-28. You have now defined your Heading style.

format codes ⟶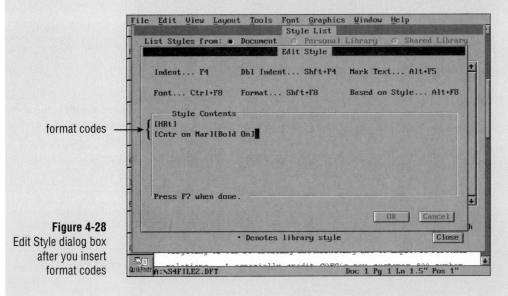

Figure 4-28
Edit Style dialog box
after you insert
format codes

④ Press **[F7]** (Exit) to exit the Style Contents box.

Normally, when you press [Enter] while using a paragraph style, WordPerfect inserts a hard return, automatically turns off the style for that paragraph, and then automatically turns it on for the next paragraph. In the style we are creating, however, we want to instruct WordPerfect that pressing [Enter] should turn off the paragraph style only, without inserting a hard return or turning the style back on for the next paragraph.

⑤ Choose **6** (**E**nter Key Action), select **2** (Turn Style Off), then choose OK.

⑥ Choose OK again to return to the Style List dialog box.

⑦ Choose Close to close the Style List dialog box. Don't press [Enter], because that will choose the default button Select. If you accidentally select the style, turn on Reveal Codes and delete the [Para Style:Heading] code.

You have finished creating the style named "Heading," which contains the codes that Steven wants for the headings in his report. In the next section, you'll use this style to format the headings in the report.

Using a Style

Steven is now ready to use the Heading style to create a section heading in his report.

To use the Heading style:

① Make sure the cursor is at the top of the first page after the title page of the report. Turn on Reveal Codes and move the cursor to the [Lft Tab] code, just to the right of the [Pg Num Set], [Just], [Tab Set], and any other codes at the beginning of that page. Your format codes might not be in this order; just be sure the cursor is on the [Lft Tab] code. Then turn off Reveal Codes.

② Choose **L**ayout, **S**tyles or press **[Alt][F8]** (Style) to display the Style List dialog box. The Style List dialog box displays the name and the description of the Heading style you just created (along with the names of the built-in styles).

③ Highlight "Heading" (see Figure 4-29) and choose **1** (**S**elect). This turns on the style and returns you to the document window. Any text that you type will be centered and boldface until WordPerfect turns off the style when it encounters a hard return. Notice that the first paragraph of the body of the report moves to the right and becomes boldface. This is only temporary; when you type the heading and press [Enter] to turn off the style, the first paragraph will return to regular text.

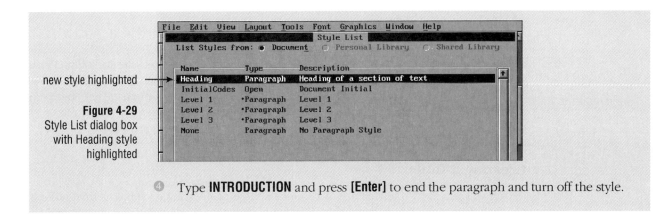

new style highlighted →

Figure 4-29
Style List dialog box
with Heading style
highlighted

④ Type **INTRODUCTION** and press **[Enter]** to end the paragraph and turn off the style.

As you can see, the heading INTRODUCTION is preceded by a blank line and is centered and in boldface type. You can now use this style to format the other headings in the report.

Using a Style with Existing Text

Steven has already typed the other headings of the report: "GROSS SALES," "CORPORATE ACCOUNTS," and "RECOMMENDATIONS." He can apply his Heading style to these headings without retyping them, just as you can apply WordPerfect's Bold command to a phrase without retyping it.

To apply a style to existing text:

① Move the cursor anywhere within the next heading, "GROSS SALES."

With a paragraph style, you don't have to block the text, nor does the cursor have to be at the beginning of the paragraph. With the cursor anywhere within the heading (which WordPerfect treats as a paragraph), you can now apply the style.

② Choose **L**ayout, **S**tyles or press **[Alt][F8]** (Style).

③ Highlight "Heading" and then choose **1** (**S**elect). Alternatively, you can double-click "Heading" in the Style List. This turns the style on.

④ Repeat these steps for the other two headings, "CORPORATE ACCOUNTS" and "RECOMMENDATIONS."

All the headings in the report now have the same format.

Using WordPerfect Tables

Steven decides to include in his report a table that summarizes his gross sales for the previous three years. WordPerfect's Tables feature allows you to specify the number of columns and rows, insert or delete columns and rows, change the width of columns, draw or remove lines between columns and rows, change the format of text and numbers within the table, and perform other tasks to make the table attractive and readable without having to retype any data.

Creating a Table

Steven will use the Tables feature to produce a table of his annual sales. His final table is shown in Figure 4-30. Let's make this table now.

TERRITORY 703 GROSS SALES (in dollars)					
Year	Qtr. 1	Qtr. 2	Qtr. 3	Qtr. 4	Total
1992	542,197	591,287	588,841	498,276	2,220,601
1993	562,422	681,647	584,892	540,699	2,369,660
1994	891,322	904,498	896,217	934,228	3,626,265

Figure 4-30
Data table for
Steven's report

To create a table:

① Move the cursor to the end of the first sentence in the section "GROSS SALES," just after the colon at the end of the phrase "during the years 1992 to 1994." This is the location in the document where you want the table to appear.

② Press **[Enter]** twice to insert two blank lines between the text and the table. See Figure 4-31.

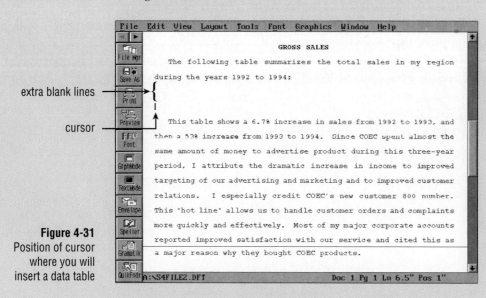

extra blank lines →

cursor →

Figure 4-31
Position of cursor
where you will
insert a data table

● Choose **L**ayout, **T**ables, **C**reate. Alternatively, press **[Alt][F7]** (Columns/Tables) to display the Column/Tabs dialog box, then choose **2** (Tables), then **1** (**C**reate).

WordPerfect prompts you for the number of columns and rows in the table. Steven's table has six columns and five rows.

● Type **6** and press **[Enter]** or **[Tab]**.

● Type **5** and press **[Enter]**, then choose OK.

The Table Edit window appears on the screen, with the table cursor in cell A1. See Figure 4-32. This window allows you to edit the table's appearance.

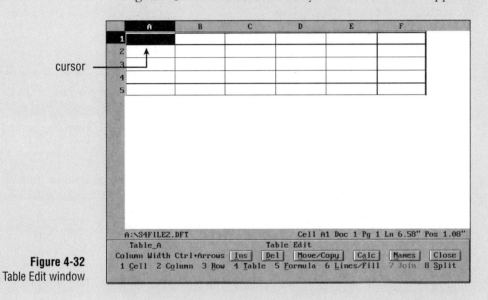

cursor

Figure 4-32
Table Edit window

In a WordPerfect table, a **cell** is a single box into which you can type a number or text. In order to identify each specific cell within a table, WordPerfect assigns letters to the columns of the table, and numbers to the rows. The first column on the left is column "A," the next column is "B," and so on in alphabetical order. The rows are numbered from top to bottom, starting with row 1. Each cell, therefore, is designated by a letter and a number. The cell in the upper-left corner is A1, the cell to its right is B1, the cell below A1 is A2, and so forth, as shown in Figure 4-33.

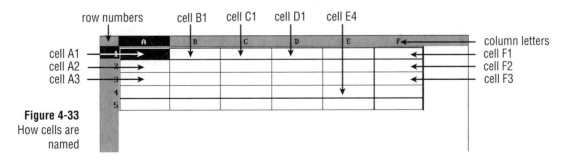

Figure 4-33
How cells are named

While the Table Edit window is active, you can move the cursor from cell to cell by using the arrow keys ([→], [←], [↑], [↓]), [Tab] (to move right), or [Shift][Tab] (to move left). You can use [End] to move to the rightmost column and [Home], [←] to move to the leftmost column. Practice using these cursor-movement keys to move the cursor around the table.

Formatting a Table

Steven realizes that he'll have to modify the format of his table to make it attractive and readable. First he'll join the cells in the top row into one large cell, so it can contain the title of the table, as shown in Figure 4-30.

To join cells in a table:

1. Make sure the cursor is in cell A1, the first cell in the group of cells you want to join.
2. Press **[Alt][F4]** or **[F12]** (Block) and **[End]** to highlight the top row of cells. Alternatively, you can drag the mouse pointer (with the left button held down) across the top row of cells to highlight them. You can't use the pull-down menus to turn Block on while the Table Edit window is active.

   If you accidentally press the right mouse button, WordPerfect will exit the Table Edit window. To return to the Table Edit window, make sure the cursor is in one of the table cells, then choose **L**ayout, **T**ables, **E**dit.
3. With the top row highlighted, choose **7** (**J**oin) to display the prompt "Join cells?"
4. Choose **Y**es to join the top row of cells into one cell. The top row is now a single cell in which you can type the title of the table.

Next Steven decides to draw a double line under the top row to separate the title from the rest of the table.

To draw a double line under a cell:

1. Make sure the cursor is still in cell A1 (which now spans the entire top row).
2. Choose **6** (**L**ines/Fill) to display the Table Lines dialog box.
3. Choose **6** (**B**ottom) to format the bottom line of the row and to display the Lines Style dialog box, where you can choose the style of the line.
4. Highlight Double Line and choose **1** (**S**elect) to select a double line.
5. Choose Close from the Table Lines dialog box. WordPerfect draws a double line along the bottom of cell A1. The double line is easy to see in text mode, but sometimes difficult to see in graphics mode or even in Print Preview. When you print the document, the double line will be clear.

Steven also wants to draw a double line below the cells of row 2. As shown in Figure 4-30, this double line will separate the column labels from the data in the columns.

To draw a double line under a row of cells:

1. With the Table edit window still on your screen, move the cursor to cell A2.
2. Press **[Alt][F4]** or **[F12]** (Block) and **[End]** to highlight the second row.
3. Choose **6** (**L**ines/Fill), **6** (**B**ottom), then highlight Double Line and choose **1** (**S**elect). Choose Close to close the Table Lines dialog box. WordPerfect draws a double line across the bottom of this row and returns to the Table Edit window. See Figure 4-34.

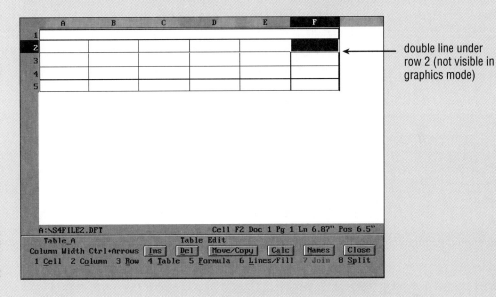

double line under
row 2 (not visible in
graphics mode)

Figure 4-34
Table Edit window
with revised table
format

Next Steven decides that the labels and the numbers in the columns should be right-justified, that is, aligned along the right side of the cells. Let's change the format of the columns to be right-justified.

To right-justify text in columns of cells:

1. Move the cursor back to cell A2.
2. Block the entire row of cells as you did before.
3. Choose **2** (**Co**lumn) to display the Column Format dialog box. See Figure 4-35 on the following page.

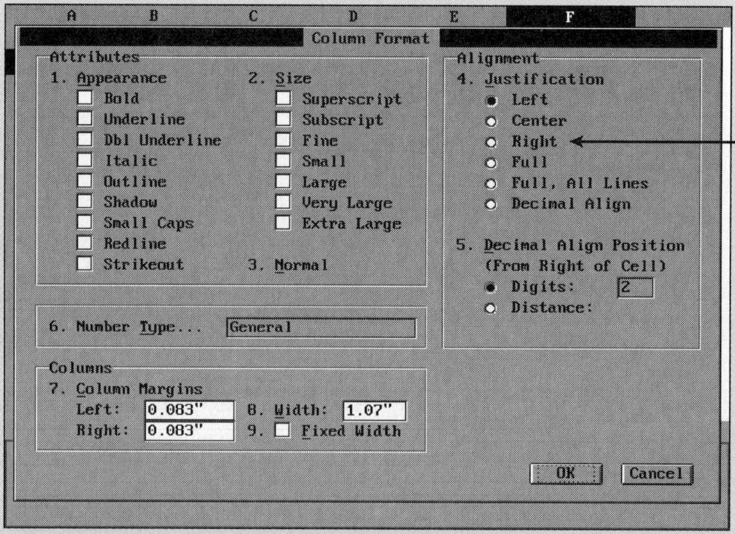

Figure 4-35
Column Format
dialog box

select this option

● Choose **4** (**J**ustification), **3** (**R**ight), and then choose OK.

This sets right justification for all the columns of the table. Any text you type into the table will be flush right in the cells.

Having set all the columns to right justification, Steven realizes that he wants the title, in cell A1, to be centered between the left and right edges of the table, as shown in Figure 4-30. Let's center-justify the text in cell A1.

To center-justify text (or numbers) in a cell:
● Move the cursor to cell A1.
● Choose **1** (**C**ell), **4** (**J**ustification), and **2** (**C**enter), so that any text typed in that cell will be centered. Choose OK.

By changing only this cell to center justification, the other cells stay set to right justification.

Notice in Figure 4-30 that the Year column is not as wide as the other columns. The keys that you press to decrease the width of a column are [Ctrl][←]. Let's decrease the width of the column now.

To decrease the width of a column:

   ① Move the cursor to cell A2 to position the cursor in the column whose width you want to change.

   ② Press **[Ctrl][←]** four times to decrease the width of the column.

Look again at Figure 4-30. The Totals column is wider than the other columns to accommodate the larger numbers. The keys that you press to increase the width of a column are [Ctrl][→]. Let's increase the column width now.

To increase the width of a column:

   ① Move the cursor to cell F2.

   ② Press **[Ctrl][→]** three times to increase the width of the column.

Now that he has completed the format changes in the table, Steven can exit the Table Edit window, return to the document window, and enter the text and data into his table.

To exit the Table Edit window:

   ① Choose Close or press **[F7]** (Exit) to exit the Table Edit window and return to the document window.

Your screen should now look similar to Figure 4-36. Notice that the status bar includes the letter and number designation of the cell in which the cursor is located.

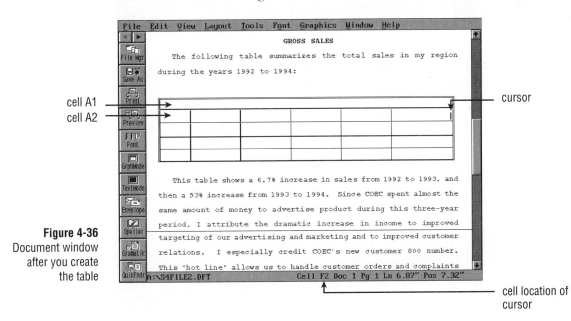

Figure 4-36
Document window
after you create
the table

cell A1

cell A2

cursor

cell location of
cursor

Entering Labels and Data into the Table

Having created and formatted the table, Steven is now ready to enter data. Although you can't change the format of the table when the cursor is in the document window, you can enter, edit, or delete information in its cells. Entering data is not difficult, because you can use most of the standard WordPerfect cursor-movement keys and deletion keys. Besides those keys, you can use [Tab] to move the cursor one cell to the right (without inserting a [Tab] code) and [Shift][Tab] to move the cursor one cell to the left. You can also click the mouse pointer in a cell to move the cursor there. Let's enter the labels and the data into the table now.

To enter data into the table:

1. Move the cursor to cell A1 and type the title of the table, as shown in Figure 4-30.
2. Press **[Tab]** or **[→]** to move to cell A2.
3. Type **Year**.
4. Press **[Tab]** or **[→]** to move to cell B2.
5. Type the data into the other cells of the table, as shown in Figure 4-30.

   Your screen should now look like Figure 4-37.

Figure 4-37
Document window
after you insert data
into the table

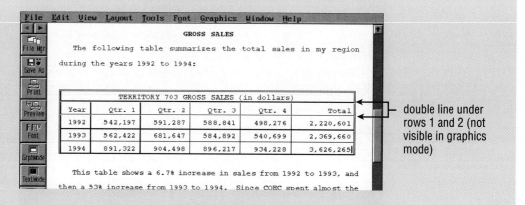

double line under
rows 1 and 2 (not
visible in graphics
mode)

Editing the Table Format

After completing the table, Steven decides that the "Total" label in column F should be centered in the column rather than right-justified; therefore, he needs to edit the table format.

To edit the table format:

1. Move the cursor anywhere within the table.
2. Choose **L**ayout, **T**ables, **E**dit or press **[Alt][F11]** (Table **E**dit). The Table Edit window appears on the screen. You can now select any of the options in the menu.
3. Move the cursor to cell F2.

④ Press **1** (**C**ell), **4** (**J**ustification), and **2** (**C**enter), then choose OK.

The text ("Total") becomes centered in the cell.

⑤ Choose **C**lose or press **[F7]** (Exit) to close the Table Edit dialog box and return to the document window.

Steven decides that he would like to avoid having any text appear below the table on the bottom of page 1, so he inserts a hard page break.

⑥ Move the cursor below the table and to the left of the tab at the beginning of the line "This table shows . . . ."

⑦ Press **[Ctrl][Enter]** (Page Break). The page break appears across the screen.

You have now completed the table. Your screen should look like Figure 4-38.

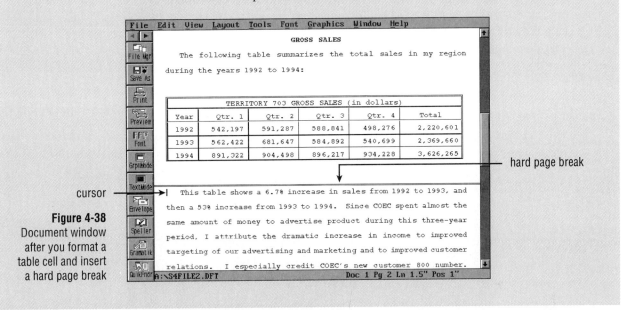

cursor

Figure 4-38
Document window
after you format a
table cell and insert
a hard page break

hard page break

Saving an Intermediate Version of the Report

Having worked on the report for another fifteen minutes or so, Steven decides to save the file again.

To save the file using the same filename:

① Choose **F**ile, **S**ave or press **[Ctrl][F12]** (Save).

WordPerfect saves the file using the current filename S4FILE2.DFT.

Using Bookmarks

Steven decides to take some time to look through the report to ensure that his narrative fits the data in the table. As he looks through the document, he wants to be able to return quickly to the location of the table, so he creates a bookmark. A WordPerfect **bookmark** is a tagged location within a document that allows you to move quickly from any place in the document to that location. Let's create a bookmark now.

To create a bookmark:

① Move the cursor to the blank line above the table and below the phrase "during the years 1992 to 1994" on page 1 of the body of the report, the location where you want a bookmark.

② Choose **E**dit, Boo**k**mark or press **[Shift][F12]** (Bookmark). WordPerfect displays the Bookmark dialog box. See Figure 4-39.

built-in bookmark

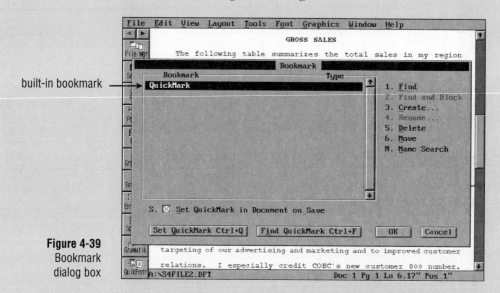

Figure 4-39
Bookmark
dialog box

WordPerfect displays a built-in bookmark called QuickMark, which we'll describe later in this section. In this example, we want to set a user-defined bookmark.

③ Choose **3** (**C**reate). The Create Bookmark dialog box appears on the screen.

④ Type **Sales Table** and choose OK. Steven names the bookmark "Sales Table" because the mark will be near the table that contains his sales data.

WordPerfect closes the Create BookMark and the Bookmark dialog boxes and inserts a bookmark at the location of the cursor.

You can turn on Reveal Codes to see that the code [Bookmark] appears in the document at the cursor. Now let's use the bookmark to quickly move the cursor to that location from anywhere else in the document.

To move the cursor to a bookmark:

① Move the cursor anywhere else in the document. For example, press **[PgDn]** two or three times. You're now ready to see how the bookmark works.

② Choose **E**dit, Boo**k**mark or press **[Shift][F12]** to display the Bookmark dialog box.

③ Highlight the "Sales Table" bookmark and press **[Enter]**. Alternatively, you can double-click the "Sales Table" name in the bookmark list.

WordPerfect closes the dialog box and moves the cursor to the Sales Table bookmark just above the table.

WordPerfect's built-in bookmark — QuickMark — is a special bookmark because you set it or move the cursor to it with simple keystrokes: Pressing [Ctrl][Q] sets the QuickMark at the current location of the cursor, and pressing [Ctrl][F] jumps the cursor to the location of the QuickMark from anywhere in the document.

You can create as many user-defined bookmarks as you want in a document. For example, if you're writing a long report — say, 40 pages — you might want to insert a bookmark at each section heading and give the bookmark the name of that section. In this way, you could easily move the cursor to any section of your report.

Setting a Conditional End of Page

As he looks through his report, Steven notices a serious formatting problem: The heading "RECOMMENDATIONS" is isolated at the bottom of page 2 (Figure 4-40). (Because of differences in type size among printers, your document might not have the heading isolated at the bottom of the page. Do the steps in this section anyway.)

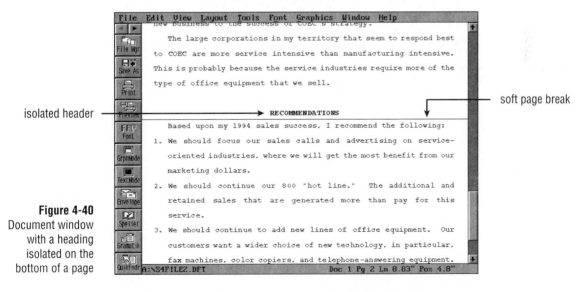

isolated header

soft page break

Figure 4-40
Document window
with a heading
isolated on the
bottom of a page

One solution to the problem would be to insert a hard page break just before the heading. The drawback to this solution is that if Steven later adds or removes text anywhere before the hard page break, the location of the page break probably would be unacceptable. For example, if Steven inserts a hard page break just before the heading and then adds three or four lines on page 2, one or two of the lines would spill over to page 3, the rest of page 3 would be blank, and "RECOMMENDATIONS" would start on page 4, as shown in Figure 4-41.

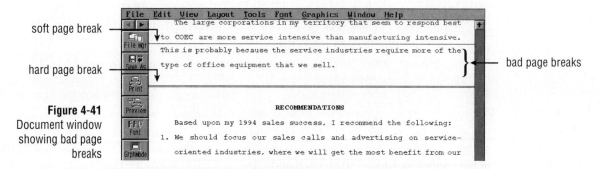

soft page break

hard page break

bad page breaks

Figure 4-41
Document window
showing bad page
breaks

A better solution is to use WordPerfect's Conditional End of Page command. The Conditional End of Page command allows you to prevent WordPerfect from inserting a soft page break that would separate a particular unit of text — such as a heading and the two lines that follow it — at an awkward point. For example, if you specify that six lines of text should be kept together, WordPerfect inserts a soft page break *above* the six lines if they would otherwise be split between two pages (Figure 4-42).

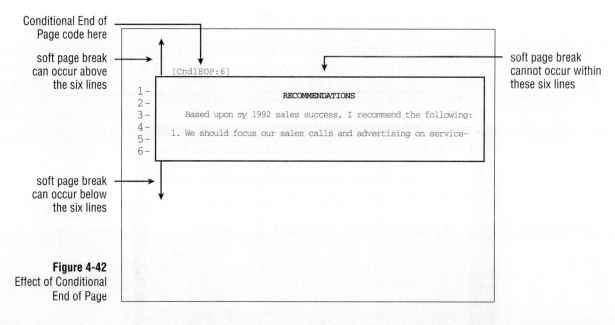

Conditional End of
Page code here

soft page break
can occur above
the six lines

soft page break
cannot occur within
these six lines

soft page break
can occur below
the six lines

Figure 4-42
Effect of Conditional
End of Page

Steven decides to use the Conditional End of Page code above the "RECOMMENDA-TIONS" heading. That way, regardless of any changes he makes to the document, the heading will never be isolated at the bottom of a page.

To set Conditional End of Page:
- ① Turn on Reveal Codes and move the cursor to the blank line below the paragraph that ends "office equipment that we sell" and above the heading "RECOMMENDATIONS."

The cursor should be on the [Para Style] code. Whenever you specify Conditional End of Page, move the cursor to the line *above* the block of text that you want kept together.

② Turn off Reveal Codes.

③ Choose **L**ayout, **O**ther or press **[Shift][F8]** (Format) and select **7** (**O**ther) to display the Other Format dialog box. See Figure 4-43.

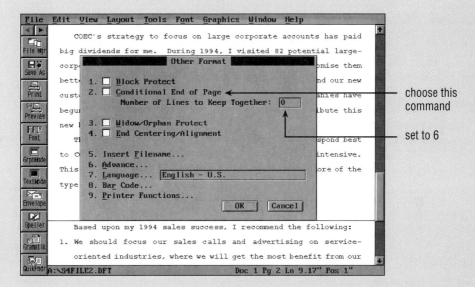

choose this command

set to 6

Figure 4-43
Other Format
dialog box

④ Choose **2** (**C**onditional End of Page). The cursor moves into the text box opposite "Number of Lines to Keep Together."

The number of lines includes the blank lines in double-spaced text. So if you want the heading and the first two lines of text under the heading to be kept together, you should specify six (three lines of double-spaced text) as the number of lines to keep together.

⑤ Type **6** and press **[Enter]**.

⑥ Choose OK to exit the Other Format dialog box. If necessary, choose Close to return to the document window. WordPerfect has inserted the format code [Condl EOP], which you can see by turning on Reveal Codes.

WordPerfect inserts a soft page break above the heading, so that the heading is now on page 3. See Figure 4-44. As you can see, a soft page break is a single line across the document window, whereas a hard page break is a double line.

Figure 4-44
Document window
with soft page break
above heading

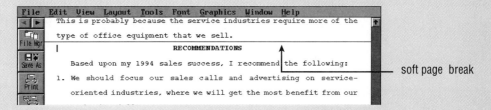

soft page break

Steven realizes that every heading in the document should have the Conditional End of Page command, so that no heading (or a heading and only one line of text) ever gets isolated at the bottom of a page. It occurs to Steven that the best way to handle this problem would be to put the Conditional End of Page code in the Heading style. The code would then take effect automatically at every heading. Let's insert the Conditional End of Page code into the Heading style.

To set Conditional End of Page in the style:

① Choose **L**ayout, **S**tyles or press **[Alt][F8]** (Style) to display the Style List dialog box.

② Highlight "Heading," choose **3** (**E**dit), and then choose **4** (Style **C**ontents), so you can edit the Heading style.

③ With the cursor at the beginning of the style codes in the Style Contents text box ([HRt] is highlighted), choose **L**ayout, **O**ther or press **[Shift][F8]** (Format) and select **7** (**O**ther) to display the Other Format dialog box.

④ Choose **2** (**C**onditional End of Page), type **6**, press **[Enter]**, and choose OK. If necessary, choose Close to exit the Format dialog box and return to the Edit Style dialog box.

The code [Condl EOP] appears in the style.

⑤ Press **[F7]** (Exit) and then choose OK and Close to move through the dialog boxes and return to the main document window.

With Conditional End of Page in the heading style, you don't need the code that you inserted above the "RECOMMENDATIONS" heading, although it won't hurt anything. (If you like, you can turn on Reveal Codes and delete the [Condl EOP] code above "RECOMMEN-DATIONS.") Because the code is in the Heading style, the six lines that include each heading and the two lines of text after it will move as one unit in the event of a soft page break.

Setting Widow/Orphan Protection

Steven realizes that long documents often have another potential formatting problem: widows and orphans. An **orphan** is the first line of a paragraph appearing alone at the bottom of a page. A **widow** is the last line of a paragraph appearing alone at the top of a page. See Figure 4-45. Widows and orphans detract from the appearance and readability of a document. Fortunately, you can solve the problem of widows and orphans by using WordPerfect's Widow/Orphan Protection. Let's set widow/orphan protection in Steven's report.

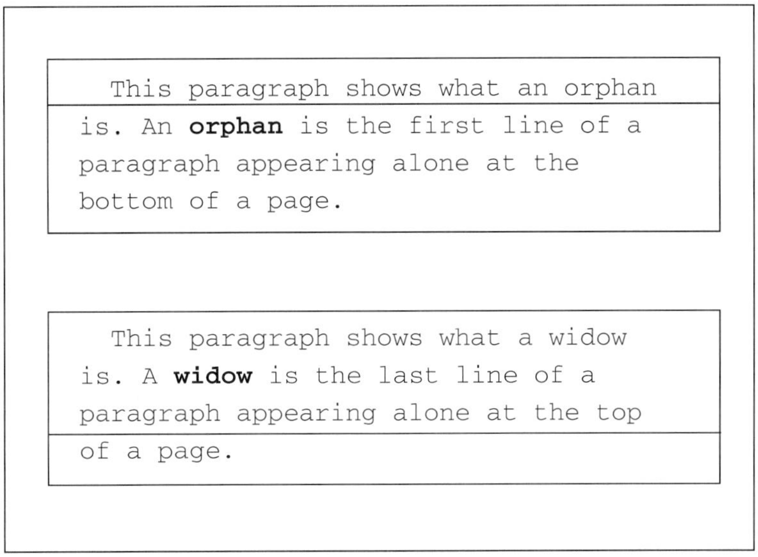

Figure 4-45
An orphan and a
widow

To set widow/orphan protection:

1. Move the cursor to the beginning of the document, before any text.
2. Choose **L**ayout, **O**ther or press **[Shift][F8]** (Format) and choose **7** (**O**ther). The Other Format dialog box appears on the screen.
3. Choose **3** (**W**idow/Orphan Protect) and choose OK. If necessary, choose Close to return to the document window.

   WordPerfect inserts the code [Wid/Orph] into the document. Now, no matter how you edit the document, no paragraph of four lines or more, when split between two pages, will ever leave only one line of the paragraph on a page.

Saving and Printing the Report

Save Steven's report as S4FILE3.REP, view the document, and then print it. Your final copy of the report should look like Figure 4-46 on the following pages.

1994 ANNUAL SALES REPORT

Steven Tanaka
Sales Representative
Territory Number 703

January 18, 1995

1994 ANNUAL SALES REPORT   Steven Tanaka

INTRODUCTION

This report summarizes my sales results in territory 703 (Arizona and New Mexico) from 1 January 1994 to 31 December 1994. In this report, I will:

1. Summarize gross sales in territory 703.
2. Compare my 1994 gross sales with gross sales for 1993 and 1992.
3. Document my success in obtaining major corporate accounts.
4. Suggest a 1995 marketing strategy for my territory and for other U.S. sales territories.

GROSS SALES

The following table summarizes the total sales in my region during the years 1992 to 1994:

TERRITORY 703 GROSS SALES (in dollars)					
Year	Qtr. 1	Qtr. 2	Qtr. 3	Qtr. 4	Total
1992	542,197	591,287	588,841	498,276	2,220,601
1993	562,422	681,647	584,892	540,699	2,369,660
1994	891,322	904,498	896,217	934,228	3,626,265

Figure 4-46
Final version of
Steven's annual
sales report

1994 ANNUAL SALES REPORT   Steven Tanaka

This table shows a 6.7% increase in sales from 1993, and then a 53% increase from 1993 to 1994. Since COEC spent almost the same amount of money to advertise product during this three-year period, I attribute the dramatic increase in income to improved targeting of our advertising and marketing and to improved customer relations. I especially credit COEC's new customer 800 number. This "hot line" allows us to handle customer orders and complaints more quickly and effectively. Most of my major corporate accounts reported improved satisfaction with our service and cited this as a major reason why they bought COEC products.

CORPORATE ACCOUNTS

COEC's strategy to focus on large corporate accounts has paid big dividends for me. During 1994, I visited 82 potential large-corporation customers in my territory. I was able to promise them better terms under our large-accounts discount program and our new customer hot line. To date, twenty-seven of these companies have begun buying their office equipment from COEC. I attribute this new business to the success of COEC's strategy.

The large corporations in my territory that seem to respond best to OOEC are more service intensive than manufacturing intensive. This is probably because the service industries require more of the type of office equipment that we sell.

1994 ANNUAL SALES REPORT   Steven Tanaka

RECOMMENDATIONS

Based upon my 1994 sales success, I recommend the following:

1. We should focus our sales calls and advertising on service-oriented industries, where we will get the most benefit from our marketing dollars.

2. We should continue our 800 "hot line." The additional and retained sales that are generated more than pay for this service.

3. We should continue to add new lines of office equipment. Our customers want a wider choice of new technology, in particular, fax machines, color copiers, and telephone-answering equipment.

4. We should consider adding office computers to our line of products. Many of the large corporations want to buy their computers from the same company that sells them their laser printers and fax machines.

Figure 4-46
(continued)

Exercises

1. Define or describe the following terms:
   a. header
   b. footer
   c. page numbering
   d. bookmark

2. How would you create a header that prints the title of your paper in the upper-right corner of every page?

3. How would you create a footer that prints your company name in the lower-left corner of every page?

4. Under what circumstances would you use each of the following features?
   a. Tables
   b. New Page Number
   c. Suppress (this page only)
   d. Style

5. What are the advantages of using a WordPerfect style to format the headings in your documents?

6. How would you set tabs every one inch (instead of the default of every half-inch) from the left margin of a document?

7. When you use WordPerfect's Tables feature to create or edit a table, how would you do each of the following?
   a. Draw double lines at the bottom of a cell
   b. Set a block of cells to right justification
   c. Create a single horizontal box that spans the entire width of the table
   d. Increase the width of a column in a table.

8. Explain the difference between the built-in bookmark called QuickMark and a user-defined bookmark.

9. What is the purpose of the following three WordPerfect commands? When would you use each of them?
   a. Conditional End of Page
   b. Widow/Orphan Protection
   c. Hard Page Break

Tutorial Assignments

Open the file T4FILE1.DFT from the data disk and do the following:

1. Change the format of the title to center justification, so that it is centered between the left and right margins.

2. Center the title page between the top and bottom margins.

3. Set the body of the report to full justification.

4. Change the line spacing to double spacing.

5. Number all the pages of the document in the upper-right corner of each page.

6. Suppress page numbering on the title page.

7. Change the tabs from 0.5-inch intervals to 0.3-inch intervals (from the left margin).

8. At the beginning of the document, turn on widow/orphan protection.

9. Create and apply a style for the headings, so they are boldface and centered.

10. In the heading style, insert a blank line at the beginning of the style, and then on that blank line, insert a Conditional End of Page code and specify that six lines should be kept together.

11. Save the file as S4FILE4.REP and print it.

Open the file T4FILE2.DFT from the data disk and do the following:

12. Create a footer that prints your name in the lower-left corner of each page and the page number in the lower-right corner. *Hint:* Within a footer, press [Ctrl][P] to insert the code for page numbers.

13. Create a character style that centers a title page top to bottom, center-justifies the lines of the title, makes the text of the title boldface, and suppresses page numbering and your footer. Then uses this style to create a title page with the title Preparing for Sales Calls, your name, and the current date. *Hint:* When you want to apply a character style, turn it on, then type the desired text, and then turn off the style.

14. Create a style that formats the headings. Each heading should include a Conditional End of Page code (with six lines kept together) and a blank line. The text of the heading should be underlined, but remain on the left. Apply this style to the three headings in the document.

15. Save the file as S4FILE5.DOC and print it.

Clear the document window and do the following:

16. Create an empty table that has three columns and seven rows.

17. Make the top row of cells into one cell, then change its justification to center. Type the heading **People to Contact in Territory 703** into the top row of the table.

18. In the second row of cells, type the following headings (one heading per cell): **Name, Company, Phone Number**. Adjust the widths of the cells so that each heading fits neatly on one line within the cell.

19. In the other five rows of the table type the following data:
Mary Fox, Kaibab Construction Co., (602) 429-8652
Carl Gallegos, Sandia Electronics Corp., (505) 322-4858
Bruno Kline, Santa Fe Travel Inc., (505) 841-2828
Sarah Dahlberg, Grand Canyon Tourist Assoc., (602) 335-8181
Candice Laake, Las Cruces Auto Parts Inc., (505) 821-7474

20. Adjust the width of the columns so that all the information fits neatly in each cell.

21. Save the file as S4FILE6.TAB and print it.

Case Problems

1. Information on Most Popular Movies

Jennifer Wong is the entertainment editor of the newspaper The Daily Review. She is writing an article about the movie industry and its popularity. She decides to include in her article a table listing the ten most popular movies in history.

Do the following:

1. Prepare a title page for the article on the popularity of the movies.
    a. Use as the title for the report, MAKE MY DAY, with the subtitle Take Me to a Movie.
    b. Also include on the title page the author of the article, the name of the newspaper, and today's date.
    c. Center-justify the lines of the title page.
    d. Center the entire page between the top and bottom margins.

2. On a second page, create a table with four columns and twelve rows.
    a. Join the cells in the top row into one cell.
    b. Insert into that cell the title ALL-TIME TOP TEN AMERICAN MOVIES.
    c. In the second row of cells, type the headings Rank, Title, Year, and Income (millions), with one heading per cell.

3. Adjust the width of the cells as follows:
    a. Make the Rank column very narrow, to fit the numbers 1 through 10.
    b. Make the Title column wide enough to fit the names of the movies. (Refer to #4, below.)
    c. Make the Year column narrower, to fit the dates.
    d. Make the Income column moderately wide.

4. Into the other ten rows, insert the following data:

1	E.T. The Extra-Terrestrial	1982	$229
2	Star Wars	1977	$194
3	Return of the Jedi	1983	$168
4	Batman	1989	$151
5	The Empire Strikes Back	1980	$142
6	Home Alone	1990	$140
7	Ghostbusters	1984	$133
8	Jaws	1975	$130
9	Raiders of the Lost Ark	1981	$116
10	Indiana Jones and the Last Crusade	1989	$116

5. Save the file as S4MOVIES.TAB and print it.

2. Report on Computer Cost and Speed

David Sokol is a graduate student at the Carlton University School of Business. As part of a class project, he must prepare a short report comparing several popular types of computers used in business offices. In his paper, he includes a table to compare each computer's cost and speed.

Do the following:

1. Open the file P4COMP.DFT from the data disk into a document window.

2. Change the line spacing to double spacing.

3. Change the tab stops so that they begin at 0.4 inches from the left margin and are spaced every 0.4 inches thereafter.

4. Set the body of the report to full justification.

5. Turn on widow/orphan protection for the entire report.

6. Create a header.
    a. Set the text of the header to flush right.
    b. Type the text of the header: **Comparison of Computers page** followed by a space. Make the title boldface.
    c. Press **[Ctrl][P]** after the text of the header to insert the code for page numbering.

7. Create a title page for the report.
    a. Insert a hard page break to separate the title page from the body of the report.
    b. On the title page, type the title A Comparison of the Speed of Common Business Computers. Press [Enter] three times after the title.
    c. Type the following information: A Report for BusMng 617. Press [Enter] twice after this information.
    d. Type by David Sokol, press [Enter] twice, and insert the current date using WordPerfect's Date Text command.
    e. Center the text of the title between the left and right margins.
    f. Center the text of the title between the top and bottom margins.

8. Suppress the header so it won't appear on the title page when you print the report.

9. Make the first page of the body of the report page number 1.

10. Create and apply a style for the four headings: INTRODUCTION, COMPUTER SYSTEMS, METHODS, and RESULTS.
    a. Within the style, insert a single-spaced line above the text of the heading.
    b. On the blank line above the heading, insert a Conditional End of Page code to keep six lines together.
    c. Make the heading underlined.

11. As David writes his report, he often has to refer to the Methods section. Immediately after the METHODS heading, insert a bookmark named Methods.

12. Look through the report. Make sure no heading is left alone at the bottom of a page. If necessary, insert a Conditional End of Page.

13. Move the cursor to the end of the report, insert two blank lines, and create the table shown in Figure 4-47. Make your table look as much like this one as possible.

Comparison of Popular PC Models				
Model	Test #1	Test #2	Test #3	Cost
286-12Mhz	35 sec	447 sec	351 sec	$700
386SX-16	27 sec	286 sec	349 sec	$950
386-20Mhz	26 sec	285 sec	240 sec	$1100
386-33Mhz	9 sec	105 sec	237 sec	$1300
486SX-25	25 sec	102 sec	162 sec	$1500
486-33Mhz	6 sec	52 sec	154 sec	$1800
486-50Mhz	5 sec	21 sec	142 sec	$2100
486DX2-66	4 sec	15 sec	142 sec	$2700

Figure 4-47

14. Save the report as S4COMP.REP and print it.

3. Investment Accounts Report

Karen Brueck is the president of Omaha Investors Group, an investment club of about 30 members. Karen asks her secretary, Christopher Manning, to prepare a quarterly report to send to each club member, telling them how each of the club's four investment accounts is doing. She tells Christopher to include in the report a table that compares each of the accounts over the last five years.

Do the following:

1. Open P4INVEST.DFT from the data disk into a document window.
2. Set the entire report to double spacing.
3. Make a header that prints the shortened title Club Q2 Report page 1, but instead of typing the 1 in page 1, press **[Ctrl][P]** to insert the page code, so that the page number will print as part of the heading.
4. Insert a hard page break after the date (and above the heading Introduction) to create a separate title page.
5. Set up the format of the title page so it is center-justified between the left and right margins.
6. Center the text of the title page between the top and bottom margins.
7. Suppress the header for the title page.
8. Turn on widow/orphan protection for the entire document.

9.   Change the page number after the title page to page 1.

10. Set the body of the report to full justification.

11. Create a style for the headings within the report. Make the headings boldface and centered between the left and right margins. Apply the style to all of the headings: Introduction, Fund Description, and Fund Performance.

12. Move the cursor to the phrase (Insert first table here). Delete the phrase, and then create the table in Figure 4-48 at that location.

Total Annual Returns(%)							
FUND NAME	1988	1989	1990	1991	1992	1993	1994
Fixed Income	9.8	9.0	9.0	9.0	9.9	9.7	9.6
Common Stock	5.3	16.6	31.2	-3.3	30.1	20.7	18.7
Windlow Stock	1.2	24.7	15.0	-5.7	25.2	17.6	37.7
Growth Stock	13.1	2.7	43.1	-19.8	65.7	31.1	21.1

Figure 4-48

13. Move the cursor to the phrase (Insert second table here). Delete the phrase, and then create the table in Figure 4-49 at that location.

The Current Value of Each Investment Fund (based on a 12/31/87 value of $1000)		
FUND NAME	Current Value	Avg. Yearly Ret.
Fixed Income	$1,755.44	9.42%
Common Stock	$2,560.44	16.23%
Windlow Stock	$2,204.87	13.49%
Growth Stock	$3,048.58	19.52%

Figure 4-49

14. Save the report as S4INVEST.REP and print it.

Tutorial 5

Using Special Word-Processing Features

Writing a Feasibility Report

Case: Connolly/Bayle Publishing Company

Since graduating last year with a degree in business management, Jonathan Lew has worked in outside sales for Connolly/Bayle (C/B) Publishing Company, which publishes computer magazines. Recently Jonathan took an in-house job as an assistant to Ann McMullen, the business manager for C/B Publishing. The company's cofounders, Stephen Connolly and John Bayle, have asked Ann to head a task force to investigate the feasibility of starting a new magazine aimed at graphic designers who use personal computers. The task force consists of Ann, Jonathan, two marketing managers, and two editors who manage other magazines at C/B Publishing.

The task force met to map out strategies for the feasibility study. They decided to send out questionnaires, conduct interviews, and, with David Palermo, an accountant at C/B Publishing, make financial projections. After completing the study, the task force met again to analyze the information, draw conclusions, and make recommendations. Ann asked Jonathan to draft an outline for the group's final report and to distribute copies of the outline to the other task force members for their approval. Once the outline has been approved, Ann will write the main body of the report and Jonathan will pre- pare the report for final distribution by adding footnotes, section headings, and other features.

OBJECTIVES

In this tutorial you will learn to:

- Use the Outline feature
- Switch between two or more document windows
- Display multiple document windows on the screen
- Record and play macros
- Create footnotes
- Use hyphenation

Planning the Document

The responsibility for planning the document rests with Jonathan, although the other members of the task force will respond to his ideas and give their final approval.

Content

The content of the feasibility report will come from the results of the feasibility study itself, from the financial analysis, and from the discussion notes Ann and Jonathan took during the task force meetings.

Organization

Jonathan will organize the feasibility report by creating an outline. He decides to have an introductory section, which will state the purposes of the report and explain how the data were gathered. He will then include sections on the target audience for the new magazine, operating expenses, and projected income. The report will conclude with a summary and the recommendation of the task force.

Style

Jonathan wants the feasibility report to conform to standard business writing style, with straight-forward logic and clear, direct sentences.

Format

C/B Publishing has no policy on how to format in-house reports. Jonathan will use Word-Perfect's default settings for margins, tabs, and justification and the standard format he learned in college for titles, headings, and page numbering.

Creating an Outline

Jonathan's task is to organize the data collected in the feasibility study and outline the report. He decides to use WordPerfect's Outline feature. In an outline, each paragraph is preceded by a paragraph number. The paragraph numbers represent levels: level-1 paragraphs (major ideas) are usually preceded by Roman numerals (I, II, III, etc.), level-2 paragraphs (supporting ideas) by uppercase letters (A, B, C, etc.), level-3 paragraphs by Arabic numerals (1, 2, 3, etc.), level-4 paragraphs by lowercase letters (a, b, c, etc.), and so forth (Figure 5-1).

Paragraph numbering in a WordPerfect outline reflects this standard hierarchy. WordPerfect's Outline feature allows up to eight levels of paragraph numbers. Notice that WordPerfect outline paragraph numbers can be numerals or letters.

```
I.    Level 1, first paragraph
      A.   Level 2
           1.  Level 3
           2.  Level 3
      B.   Level 2
           1.  Level 3
               a.  Level 4
               b.  Level 4
           2.  Level 3
II.   Level 1, second paragraph
      A.   Level 2
      B.   Level 2
III.  Level 1, third paragraph
```

Figure 5-1
Standard outline
levels and
paragraph numbers

The advantage of WordPerfect's Outline feature is that paragraph numbering is automatic. When Outline is on and you press [Enter] to end one paragraph and start a new one, WordPerfect automatically inserts the appropriate number or letter for the next paragraph in the outline. With a simple keystroke, you can change a paragraph number from a higher level to a lower level or from a lower level to a higher level. When you move a paragraph or a group of paragraphs in the outline, WordPerfect automatically renumbers them.

The first draft of Jonathan's outline is shown in Figure 5-2. In the following steps, you'll use WordPerfect's Outline feature to create this outline.

```
                                  OUTLINE

            Report on the Feasibility of Publishing a New Magazine
                           The Computer Artist

       I.     Introduction
              A.    Purposes of report
                    1.  Potential size of the market
                    2.  Competing magazines
                    3.  Projected costs of starting and running
                        the magazine
                    4.  Potential profitability of the magazine
              B.    Information upon which decision will be based
       II.    Target audience
              A.    Description of target audience
              B.    Estimated size of target audience
       III.   Expenses
              A.    Start-up expenses
              B.    Total first-year expenses
              C.    Sustaining cost
       IV.    Projected income
              A.    Estimate of number of subscribers
              B.    Estimate of income from advertising
              C.    Estimate of income from subscriptions
       V.     Summary and recommendation
```

Figure 5-2
Jonathan's outline
of the report

First you need to create the title of the outline.

To create the outline title:

① Make sure the WordPerfect document window is clear.

② Choose **L**ayout, **A**lignment, **C**enter or press **[Shift][F6]** (Center), then type **OUTLINE** and press **[Enter]** twice.

③ Type the next two lines of the title, as shown in Figure 5-2. Choose **L**ayout, **A**lignment, **C**enter or press **[Shift][F6]** (Center) to center these lines.

④ Press **[Enter]** twice to double-space after the title. See Figure 5-3.

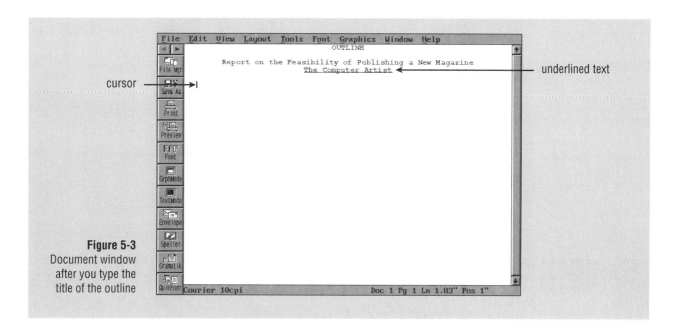

Figure 5-3
Document window
after you type the
title of the outline

cursor

underlined text

Now you're ready to turn on WordPerfect's Outline feature and create the outline. With Outline on, whenever you press [Enter], WordPerfect automatically inserts a new paragraph number into the document. You can then type the text of the paragraph; change the paragraph to a lower level (for example, from II to A) by pressing [Tab] or to a higher level (for example, from A to II) by pressing [Shift][Tab]; or delete the paragraph number entirely by pressing [Backspace]. As you work through the following steps, you'll see how these commands work to help you create an outline quickly and efficiently.

To create an outline:

① With the cursor at the left margin on the first line after the title, choose **T**ools, **O**utline, **B**egin New Outline or press **[Ctrl][F5]** (Outline) and choose **1** (**B**egin New Outline).

WordPerfect displays the Outline Style List dialog box, from which you can choose the outline style you want to use. See Figure 5-4 on the following page. WordPerfect supports several different types of paragraph numbering styles, such as Paragraph, which uses the paragraph numbers "1., a., i., (1), (a), (i), 1), a)," and Legal, which uses decimal numbers "1, 1.1, 1.1.1, etc.," as shown in the dialog box in Figure 5-4 on the following page. We want to choose the Outline paragraph numbering style, which uses the paragraph numbers "I., A., 1., a., (1), (a), i), a)."

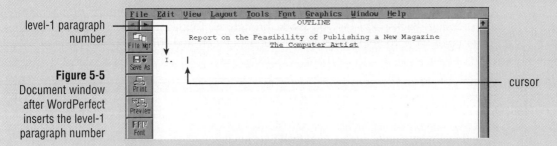

choose this
command

Figure 5-4
Outline Style List
dialog box

② Highlight **Outline** and choose **1** (**S**elect).

WordPerfect turns Outline on, inserts the format code for the type of outline style you chose, inserts the paragraph number I, and automatically indents to the next tab stop. See Figure 5-5. (If you like, you can see these codes by turning on Reveal Codes. After looking at the codes, turn off Reveal Codes.)

level-1 paragraph
number

Figure 5-5
Document window
after WordPerfect
inserts the level-1
paragraph number

cursor

You are now ready to type the text of Jonathan's draft outline.

③ Type **Introduction** and press **[Enter]**. See Figure 5-6.

Figure 5-6
Document window
after WordPerfect
inserts the second
level-1 paragraph
number

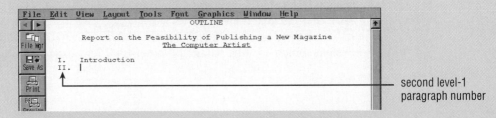

second level-1
paragraph number

Because the Outline feature is on, pressing [Enter] moves the cursor down one line and automatically inserts the next level-1 paragraph number (II). However, you want the level-2 paragraph number A, not II, on this line, as shown in Figure 5-2. To indent and change the paragraph number, you press [Tab].

❹ Press **[Tab]** to change from the level-1 paragraph number I to the level-2 paragraph number A and indent to the next tab stop.

You're now ready to type the text of the level-2 paragraph.

❺ Type **Purposes of report** and press **[Enter]**. See Figure 5-7.

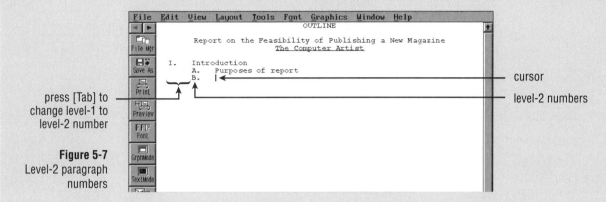

press [Tab] to change level-1 to level-2 number

cursor

level-2 numbers

Figure 5-7
Level-2 paragraph numbers

Notice that, when you press [Enter], WordPerfect again automatically inserts a paragraph number, but this time it is a level-2 number, because that is the *current* level.

❻ With the cursor to the right of paragraph B, press **[Tab]** to change from level 2 to level 3 and to indent to the next tab stop. The "B" changes to "1."

❼ Type **Potential size of the market** and press **[Enter]**. When you press [Enter] here, the cursor moves to the next line, and WordPerfect inserts the next paragraph number in the current level — in this case, the level-3 number 2.

❽ Type **Competing magazines**, press **[Enter]** to insert the next paragraph number (3), and type **Projected costs of starting and running the magazine**. Press **[Enter]** again and type **Potential profitability of the magazine**. See Figure 5-8.

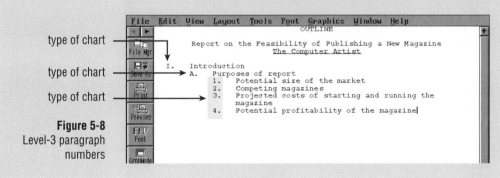

type of chart

type of chart

type of chart

Figure 5-8
Level-3 paragraph numbers

You have now completed four items at level 3. In the next steps, you'll instruct WordPerfect to change a lower-level paragraph number to a higher-level paragraph number. To change to a higher level paragraph number, you press [Shift][Tab] (Left Margin Release).

To change to a higher level:

1. Press **[Enter]**. WordPerfect inserts the level-3 paragraph number 5, which you don't want.

2. Press [Shift][Tab] (Left Margin Release) to return to the next higher level of paragraph numbering. The level-3 paragraph number 5 changes to the level-2 paragraph number B.

3. Type **Information upon which decision will be based**. Your screen should now look like Figure 5-9.

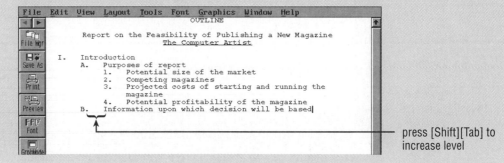

Figure 5-9
Using [Shift][Tab] to increase the paragraph level

press [Shift][Tab] to increase level

4. Complete the outline shown in Figure 5-2. Remember that when you want to change to a lower level in the outline, press [Tab], and when you want to change to a higher level, press [Shift][Tab]. Do not press [Enter] after typing the last line.

5. Save this intermediate version of the outline as S5OUTLIN.DFT.

Your screen should now look like Figure 5-10.

Figure 5-10
Document window with the completed outline

cursor

Moving the Cursor Through an Outline Using the Keyboard

In addition to the standard WordPerfect cursor-movement commands, WordPerfect provides four special cursor-movement commands to use in an outline (Figure 5-11). These special cursor-movement commands require an enhanced keyboard with separate cursor-movement keys. (If you don't have an enhanced keyboard, go to the next section.) Let's practice using the special cursor-movement commands.

SPECIAL OUTLINE CURSOR-MOVEMENT KEYS	
Keys	**Description**
[Alt][→]	Move cursor to next paragraph
[Alt][←]	Move cursor to previous paragraph
[Alt][↓]	Move cursor to next paragraph at same outline level or higher
[Alt][↑]	Move cursor to previous paragraph at same outline level or higher

Figure 5-11
Special outline
cursor-movement
keys

To use the special cursor-movement commands to move the cursor through the outline:

1. Make sure the intermediate version of the outline, S5FILE1.DFT, is in a WordPerfect document window.

2. Use the standard cursor-movement keys to move the cursor to the "I" in "Introduction," to the right of Roman numeral I.

3. Press **[Alt][→]** ten times and then **[Alt][←]** ten times. Observe the movement of the cursor.

    As you can see, the cursor moves to the beginning of the text of the next paragraph each time you press [Alt][→] and to the beginning of the text of the previous paragraph each time you press [Alt][←].

4. Make sure the cursor is at the "I" in "Introduction" once again. Press **[Alt][↓]** four times. Then press **[Alt][↑]** four times. Observe the movement of the cursor.

    As you can see, pressing [Alt][↑] moves the cursor to the previous paragraph number of the same level or higher, and pressing [Alt][↓] moves the cursor to the next paragraph number of the same level or higher.

Inserting New Paragraph Numbers into an Outline

Jonathan gives the task force members a copy of the outline at their next meeting. The task force decides to add a new section on competing magazines, as shown in Figure 5-12. They also suggest that item III ("Expenses") and item IV ("Projected income") be switched, so that projected income is presented before expenses. Finally, they suggest that items B and C under "Projected income" be switched, so that the estimate of income from subscriptions comes immediately after the estimate of the number of subscribers. Jonathan will use WordPerfect's outline editing features to make these changes.

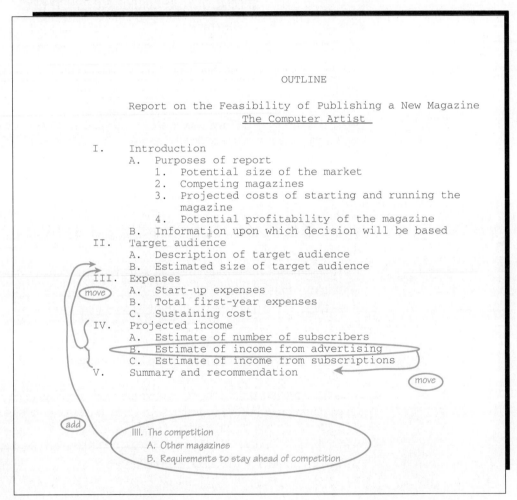

Figure 5-12
The task force's
suggested changes
to the outline

After the task force meeting, Jonathan returns to his office and edits the outline according to the committee's suggestions. First let's insert the text on competing magazines, which begins with outline paragraph number III.

To insert new paragraph numbers into an outline:

1. Move the cursor to the end of item II.B., "Estimated size of target audience," that is, to the end of the line above the point at which you want to make the insertion.

2. Press **[Enter]**. WordPerfect inserts a hard return, moves the cursor down a line, and inserts the paragraph number "C" under the "B."

   Because Jonathan wants a level-1 paragraph number (III) here, he must change the paragraph number "C" to a higher level.

3. Press **[Shift][Tab]** (Left Margin Release) to change the paragraph number to a higher level.

   The "C" disappears, the cursor moves one tab stop to the left, and "III" appears on the screen. WordPerfect automatically increments the subsequent level-1 paragraph numbers.

4. Type **The competition**.

Next you'll insert the two level-2 paragraphs into the revised outline.

5. Press **[Enter]** to insert a hard return and a new paragraph number, press **[Tab]** to change to a lower level (A), and type **Other magazines**.

6. Press **[Enter]** and type **Requirements to stay ahead of competition**.

   Your screen should now look like Figure 5-13. WordPerfect automatically renumbered the outline paragraphs below the newly inserted text.

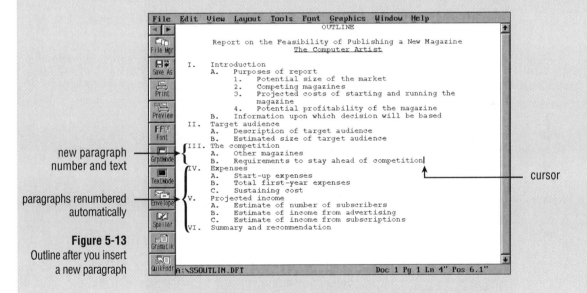

new paragraph
number and text

paragraphs renumbered
automatically

cursor

Figure 5-13
Outline after you insert
a new paragraph

Using the Outline Bar

WordPerfect provides another method for editing an outline, called the Outline Bar. Let's display and then use this feature.

To display the Outline Bar:

① Choose **V**iew, **O**utline Bar or press **[Ctrl][F5]** (Outline) to display the Outline dialog box, then choose **7** (**D**isplay Outline Bar). WordPerfect displays the Outline Bar shown in Figure 5-14.

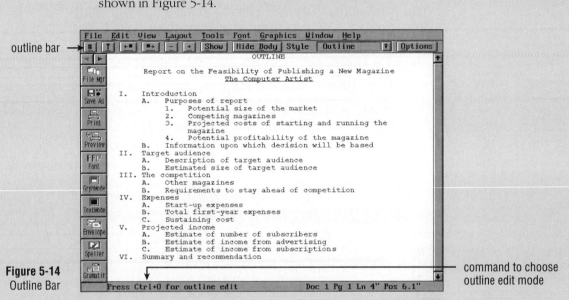

outline bar →

Figure 5-14
Outline Bar

command to choose
outline edit mode

Let's try a few of the options available on the Outline Bar. The Outline Bar is designed primarily for use with a mouse. If you do not have a mouse, skip this series of steps.

Suppose you want to see just main (level-1) headings and text.

To use the options on the Outline Bar:

① Click the Show button on the Outline Bar. A menu displaying the outline levels appears on the screen. See Figure 5-15.

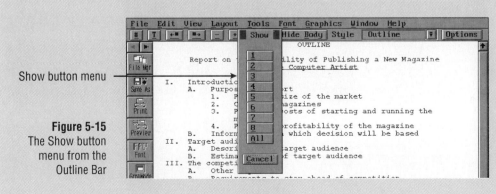

Show button menu →

Figure 5-15
The Show button
menu from the
Outline Bar

② Choose **1**. The outline collapses to display only level-1 paragraphs. See Figure 5-16. The text of the lower-level paragraphs is not lost, just hidden.

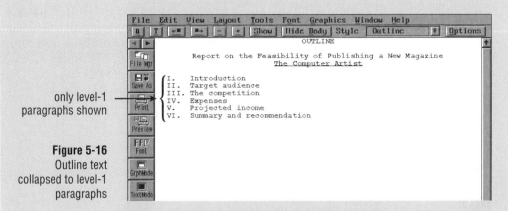

only level-1 paragraphs shown

Figure 5-16
Outline text collapsed to level-1 paragraphs

③ Click the Show button and choose All to redisplay all levels of the outline.

Next we'll convert an outline paragraph into regular text.

④ Move the cursor (for example, by pressing **[Alt][↑]** or **[Alt][↓]**) to the beginning of paragraph III, "The competition."

⑤ Click the **T** button on the Outline Bar. The phrase, "The competition," no longer has a number, and WordPerfect has renumbered the paragraphs below it. See Figure 5-17.

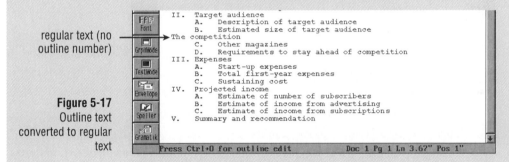

regular text (no outline number)

Figure 5-17
Outline text converted to regular text

⑥ Without moving the cursor, choose **#** from the button bar. WordPerfect converts the normal text into a numbered paragraph. It numbers the paragraph at the same level as the numbered paragraph above it.

⑦ Press **[Shift][Tab]** to convert "C. The competition" from level 2 back to level 1 — "III. The competition."

With the Outline Bar on the screen, you can insert and delete text and do most of the other editing commands available in a normal document window, as long as WordPerfect is not in Outline Edit mode, as explained later.

Using Outline Edit Mode

You've already discovered how easy it is to insert new paragraph numbers and text into your outline. Revising the hierarchy of your outline is just as easy. WordPerfect provides an easy way to delete, copy, or move entire outline families. An outline **family** is a group of paragraph numbers and accompanying text that includes the level where the cursor is located and all levels subordinate to it, as shown in Figure 5-18.

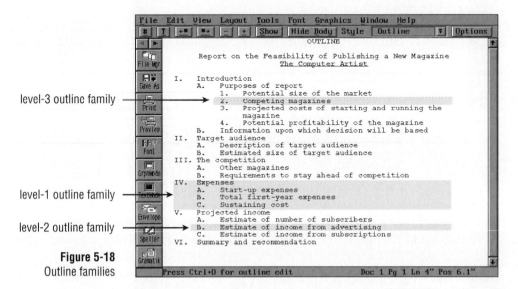

level-3 outline family

level-1 outline family

level-2 outline family

Figure 5-18
Outline families

The key to quick editing of outline families is WordPerfect's Outline Edit mode. In Outline Edit mode you can:

- Change an outline paragraph to a higher or lower level
- Change the level of an outline family with one command
- Move or copy an entire outline family
- Change the outline style to modify the numbering method or convert from numbered paragraphs to headings
- Show or hide specific levels of your outline

To use the Outline Edit mode, the Outline Bar *must* be active. In Outline Edit mode, you can use the keyboard, as well as the mouse, to execute Outline Bar commands. You cannot insert or delete text in Outline Edit mode.

To activate and use Outline Edit mode:

1 With the Outline Bar still in the document window, press **[Ctrl][O]**. Your document window now looks something like Figure 5-19, with one of the outline families highlighted. Along the left edge of the outline, you can see a column of minus signs (dashes). You can now use the keyboard, as well as the mouse, to execute an Outline Bar command, either by pressing the letter key that corresponds to the mnemonic (underlined) letter on the Outline Bar or by clicking with the mouse.

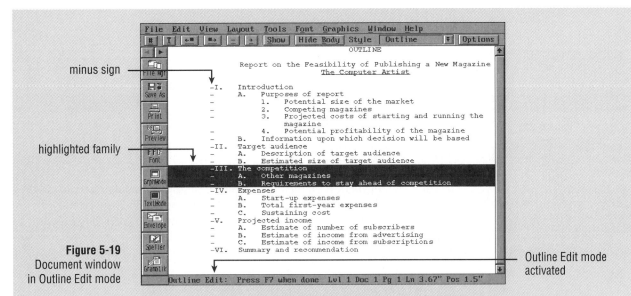

minus sign

highlighted family

Figure 5-19
Document window
in Outline Edit mode

Outline Edit mode
activated

❷ Press [↑] several times and then press [↓] several times. Alternatively, you can click the mouse pointer on a paragraph number to move the highlight to that location. Notice how the highlight moves to the next outline family, not necessarily just the next line. Now press [↑] until the highlighted text blocks the entire first outline family. See Figure 5-20.

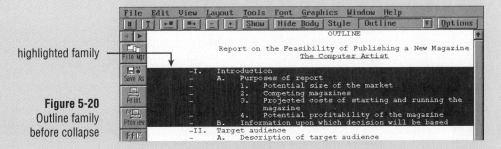

highlighted family

Figure 5-20
Outline family
before collapse

As you can see, the highlight (block) selects an outline paragraph or an outline family, depending on the location of the cursor. The blocked text is always an outline paragraph and all paragraphs (if any) that are subordinate to it. For example, when the highlighted block begins at "I. Introduction," WordPerfect extends the highlight to the "A" and "B" paragraphs below it, as shown in Figure 5-20.

The minus signs along the left edge of the outline tell you that, if you click the minus sign button on the Outline bar or press dash (minus sign), WordPerfect will collapse that family. In other words, the highest level paragraph will remain on the screen, but all paragraphs subordinate to it will be hidden. Let's try it.

❸ Click the minus sign (-) button on the Outline Bar or press the dash key on the main keyboard or the minus sign key on the numeric keypad. This hides the subordinate paragraphs and changes the minus sign to a plus sign. See Figure 5-21 on the following page.

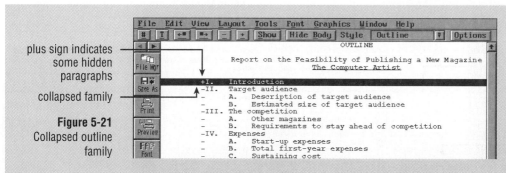

plus sign indicates some hidden paragraphs

collapsed family

Figure 5-21
Collapsed outline family

④   Click the plus sign (**+**) button on the Outline Bar or press the plus sign key on either the numeric keypad or the main keyboard to redisplay the subordinate paragraphs. The minus sign reappears next to the Roman numeral I, and the entire outline family reappears.

Moving an Outline Family

Jonathan's next task is to move the outline family that begins with paragraph number V ("Projected income") and includes subordinate paragraphs A, B, and C. Let's use Outline Edit mode to move this outline family.

To move an outline family using Outline Edit mode:

①   In Outline Edit mode, use the arrow keys or the mouse pointer to highlight family V, as shown in Figure 5-22.

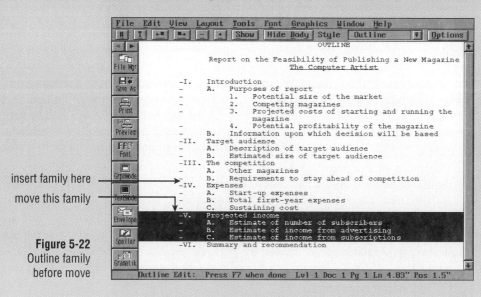

insert family here

move this family

Figure 5-22
Outline family before move

② From the Outline Bar, choose **O**ptions to display the Outline dialog box. Because you cannot insert or delete text within Outline Edit mode, you do not need to press [Alt] to access the Outline Bar with the keyboard. See Figure 5-23.

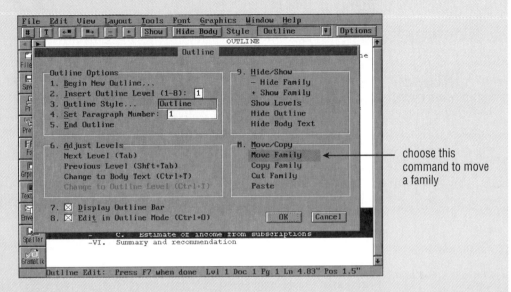

choose this command to move a family

Figure 5-23
Outline dialog box

③ Choose **M** (**M**ove/Copy) and **1** (**M**ove Family).

WordPerfect removes (cuts) the highlighted family from the outline and displays the prompt "Move cursor; press Enter to retrieve" on the status bar at the bottom of the document window. See Figure 5-24.

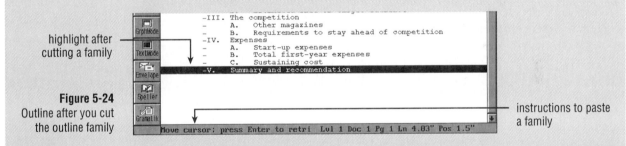

highlight after cutting a family

Figure 5-24
Outline after you cut the outline family

instructions to paste a family

④ Highlight the "IV. Expenses" outline family, and press **[Enter]**. WordPerfect inserts the "Projected income" family above the "Expenses" family. WordPerfect automatically renumbers the outline so that "Projected income" becomes number IV, and "Expenses" becomes number V.

You have now moved the "Projected income" family above the "Expenses" family. Your next task is to move item "B. Estimate of income from advertising" underneath item "C. Estimate of income from subscriptions." Let's use a simpler method for moving an outline family.

To move a family in Outline Edit mode:

① Move the highlight to "B. Estimate of income from advertising," as shown in Figure 5-25.

highlighted family to move

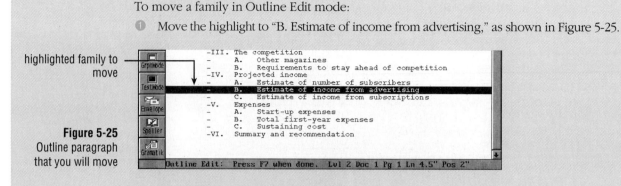

Figure 5-25
Outline paragraph
that you will move

② Press **[Ctrl][↓]**. The highlighted paragraph moves down one position, so that it becomes paragraph C.

As usual, WordPerfect automatically renumbers the outline. Pressing [Ctrl][↓] moves the highlighted family below the next family; pressing [Ctrl][↑] moves it above the previous family.

Exiting Outline Edit Mode and Turning Off the Outline Bar

You have now made all the requested changes to the outline. You're ready to exit Outline Edit mode and turn off the Outline Bar.

To exit Outline Edit mode:

① Press **[F7]** (Exit) to exit Outline Edit mode. The minus signs at the left edge of the outline disappear.

Now let's turn off the Outline Bar.

To turn off the Outline Bar:

① Choose **V**iew, **O**utline Bar to turn off the Outline Bar. Alternatively, you could choose **T**ools, **O**utline, Out**l**ine Options to display the Outline dialog box, and then choose **7** (**D**isplay Outline Bar) to toggle off the Outline Bar.

Your document window no longer displays the Outline Bar.

Turning Off the Outline Feature

If your document doesn't contain any text after the outline, you don't have to turn off the Outline feature. But if you want to insert additional text below the outline, you must turn off the Outline feature.

To turn off the Outline feature:

1. Move the cursor to the end of the outline.
2. Choose **T**ools, **O**utline, **E**nd Outline or press **[Ctrl][F5]** (Outline) and choose **5** (**E**nd Outline). Now when you press [Enter] or edit text below the outline, WordPerfect will no longer display outline paragraph numbers.

Now let's save and print the completed outline.

3. Save the outline as S5OUTLIN.DOC and print it.

    The final version of your outline should now look like Figure 5-26.

```
                            OUTLINE

        Report on the Feasibility of Publishing a New Magazine
                      The Computer Artist

    I.   Introduction
         A.   Purposes of report
              1.  Potential size of the market
              2.  Competing magazines
              3.  Projected costs of starting and running the
                  magazine
              4.  Potential profitability of the magazine
         B.   Information upon which decision will be based
   II.   Target audience
         A.   Description of target audience
         B.   Estimated size of target audience
  III.   The competition
         A.   Other magazines
         B.   Requirements to stay ahead of competition
   IV.   Projected income
         A.   Estimate of number of subscribers
         B.   Estimate of income from subscriptions
         C.   Estimate of income from advertising
    V.   Expenses
         A.   Start-up expenses
         B.   Total first-year expenses
         C.   Sustaining cost
   VI.   Summary and recommendation
```

Figure 5-26
Final version of
Jonathan's outline

You may now close the document window, exit WordPerfect, and take a break, or you can leave the document in the document window for use in the next exercise.

Using Multiple Document Windows

After approving Jonathan's revised outline, the task force agrees that Ann should begin writing the first draft of the report.

Opening a Second Document Window

Ann wants to have the approved outline handy at all times without cluttering her desk; therefore, she decides to use WordPerfect's multiple document window feature. The **multiple document window** feature allows you to have up to nine document windows open at once. You can then easily switch back and forth among them. This is helpful if you want to read one document while creating another, copy text from one document to another, or edit two or more documents together. In this case, Ann will write her report in document window 2 (labeled "Doc 2" on the status line) while keeping the outline in document window 1 (labeled "Doc 1" on the status line). In that way, she will always have access to the approved outline in WordPerfect. Let's use WordPerfect's multiple document feature to begin writing the report.

To use document window 2:

1. Make sure the final version of the outline (S5OUTLIN.DOC) is in document window 1. If it isn't, open S5OUTLIN.DOC now.

2. Choose **W**indow, **Sw**itch to or press **[F3]** (Switch To). WordPerfect displays the Switch to Document dialog box. See Figure 5-27.

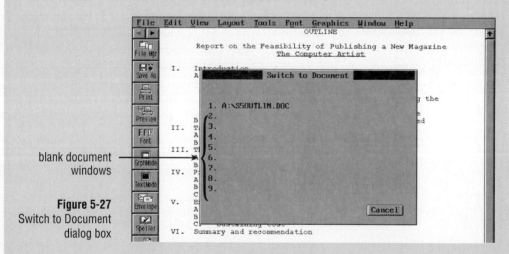

blank document windows

Figure 5-27
Switch to Document
dialog box

The dialog box shows you which windows are open and the name of the file (if any) in each of the windows. In our case, only document window 1 is open.

3. Choose **2**. WordPerfect switches to document window 2. The right side of the status line shows "Doc 2" instead of "Doc 1."

With blank document window 2 open, Ann is ready to start writing the report.

Copying Text Between Document Windows

Ann can now use Doc 2 to write her report and switch to Doc 1 whenever she wants to see the outline. She will use [F3] (Switch To) and other methods we'll present in the following procedure to switch between the two documents.

So that she doesn't have to retype the title of the report, Ann decides to copy it from the outline. Let's copy the title from Doc 1 to Doc 2 using a block operation.

To copy text from Doc 1 to Doc 2:

① Switch back to Doc 1 by choosing **W**indow, **S**witch or by pressing **[Shift][F3]** (Switch). These commands automatically switch you to the next open document window.

② Move the cursor to the left margin of the line that begins "Report on the Feasibility."

③ Turn the Block command on by choosing **E**dit, **B**lock or by pressing **[Alt][F4]** or **[F12]** (Block).

④ Move the cursor to the end of the second line of the title, after "The Computer Artist," to highlight the title.

⑤ Choose **E**dit, **C**opy or press **[Ctrl][C]**.

Now you want to switch to Doc 2 and paste the title there.

⑥ Choose **W**indow, **S**witch or choose **W**indow, S**w**itch to and choose **2**. Alternatively, press **[Shift][F3]** (Switch) or press **[F3]** (Switch to) and choose **2**. Simplest of all, press **[Home]**, **2**. (Pressing [Home] and 2 is a shortcut for choosing **W**indow, S**w**itch to, **2**.) Any one of these methods will switch you from Doc 1 to Doc 2.

⑦ Choose **E**dit, **P**aste or press **[Ctrl][V]**. A copy of the title is pasted into Doc 2. See Figure 5-28.

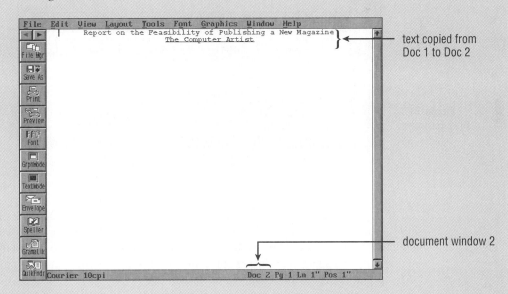

Figure 5-28
Document window
2 after you copy text

These steps demonstrate that you can use the familiar copy and cut-and-paste operations to copy and move text, not only within a document, but also between documents.

Using Tiled Windows

Ann decides that she would like to be able to see the outline while she is typing her report. Using the Switch command, she can easily switch between the two documents, but she can't see them both on the screen at once. To view the documents simultaneously, she will use the Tile Window feature.

To use the Tile Window feature:

1 Make sure that Doc 2 still appears on your screen.

2 Choose **W**indow, **T**ile. WordPerfect puts a frame around each of the two windows, reduces their size, and fits them onto the screen, like tiles on a bathroom floor. See Figure 5-29. The active window — the one with the cursor in it, where all editing takes place — has a highlighted title bar. In our case, "2-(Untitled)" is active; "1-A:\S5OUTLIN.DOC" is inactive.

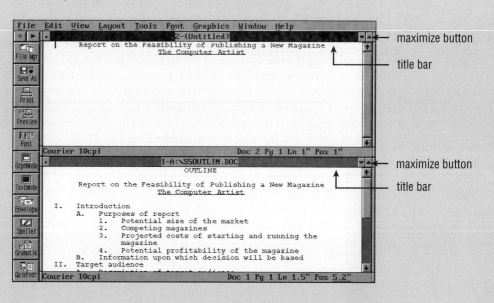

Figure 5-29
Tiled document windows

Now Ann can see both documents simultaneously. She can edit only one document at a time because the cursor must be in either one window or the other. She can, however, move the cursor between the two windows using any of the commands demonstrated for switching from one document window to another. She can also simply click the mouse pointer in the window she wants to activate.

Ann decides that her report should be double-spaced, so her next task is to set double spacing for the document in Doc 2. Let's insert the format code for double spacing.

To double-space the document in Doc 2:

1. If necessary, move the cursor to the beginning of document window 2, before the title.

2. Choose **L**ayout, **L**ine or press **[Shift][F8]** (Format) and choose **1** (Line). The Line Format dialog box appears on the screen.

3. Choose **3** (Line **S**pacing), type **2** for double spacing, and press **[Enter]**.

4. Choose OK and Close if necessary or press **[F7]** (Exit) once or twice to return to the document window.

Next Ann wants to type a heading for the first section of her report.

To insert a heading:

1. In Doc 2, move the cursor to the end of the title, after "The Computer Artist" and after the Underline code. Choose F**o**nt, **U**nderline or press **[F8]** (Underline), if necessary, to make sure Underline is off, then press **[Enter]** to double-space after the title.

2. Choose F**o**nt, **B**old or press **[F6]** (Bold) to turn on boldfacing, type **Introduction**, choose F**o**nt, **B**old or press **[F6]** (Bold) again to turn off boldfacing, and press **[Enter]**.

Ann continues to type her report in Doc 2. The WordPerfect commands she carries out in the report don't affect the outline in Doc 1.

In the next steps, you'll retrieve the remainder of Ann's draft of the report into document window 2 and maximize the document windows. To **maximize** a window means to make it fill the entire WordPerfect screen. A maximized window no longer has a frame around it.

To retrieve the report and maximize the windows:

1. With the cursor underneath the first heading ("Introduction") in Doc 2 and the WordPerfect data disk in drive A, choose **F**ile, **R**etrieve to display the Retrieve Document dialog box. See Figure 5-30. Alternatively, press **[Shift][F10]** (Open/Retrieve) to display the Open Document dialog box, then press **[Shift][F10]** again to change it to the Retrieve Document dialog box.

retrieve

Figure 5-30
Retrieve Document
dialog box

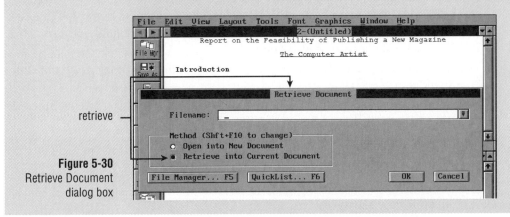

In WordPerfect 6.0, "Open" means to load a file from the disk and insert it into its own document window. Retrieve means to load a file from the disk and insert it into the current (already open) document window. In this case, we want to *retrieve* a document file.

② Type **a:\c5file1.dft** and press **[Enter]**. WordPerfect inserts the document file into document window 2.

Now that you're ready to work on the retrieved document, you don't need to see the outline in document window 1. So let's maximize the windows.

③ Choose **W**indow, **M**aximize. Alternatively, click the maximize button (the up-arrow-head) in the upper-right corner or the document window, as shown in Figure 5-29. Document window 2 now fills the entire WordPerfect screen.

④ Press **[Home]**, **1** or use another method to switch to document window 1, the outline.

Notice that document window 1 is still framed. Let's maximize it.

⑤ Choose **W**indow, **M**aximize or click the maximize button. WordPerfect maximizes document window 1.

⑥ Switch back to document window 2, the draft of the report.

⑦ Take a few minutes to read the report, so you'll be familiar with its contents. Notice that the title of the magazine is missing from the first paragraph. You'll fix that problem later.

Using Macros

Ann knows that while writing the feasibility study she will have to type the name of the proposed magazine, "The Computer Artist," many times. For any word-processing procedure that you have to repeat several times — such as a series of WordPerfect commands, a word, a phrase, or a combination of commands and text — you can record a macro to perform the procedure for you. A **macro**, in its simplest sense, is a "recording" of keystrokes that you can "play back" at any time by pressing just a few keys.

Recording a macro to play back frequently pressed keystrokes has several advantages:

- Macros save time. By playing a macro, you can save many keystrokes, which means you can complete your document faster.

- Macros are accurate. When you play a macro, you don't have to worry about typos or other mistakes. If you record the macro correctly, every time you use it the keystrokes will play back without error.

- Macros are consistent. Macros that insert text and formatting codes create the same text and format each time.

To record a macro you must perform four steps similar to recording on a cassette recorder (Figure 5-31):

- Turn on the "recording," that is, turn on Record Macro.
- Give the macro a name.
- Record the desired keystrokes.
- Turn off Record Macro.

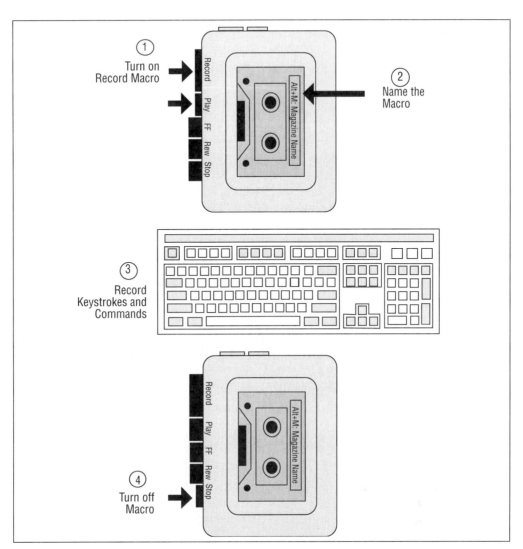

Figure 5-31
Four steps required
to record a macro

When you record a macro, you can select one of three ways of naming it. An **Alt macro** is a macro you name by pressing [Alt] and a letter, for example, [Alt][M]. You can use any one of the 26 letters of the alphabet, but you can't use any other type of character, that is, no numerals or symbols. To play an Alt macro, that is, to "play back" the recorded keystrokes, you simply press [Alt] and the letter.

A **named macro** is a macro you name by typing a legal DOS filename. To play a named macro, you issue the Play Macro command, type the filename of the macro, and choose OK.

An **Enter macro** is a macro without a name. When WordPerfect asks you for the name of the macro to record or play, you just press [Enter]. In the steps that follow, you'll record and play each of these three types of macros.

Before you record any macros, however, you should instruct WordPerfect where you want the macros saved. Because you will want WordPerfect to save your macros to your data disk, let's specify drive A as the storage location. This is necessary only because you are recording macros as part of your classwork and want the macros saved to drive A. Under normal circumstances, however, you would want your macros saved to your hard disk, in the default directory specified by WordPerfect.

To specify the storage location of your macros:

① Make sure your WordPerfect data disk is in drive A.

② Choose **F**ile, Se**t**up, **L**ocation of Files. Alternatively, press **[Shift][F1]** (Setup) and select **5** (Location of Files). WordPerfect displays the Location of Files dialog box. See Figure 5-32.

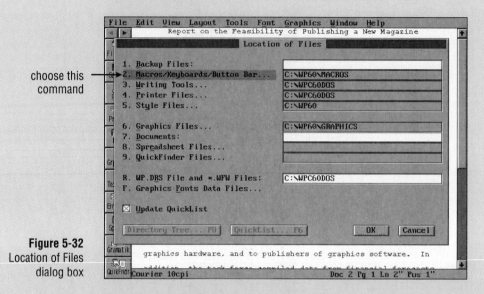

choose this
command

Figure 5-32
Location of Files
dialog box

③ Choose **2** (**M**acros/Keyboards/Button Bar) and then choose **1** (**P**ersonal Path).

④ Type **a:** and press **[Enter]**, then choose OK.

⑤ Choose OK and Close or press **[F7]** (Exit) until you return to the document window. From now on, any macro you record will be saved to the disk in drive A.

Recording an Alt Macro

In the following steps, you'll define a macro that inserts the name of the proposed magazine into Ann's report.

To record an Alt macro:

① Move the cursor to the right of the space after the words "tentatively entitled" in the second line of the first paragraph. The cursor should be at the comma.

When you create a macro, the keystrokes you record are executed in the document. If the macro inserts text, move the cursor to the position in the document where you want that text before you create the macro.

② Choose **T**ools, **M**acro, **R**ecord or press **[Ctrl][F10]** (Record Macro). The Record Macro dialog box appears on the screen. See Figure 5-33.

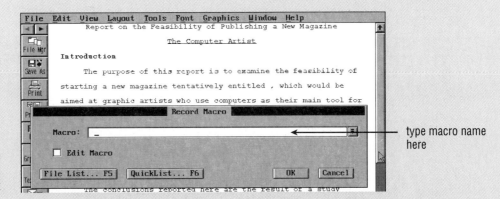

type macro name
here

Figure 5-33
Record Macro
dialog box

You type the name of the macro in this dialog box. Because you are going to record an Alt macro to insert the name of the magazine, you'll use the name "ALTM," where "M" stands for magazine.

Note: If you use the keyboard to access the items on the main menu (File, Edit, View, Layout, and so forth), you should avoid creating an Alt macro that uses any of the mnemonic letters in the pull-down menu names (F, E, V, L, T, O, G, W, or H). The Alt macro takes precedence over the keyboard pull-down menu letters, so it's possible that you could inadvertently execute a macro when what you want is to access a pull-down menu.

③ Press **[Alt][M]** or type **altm** to name the macro. This creates an Alt macro, which WordPerfect saves using the filename ALTM.WPM.

④ Choose OK. The cursor returns to the document window, and the message "Recording Macro" appears in the status bar in the lower-left corner of the screen. Now you're ready to record the keystrokes of the macro.

⑤ Press **[F8]** (Underline), type **The Computer Artist**, and press **[F8]** (Underline) again. You could also use the pull-down menu to turn Underline on and off. These commands, which create the underlined title of the proposed magazine, are now recorded as the Alt-M macro.

Now that you have recorded the keystrokes for the Alt-M macro, you need to stop recording the macro.

⑥ Choose **T**ools, **M**acro, **S**top or press **[Ctrl][F10]** (Record Macro) to stop recording the macro. The message "Recording Macro" disappears from the status bar. WordPerfect now **compiles** the macro, which means that the macro is translated into a form that WordPerfect can play back. WordPerfect also saves the completed macro as ALTM.WPM on the data disk in drive A.

You can use this same procedure to record virtually any sequence of keystrokes or commands, such as your company name, your own name and address, or the commands for setting double spacing.

Correcting an Error in a Macro

Take a moment to look at your document. Did you spell "The Computer Artist" correctly? Is it underlined? Did you remember to turn off underlining after you typed the magazine name? If you made a mistake, you can record the macro again. Let's assume you made a typing error and have to re-record the Alt-M macro.

To correct an error in a macro:

① Delete any text you typed while creating the macro and move the cursor to the point where you want the macro to insert the text. In this case, delete "The Computer Artist" and the underline code that you inserted while creating the macro.

② Choose Tools, Macro, Record or press **[Ctrl][F10]** (Record Macro) to display the Record Macro dialog box.

③ Press **[Alt][M]** to name the macro and choose OK. WordPerfect displays a prompt telling you that a macro named ALTM.WPM already exists. See Figure 5-34.

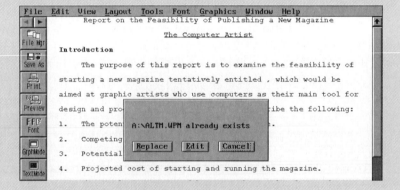

Figure 5-34
Macro already exists
dialog box

④ Choose Replace to instruct WordPerfect to replace the existing (erroneous) macro with a new one of the same name. WordPerfect erases the old macro file from the disk and displays "Recording Macro" on the status bar.

⑤ Carefully type the correct keystrokes that you want to record in the macro. In this case, press **[F8]** (Underline), type **The Computer Artist**, and press **[F8]** (Underline) once again.

⑥ Choose Tools, Macro, Stop or press **[Ctrl][F10]** (Record Macro) to stop recording the macro.

In general, any time you make a mistake while you are creating a simple macro, just press [Ctrl][F10] (Record Macro) to stop recording the macro, then start over.

Executing an Alt Macro

Now that you've correctly recorded an Alt macro, you're ready to use it to insert the magazine name into the document. To play an Alt macro, you press [Alt] and, while holding it down, press the letter you used to name the macro.

To play an Alt macro:

1. Move the cursor to the location in your document where you want the macro executed. In this case, move the cursor just to the right of the phrase "target audience" on the first line under the heading "The Target Audience." (Remember, you've already inserted the magazine title in the introductory paragraph.)

2. Press **[Spacebar]**, type **of**, and press **[Spacebar]**.

   Now you're ready to insert the underlined name of the magazine. But instead of using the Underline command and typing the text, you'll simply execute the macro you just recorded.

3. Press **[Alt][M]**. The underlined magazine title appears in the document at the cursor position.

   You may see a warning box with the message, "No button bar files found." This appears here because, in an earlier procedure, you changed the path where WordPerfect looks for macros, keyboard layouts, and button bars. The new path you selected is drive A, which has no button bar files. If the warning box appears, choose OK and continue. Your button bar will disappear from the screen. (You will restore it later in this tutorial.)

4. Now move the cursor after "The potential audience" at the beginning of the second sentence of the next paragraph.

5. Insert the phrase "for The Computer Artist" using the Alt-M macro. Your screen should look similar to Figure 5-35.

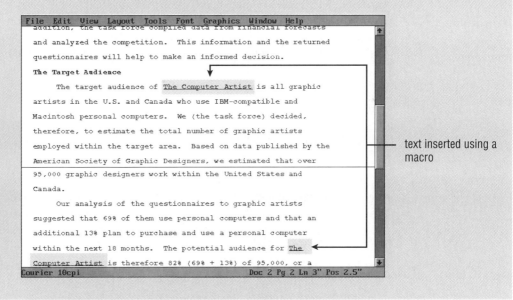

Figure 5-35
Document window after you use a macro to insert text

Although Ann recorded and played the Alt-M macro while writing her feasibility report, the macro is not associated exclusively with the report, but is saved to the disk as a separate file. She can use the Alt-M macro in this report and in any future documents she writes using the disk on which the macro is stored.

Creating and Executing a Named Macro

Ann knows that in this report and in other documents, she will frequently have to type the abbreviated name for Connolly/Bayle Publishing Company — C/B Publishing — so she decides to record a macro for it.

As you record this macro, you'll insert the name "C/B Publishing" into the document at the beginning of the title; later, you'll play the macro to insert the name elsewhere in the document. First let's insert a new title line.

To insert a new title line:

① Move the cursor to the beginning of Ann's report, so that the cursor is located after the initial formatting codes but before the title. You may have to turn on Reveal Codes to make sure that the cursor is on the first [Cntr on Mar] code. Turn off Reveal Codes after you position the cursor.

② Press **[Enter]** to insert a blank line at the beginning of the document. Then move the cursor back to the beginning of the blank line.

③ Choose **L**ayout, **A**lignment, **C**enter or press **[Shift][F6]** (Center) to center the title line.

You're now ready to record the macro that will insert the abbreviated company name. Ann decides to create a named macro using the name "CB," which stands for "C/B Publishing." In a named macro you can use any legal DOS filename, but don't add an extension; WordPerfect automatically adds .WPM. Let's record the named macro. Remember, if you make a mistake while recording keystrokes in a macro, turn off Record Macro and start again.

To record a named macro:

① Choose **T**ools, **M**acro, **R**ecord or press **[Ctrl][F10]** (Record Macro) to display the Record Macro dialog box.

② Type **cb** and press **[Enter]** to name the macro. The message "Recording Macro" appears on the status bar.

③ Type **C/B Publishing** but do *not* press [Enter]. (If you do press [Enter], the macro will record it, and every time you play the CB macro, a hard return will be inserted into the document.) If you make a mistake, turn off Record Macro and start over, replacing the original CB macro with the correct version.

④ Choose **T**ools, **M**acro, **S**top or press **[Ctrl][F10]** (Record Macro) to stop recording the macro. The message "Recording Macro" disappears from the status bar, and WordPerfect automatically saves the macro as CB.WPM.

Your screen should now look like Figure 5-36.

newly inserted text ⟶

Figure 5-36
Document window after
you add a title line

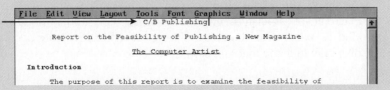

Before playing the CB macro or any other macro that inserts format codes or text, you have to move the cursor to the location in your document where you want the code or text.

To play a named macro:

1. Move the cursor to the right of the words "will help," just above the heading "The Target Audience" and press **[Spacebar]**. This places the cursor where you want the name "C/B Publishing" inserted.

2. Choose **T**ools, **M**acro, **P**lay or press **[Alt][F10]** (Play Macro). The Play Macro dialog box appears on the screen.

3. Type **cb** and press **[Enter]**. The macro inserts the name of the company into the document at the location of the cursor.

Next let's use the CB macro to insert the company name elsewhere in the document.

4. Move the cursor to the "b" in "board of directors" in the middle of the paragraph titled "The Competition." You might want to use the Search command to find "board of directors," and then move the cursor back to the "b."

5. Choose **T**ools, **M**acro, **P**lay or press **[Alt][F10]** (Play Macro), type **cb**, and press **[Enter]**. Press **[Spacebar]** to leave a space after the company name.

Ann has now completed her work on this draft of the document and is ready to save the intermediate version to the disk.

6. Save the document as S5FILE2.DFT.

So far you have seen how to define two types of macros, Alt macros and named macros. The advantage of a named macro over an Alt macro is that the named macro is mnemonic — you can use easy-to-remember names for it. The advantage of the Alt macro is that it takes fewer keystrokes to play than a named macro. For example, to play the CB macro, you have to press [Alt][F10] (Play Macro), type "CB," and press [Enter] — a total of five keystrokes. To play the Alt-M macro, you simply press [Alt][M] — two keystrokes.

Creating and Executing an Enter Macro

Ann gives Jonathan a disk that contains a copy of the file S5FILE2.DFT and asks him to make any formatting changes he feels would improve the appearance of the report. Jonathan decides that each heading should be preceded by three blank lines (not just the two lines currently in the double-spaced document), and to simplify editing, a Conditional End of Page command should be inserted just before each heading. Making these changes for the six headings would require many keystrokes, so Jonathan decides to record a macro to make the changes quickly and accurately.

Such a macro is applicable only to this report, because Jonathan doubts he would use it in future documents. He therefore decides to record an Enter macro instead of an Alt or a named macro. Unlike an Alt or a named macro, an Enter macro doesn't have a name; therefore, you should not create an Enter macro if you plan to use it in more than one document. To record or play an Enter macro, you simply press [Enter] when WordPerfect prompts you for the macro name.

Let's record an Enter macro to format the headings of Ann's report. As you record the macro, you'll actually be formatting the first heading. Later, you'll use the macro to format the other headings in the document.

As you record an Enter macro (or any other kind of macro), *the keystrokes are executed as you enter them*, thus modifying your document. If you press the wrong keys, your document could be altered *beyond repair*. Therefore, always save your document before you record or play a complex macro. Make sure you have saved this document as S5FILE2.DFT.

To start recording an Enter macro:

① Move the cursor to the beginning of the document. Because this Enter macro will search for the first occurrence of a heading, it must start at the beginning of the document.

② Choose **T**ools, **M**acro, **R**ecord or press **[Ctrl][F10]** (Record Macro) to begin recording the macro.

③ Press **[Enter]**. Pressing [Enter] without typing a macro name automatically makes this an Enter macro. The message "Recording Macro" appears on the status bar.

You're now ready to record the keystrokes and commands of the macro. Because the headings contain the only boldface characters in the report, you'll begin the macro by searching for the [Bold On] code, then setting the Conditional End of Page code.

To continue recording an Enter macro:

① Choose **E**dit, Searc**h** or press **[F2]** (Search). WordPerfect displays the Search dialog box.

② Choose F**o**nt, **B**old or press **[F6]** (Bold) to insert the [Bold On] code, press **[Enter]**, and choose Searc**h** ([F2]).

The cursor moves to the first occurrence of boldface text, which is the heading "Introduction," just after the invisible [Bold On] code. To format the heading, you want the cursor *before* the [Bold On] code. In the keystrokes that follow, you'll move the cursor to the left of the [Bold On] code, then set Conditional End of Page.

③ Press **[Home]**, **[Home]**, **[Home]** **[←]** to move the cursor to the left margin (and to the left of any text or format codes).

④ Choose **L**ayout, **O**ther or press **[Shift][F8]** (Format) and select **7** (**O**ther) to display the Other Format dialog box.

⑤ Choose **2** (**C**onditional End of Page), type **6** (the number of lines that you want kept together), and press **[Enter]**.

⑥ Choose OK and then, if necessary, choose Close to return to the document window.

Next you want to add the codes necessary to insert one blank line above the heading. You can't just press [Enter], because with the line spacing set to double, [Enter] would insert two blank lines. Therefore, you must first set the spacing to single, press [Enter], then reset the spacing to double.

To insert a blank line above the heading in the Enter macro:

❶ Choose **L**ayout, **L**ine or press **[Shift][F8]** (Format) and select **1** (**L**ine) to display the Line Format dialog box.

❷ Choose **3** (Line **S**pacing), type **1**, press **[Enter]**, and choose OK and close if necessary or press **[F7]** (Exit) once or twice to return to the document window.

❸ Press **[Enter]** to insert a single blank line above the heading.

Now you have to set the line spacing back to double.

❹ Choose **L**ayout, **L**ine or press **[Shift][F8]** (Format) and select **1** (**L**ine).

❺ Choose **3** (Line **S**pacing), type **2**, press **[Enter]**, and exit all dialog boxes to return to the document window.

Now you have to move the cursor *below* the heading, so that when you play the macro, the cursor will be past the heading you've just edited and will find the next heading.

To finish recording the Enter macro:

❶ Press [↓] to move the cursor below the heading you just edited.

❷ Choose **T**ools, **M**acro, **S**top or press **[Ctrl][F10]** (Record Macro) to stop recording the macro.

The complete sequence of keystrokes needed to format the heading is long and tedious, which is why you want to do it only once, not at every heading. Having formatted the first heading while he was creating the Enter macro, Jonathan is now ready to use the macro to format the other five headings in the report. Since the only boldfacing in this document is in the headings, the Enter macro can easily find them. Don't use this macro in documents that may have boldfacing other than in headings.

To play an Enter macro:

❶ Choose **T**ools, **M**acro, **P**lay or press **[Alt][F10]** (Play Macro). WordPerfect displays the Play Macro dialog box.

❷ Press **[Enter]**.

The macro finds the next [Bold On] code, which occurs only in headings in this document, and inserts the desired formatting codes. See Figure 5-37. You now want to repeat these steps four times to edit the other four headings. Let's use WordPerfect's Repeat feature.

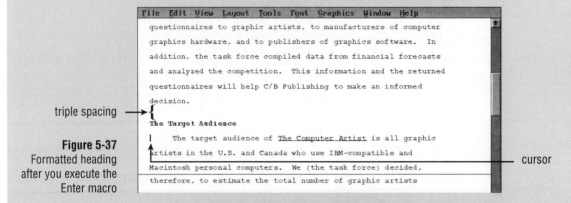

triple spacing ⟶

Figure 5-37
Formatted heading
after you execute the
Enter macro

cursor

③ Choose **E**dit, **R**epeat or press **[Ctrl][R]**. WordPerfect displays the Repeat dialog box. See Figure 5-38.

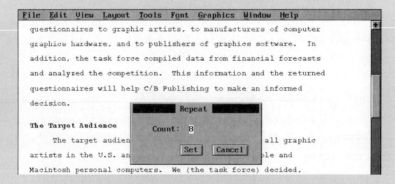

Figure 5-38
Repeat dialog box

④ Type **4** to set the repeat count, but do not press [Enter] or choose Set.

Choosing Set from the Repeat dialog box sets the repeat number for subsequent repeats but does not produce a repeat in the current operation.

⑤ With the Repeat dialog box still on the screen, press **[Alt][F10]** (Play Macro) and press **[Enter]** to execute the Enter macro four times.

Your screen should now look like Figure 5-39.

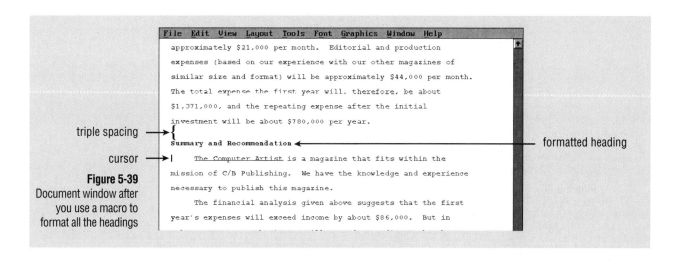

triple spacing →

cursor →

Figure 5-39
Document window after
you use a macro to
format all the headings

formatted heading

Having completed the macros in this tutorial, you can now reset the default location of the macro files and restore your button bar to the screen. Under normal circumstances, you would save your macros to the default path on your hard drive, and the following steps would be unnecessary. They are necessary here only because you created macros as part of your classwork and wanted them saved to drive A.

To reset the location of macro files and restore the button bar:

1. Choose **F**ile, Se**t**up, **L**ocation of Files or press **[Shift][F1]** (Setup) and choose **5** (Location of Files) to display the Location of Files dialog box.

2. Choose **2** (**M**acros/Keyboards/Button Bar) to display the Macros/Keyboards/Button Bar dialog box.

3. Choose **1** (**P**ersonal Path) and type the complete default path for WordPerfect macro files, then press **[Enter]**. Normally, you would type **c:\wp60\macros**. If necessary, consult your instructor or technical support person.

4. Choose OK twice and, if necessary, choose Close to return to the document window.

   You have reset the default location for WordPerfect macros and button bars, but you still have to restore the button bar to the screen.

5. Choose **V**iew, **B**utton Bar.

   The button bar appears on the screen along the left edge of the document window.

Using Footnotes

Jonathan prints and distributes a copy of the feasibility report to the members of the task force, who then suggest some minor revisions. They think the report should include three footnotes: the first giving the source of the data published by the American Society of Graphic Designers, the second explaining how the task force arrived at the proposed subscription rate of $55, and the third giving the source of the expenses required to start up the proposed magazine (Figure 5-40). Let's create these footnotes now.

Jonathan, please add these footnotes to the text:

After "American Society of Graphic Designers" add the footnote:
> Report of the American Society of Graphic Designers, Arbol Press, March 1992, p. 84.

After "$55 per year" add the footnote:
> Our questionnaire indicated that specialty magazines of this type have subscription rates typically in the range of $35 to $95 per year.

After "$721,000" add the footnote:
> For a detailed breakdown of these expenses, contact David Palermo in the Financial Office.

Figure 5-40
The task force's footnotes for the report

To create a footnote:

① Move the cursor to the location in the text where you want the footnote number to appear. In this case, move the cursor to the right of the comma that follows the phrase "American Society of Graphic Designers" in the paragraph under "The Target Audience."

② Choose **L**ayout, **F**ootnote, **C**reate or press **[Ctrl][F7]** (Notes) to display the Notes dialog box (see Figure 5-41), then choose **1** (**F**ootnote) and **1** (**C**reate).

choose this command →

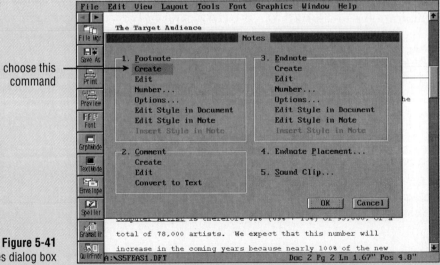

Figure 5-41
Notes dialog box

WordPerfect now displays the Footnote window, as shown in Figure 5-42. The window contains an automatic tab and a superscript footnote number as part of the Footnote style.

footnote number

cursor

blank footnote edit
window

Figure 5-42
Footnote edit
window

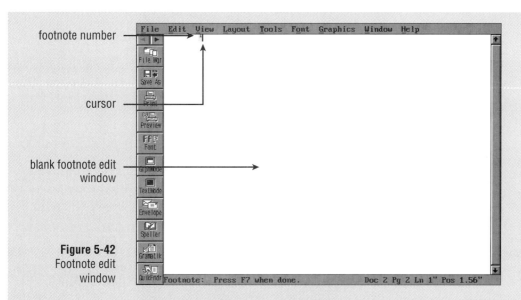

③ Without pressing [Spacebar] or [Tab], type the text of the first footnote, as shown in Figure 5-40. Do not press [Enter].

④ Press **[F7]** (Exit) to return to the document window.

WordPerfect automatically inserts the correct footnote number into the body of the report and formats the text of the footnote at the bottom of the page.

⑤ Choose **F**ile, Print Pre**v**iew or press **[Shift] [F7]** then choose **7** (Print Preview) or click the Preview button to display the Print Preview window, then choose **V**iew, **F**ull Page or click the Full Page button to see the entire page containing the footnote. See Figure 5-43.

Figure 5-43
Print Preview
screen showing the
new footnote

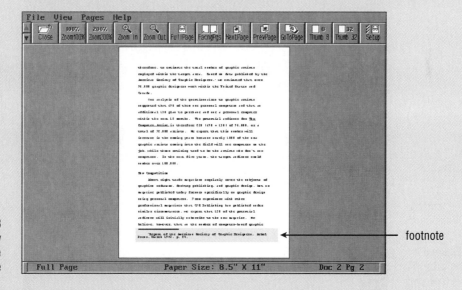

footnote

The text of the footnote appears at the bottom of the page with a short horizontal line separating it from the body of the text.

⑥ Exit the Print Preview window and return to the document window.

Editing a Footnote

After typing the first footnote, Jonathan remembers that the report cited in the footnote was published in 1993, not in 1992. The footnote given to him by the task force is incorrect. Thus, he needs to edit the footnote to make this correction.

To edit a footnote:

① Choose **L**ayout, **F**ootnote, **E**dit. Alternatively, press **[Ctrl][F7]** (Notes) to display the Notes dialog box, choose **1** (**F**ootnote), **2** (**E**dit). WordPerfect displays the Footnote Number dialog box, prompting you to enter the number of the footnote you want to edit.

② Type **1** and choose OK.

The Footnote window appears with the footnote text you previously typed.

③ Using the WordPerfect cursor-movement and edit keys, change "1992" to "1993."

④ Press **[F7]** (Exit) to return to the document window.

The text of footnote 1 is now correct.

Adding a New Footnote

Jonathan now wants to add the second and third footnotes.

To add a footnote:

① Move the cursor to the space after the final "r" in the phrase "$55 per year" in the second paragraph under "Projected income."

② Choose **L**ayout, **F**ootnote, **C**reate or press **[Ctrl][F7]** (Notes), then choose **1** (**F**ootnote), **1** (**C**reate).

③ Type the text of the second footnote, as shown in Figure 5-40. Your screen should now look like Figure 5-44. Then press **[F7]** (Exit) to return to the document window.

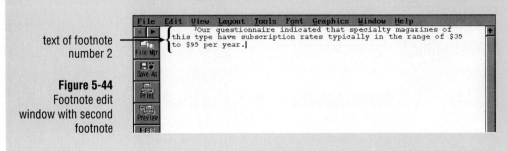

text of footnote number 2

Figure 5-44
Footnote edit window with second footnote

④ Use steps 1 through 3 to create the third footnote shown in Figure 5-40. Put this footnote after the period following the number "$721,000" in the paragraph headed "Expenses."

Benefits of the Footnotes Feature

Using the Footnotes feature provides three benefits:

- WordPerfect automatically numbers the footnotes. If you add a footnote anywhere in the document, delete a footnote, or move a footnote, WordPerfect automatically renumbers all the footnotes so they appear consecutively.
- WordPerfect automatically formats the footnote text at the bottom of the page.
- WordPerfect allows you to edit the footnote.

What is true of footnotes is also true of **endnotes**, which are notes printed at the end of the document rather than at the bottom of each page. You can create and edit endnotes the same way you create and edited footnotes, except that you would select Endnotes rather than Footnotes from the Layout menu or from the dialog box that appears after you press [Ctrl][F7] (Notes).

To delete a footnote, you move the cursor to the footnote number in the document and use the usual deletion keys to delete the footnote code. When you delete a footnote number, WordPerfect automatically deletes the text of the footnote and renumbers the remaining footnotes consecutively.

To move a footnote, you move the cursor to the footnote, turn on Reveal Codes, block the footnote code, and use a regular cut-and-paste block operation to move the footnote to another point in your document. Again, WordPerfect automatically renumbers the footnotes.

Using Hyphenation

When text is fully justified, WordPerfect inserts small spaces between words and characters to keep the lines of text aligned along the right margin. Sometimes this causes unsightly "rivers," or blank areas, in the text, which distract the reader. Similarly, when text is left-justified, an extremely ragged right edge may occur (Figure 5-45). To solve these problems, you can use WordPerfect's automatic hyphenation feature. With hyphenation on, long words that would otherwise wrap to the next line are divided in two, so that part of the word stays on the original line. Thus, the occurrence of "rivers" or extremely ragged right margins is decreased.

rivers

full justification

excessively ragged
margin

left justification

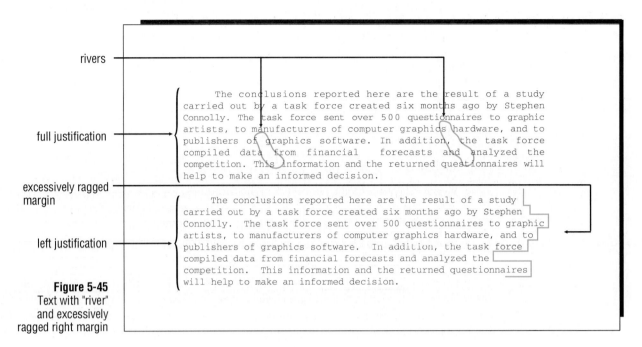

Figure 5-45
Text with "river"
and excessively
ragged right margin

When you turn on hyphenation and then move the cursor through your document, WordPerfect analyzes each word that falls at or near the end of a line and checks to see if it should be wrapped to the next line, kept on the same line without hyphenation, or hyphenated. If WordPerfect needs help in deciding how to hyphenate a word, a Position Hyphen dialog box appears on the screen to ask you where or if you want the word hyphenated.

As the final step in formatting his document, Jonathan decides to turn on hyphenation to minimize raggedness along the right margin. You should turn on hyphenation as the *last step* in preparing the final version of a document; otherwise, WordPerfect will constantly interrupt you with hyphenation prompts as you type and modify the text.

To turn on hyphenation:

❶ Move the cursor to the beginning of the document.

Hyphenation occurs only from the point in the document where you position the cursor and turn on hyphenation to the end of the document. Since you want to hyphenate the entire document in this case, you should move the cursor to the beginning of the document.

❷ Choose **L**ayout, **L**ine, or press **[Shift][F8]** (Format) and choose **1** (**L**ine).

WordPerfect displays the Line Format dialog box.

❸ Choose **6** (**Hy**phenation) to click the Hyphenation checkbox, then choose OK and close if necessary or press **[F7]** (Exit) once or twice to return to the document window.

❹ Press **[Home]**, **[Home]**, **[↓]** to move the cursor to the end of the document, forcing WordPerfect to hyphenate the entire document, as necessary.

As the cursor moves through the document, WordPerfect automatically hyphenates some words. The words that WordPerfect selects for hyphenation depend on the size of the font you're using.

If WordPerfect's hyphenation dictionary doesn't recognize a particular word that needs hyphenation, WordPerfect stops and asks you for help in positioning the hyphen. You can then instruct WordPerfect where to hyphenate, or you can choose not to hyphenate the word at all. For example, WordPerfect might stop at a word like "Stanislowski" and display the Position Hyphen dialog box, shown in Figure 5-46.

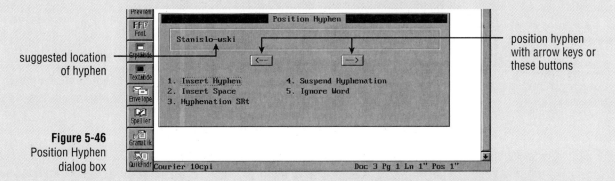

suggested location of hyphen

position hyphen with arrow keys or these buttons

Figure 5-46
Position Hyphen
dialog box

If the Position Hyphen dialog box appears on your screen, you should position the hyphen where you want it or choose to skip hyphenation.

⑤ If WordPerfect displays a Position Hyphen dialog box and you want to accept WordPerfect's suggested position of the hyphen, choose **1** (Insert Hyphen). If you want to change the location of the hyphen in the word, press [→] or [←] to move the position of the hyphen, and then choose **1** (Insert Hyphen). If you don't want to hyphenate the word, choose **5** (Ignore Word).

For example, if WordPerfect stopped at "Stanislowski," you would press [←] to move the hyphen so the word in the dialog box is "Stani-slowski." If you press [→] and the hyphen doesn't move to the right, WordPerfect is telling you that you have reached the maximum size for the partial word to fit on the current line.

If you make a mistake in hyphenating a word, move the cursor to the word and delete the hyphen.

This completes the feasibility report, the final version of which is shown in Figure 5-47 on the following pages. Your document may look slightly different because of differences in font size and hyphenation. You are now ready to save and print the document and exit WordPerfect. Exiting WordPerfect with two (or several) document windows open is simple if you use the Exit WordPerfect command.

C/B Publishing
Report on the Feasibility of Publishing a New Magazine
The Computer Artist

Introduction

The purpose of this report is to examine the feasiblity of starting a new magazine tentatively entitled The Computer Artist, which would be aimed at graphic artists who use computers as their main tool for design and production. This report will describe the following:

1. The potential size of the market audience.
2. Competing magazines.
3. Potential profitability of the magazine.
4. Projected cost of starting and running the magazine.

The conclusions reported here are the result of a study carried out by a task force created six months ago by Stephen Connolly and John Bayle. The task force sent over 500 questionnaires to graphic artists, to manufacturers of computer graphics hardware, and to publishers of graphics software. In addition, the task force compiled data from financial forecasts and analyzed the competition. This information and the returned questionnaires will help C/B Publishing to make an informed decision.

The Target Audience

The target audience of The Computer Artist is all graphic artists in the U.S. and Canada who use IBM-compatible and Macintosh personal computers. We (the task force) decided,

---

therefore, to estimate the total number of graphic artists employed within the target area. Based on data published by the American Society of Graphic Designers,[1] we estimated that over 95,000 graphic designers work within the United States and Canada.

Our analysis of the questionnaires to graphic artists suggested that 69% of them use personal computers and that an additional 13% plan to purchase and use a personal computer within the next 18 months. The potential audience for The Computer Artist is therefore 82% (69% + 13%) of 95,000, or a total of 78,000 artists. We expect that this number will increase in the coming years because nearly 100% of the new graphic artists coming into the field will use computers on the job, while those retiring tend to be the artists who don't use computers. In the next five years, the target audience could number over 100,000.

The Competition

About eight trade magazines regularly cover the subjects of graphics software, desktop publishing, and graphic design, but no magazine published today focuses specifically on graphic design using personal computers. From experience with other professional magazines that C/B Publishing has published under similar circumstances, we expect that 12% of the potential audience will initially subscribe to the new magazine. We believe, however, that as the number of computer-based graphic designers increases,

---

[1] Report of the American Society of Graphic Designers, Arbol press, March 1993, p.84.

Figure 5-47
Final version of the
feasibility report

other publishers will certainly recognize this growing market and launch new magazines of their own. For this reason, the success of The Computer Artist will largely depend on our securing a commitment from the C/B Publishing board of directors to aggressive marketing and adherence to high publication standards. We must secure this commitment if we hope to increase or even maintain our subscription level two or three years into circulation. Being the first magazine to tap this market will help us, but we must be ever vigilant of the competition.

Projected Income

Our income from The Computer Artist has two sources, subscriptions and advertising.

From the estimated size of the potential audience (78,000 graphic designers in the U.S. and Canada) and the expected percentage of subscribers (12%), we project that we will have 9400 subscribers within the first year of publication. Assuming a subscription rate of $55 per year[2] and 9400 subscribers, the potential income from subscriptions will be $517,000.

Results of the questionnaires sent to manufacturers of computer graphics hardware and to publishers of graphics software were very encouraging. We have verbal commitments for full-page, half-page, and quarter-page advertisements from several large hardware and software companies who market graphics programs, laser printers, plotters, soft fonts, printer cartridges, and

---

[2]Our questionnaire indicated that specialty magazines of this type have subscription rates typically in the range of $35 to $95 per year.

optical character recognition software. The marketing members of the task force are confident that with effort and focus, they can sell all of our advertisement space in The Computer Artist.

We have budgeted 16 of the 64-page issues for ad space. If we fill all 16 pages in 12 issues per year, and if we assume an average gross income per page of $4000, the total revenues from page advertisements will be approximately $768,000 per year.

The total projected income from publication of the magazine will, therefore, be approximately $1,285,000 per year.

Expenses

The cost of starting the magazine (including hiring six new staff members, renovating office space, meeting additional office expenses and other overhead costs, marketing expenses for the first two issues, and producing the first two issues) will be approximately $721,000.[3] Continued marketing expenses will be approximately $21,000 per month. Editorial and production expenses (based on our experience with our other magazines of similar size and format) will be approximately $44,000 per month. The total expense the first year will, therefore, be about $1,371,000, and the repeating expense after the initial investment will be about $780,000 per year.

Summary and Recommendation

The Computer Artist is a magazine that fits within the mission of C/B Publishing. We have the knowledge and experience

---

[3]For a detailed breakdown of these expenses, contact David Palermo in the Financial Office

Figure 5-47
(continued)

```
necessary to publish this magazine.
        The financial analysis given above suggests that the first
year's expenses will exceed income by about $86,000.  But in
subsequent years, the income will exceed expenditures by about
$505,000.
        Based on the above analysis, we recommend publication of the
new magazine The Computer Artist.
```

Figure 5-47
(continued)

To save and print the document and exit WordPerfect:

1. Save the document as S5FILE3.REP and print it.

2. Choose **F**ile, E**x**it WP or press **[Home]**, **[F7]** (Exit). The Exit WordPerfect dialog box appears on the screen. See Figure 5-48.

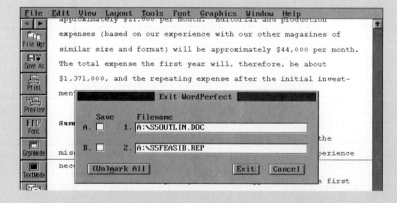

Figure 5-48
Exit WordPerfect
dialog box

The dialog box lists all currently open windows. Any document that you haven't saved since it was last edited has an "X" in the Save checkbox next to the filename box. In our case, both files have been saved, so they don't need saving again. In general, you should make sure the Save checkbox is checked for each of the documents you want saved.

3. Choose E**x**it or choose **S**ave and E**x**it. If a Save As dialog box appears on the screen, type the name of the file you want to save, and choose OK.

Exercises

1. Define or describe each of the following terms:
   a. paragraph number in an outline
   b. outline level
   c. outline family
2. How would you begin an outline?
3. What is Outline Edit mode?
4. What is the Outline Bar?
5. How would you turn on hyphenation?
6. List the four steps used in recording a macro.
7. Describe how to execute each of the following types of macros:
   a. Alt macro
   b. Named macro
   c. Enter macro
8. Name one advantage and one disadvantage of each of the three types of macros.
9. What would you do to have two different documents open at the same time?
10. How would you view two different documents on the screen simultaneously?
11. Suppose you needed to copy several nonconsecutive sentences and paragraphs from one document to another. How would you perform that task?
12. How would you create a footnote?
13. If WordPerfect needs help in positioning the hyphen when hyphenation is on, the Position Hyphen dialog box appears on the screen with a suggested position for the hyphen. What would you do to change the position of the hyphen and instruct WordPerfect to continue checking through the document?

Tutorial Assignments

Open the file T5FILE1.DFT from your WordPerfect data disk and do the following:

1. With T5FILE1.DFT in Doc 1, write an outline of the report in Doc 2, switching between your outline and the report as needed and using WordPerfect's Outline feature. Use the headings and subheadings of the report to help you in preparing the outline.
2. Save the outline as S5ALDUS.OTL.
3. Print the outline.
4. In Doc 1, position the cursor at the beginning of the report and turn on automatic hyphenation. Move the cursor to the end of the document and respond to any Position Hyphen dialog boxes that WordPerfect displays.
5. Create a macro named TITLE.WPM that makes a heading boldface and switches it to all uppercase letters (for example, "Introduction" to "**INTRODUCTION**"). *Hint:* To bold or capitalize existing text, you have to use a block operation.
6. Use the macro you just created to bold and capitalize the other four major headings in the report in Doc 1.

7. Change the location of macro files to your data disk in drive A. Record an Alt macro (Alt-A) that inserts the magazine name <u>Aldus Magazine</u> (with underlining). Use the macro to insert the magazine name at the location of double question marks (??) in the report in Doc 1. Then delete the double question marks. Restore the default location of macro files to C:\WP60\MACROS or to the path given by your instructor or technical support person.

8. Save the report as S5ALDUS.DFT.

9. Print the report.

10. Move the cursor to the right of the comma after the phrase "<u>Aldus Magazine</u>" in the first paragraph of the report. Insert the following footnote: <u>Aldus Magazine</u> is published by Aldus Corporation, 411 First Avenue South, Seattle, WA 98104-2871.

11. Move the cursor to the right of the article title "Pattern Recognition" (and just after the close quote) and insert the following footnote: Olav Martin Kvern, "Pattern Recognition," <u>Aldus Magazine</u>, Vol. 4, No. 2, 1993, p. 64.

12. Move the cursor to the right of the article title "Beating Banding" (and just after the close quote) and insert the following footnote: Greg Stumph, "Beating Banding," <u>Aldus Magazine</u>, Vol. 4, No. 2, 1993, p. 41.

13. Save the document as S5ALDUS.REP.

14. Print the final version of the document.

Open the file T5FILE2.DFT from your WordPerfect data disk and do the following:

15. With T5FILE2.DFT in Doc 1, write an outline of the report in Doc 2, switching between your outline and the report as needed and using WordPerfect's Outline feature. Use the headings and subheadings of the report to help you in preparing the outline.

16. Save the outline as S5FREHND.OTL.

17. Print the outline.

18. In Doc 1, position the cursor at the beginning of the report and turn on automatic hyphenation. Move the cursor to the end of the document and respond to any Position Hyphen dialog boxes that WordPerfect displays.

19. Change the location of macro files to your data disk in drive A.

20. Move the cursor to the first occurrence of "??" in the document, delete the double question marks, and then record a macro named FH.WPM that inserts the phrase "Aldus FreeHand" into the document.

21. Use the macro to insert "Aldus FreeHand" at the other locations of "??" in the document.

22. Restore the default location of macro files to C:\WP60\MACROS or to the path given by your instructor or technical support person.

23. Move the cursor immediately to the right of the first occurrence of "Aldus FreeHand" in the first paragraph of the report and insert the following footnote: "Aldus FreeHand is published by Aldus Corporation, 411 First Avenue South, Seattle, WA 98104-2871."

24. Move the cursor immediately to the right of "EPS" in the first paragraph of the report and insert the following footnote: "EPS stands for Encapsulated PostScript. PostScript is a printer language developed by Adobe Systems, Inc."

25. Move the cursor immediately to the right of "TIFF" in the first paragraph of the report and insert the following footnote: "TIFF stands for Tag Image File Format."

26. Save the report as S5FREHND.REP.

27. Print the report.

Case Problems

1. Justification Report for New Office in San Jose

Charles Mataoa is an assistant business manager for the Custom Cables and Connectors Company. He wants to write a justification report, in memorandum format, to propose that the company open a new business office in San Jose, California.

Do the following:

1. Open the document P5SANJOS.DFT, the first few paragraphs of a draft of the justification report.
2. Write a short outline of the contents of the report to this point, using the headings of the report as your guide. Be sure to use WordPerfect's Outline feature in creating your outline.
3. Save the outline as S5SANJOS.OTL.
4. Print the outline.
5. Move the cursor to the right of the [Lft Tab] code on the "SUBJECT:" line in the heading of the memo. Type **A proposal for** and press **[Spacebar]**.
6. Change the location of macro files to your data disk in drive A.
7. Record a macro that now inserts the phrase "a new office in San Jose."
8. Move the cursor to all occurrences of double question marks (??) in the document, delete the double question marks, and use your macro to insert the phrase "a new office in San Jose."
9. Using the first level-1 heading ("Executive Summary"), create a macro you can use to convert level-1 headings to boldface and all uppercase letters, for example, "**EXECUTIVE SUMMARY**."
10. Use the heading macro to format the other level-1 headings in the report.
11. Restore the default location of macro files to C:\WP60\MACROS or to the path given by your instructor or technical support person.
12. After the period at the end of the phrase "is well documented," insert a footnote reference. The text for the footnote is the following:
    See the report, "Networking Hardware Needs in the San Jose Area," attached.
13. Save the report (in its unfinished format) as S5SANJOS.DFT.
14. Print the draft of the report.

2. Outline for a Presentation on Time Management

Valerie Mitchell graduated six years ago with a bachelor's degree in business management and started working as a consultant for T.I.M.E. (Training In Management Excellence), a company that gives management training seminars, especially on time management. Besides giving time-management seminars as part of her job, she also speaks frequently on a voluntary basis at local service organizations, self-help groups, churches, and not-for-profit foundations. Right now, she is creating an outline for a speech she will give to United Way workers in two weeks.

Do the following:

1. Open the draft of the outline of Valerie's time-management speech, P5TIME.OTL, from your WordPerfect data disk.

2. Move the outline family that begins with the paragraph "IV. Time is Money" to paragraph II. (The current paragraph II, "The Ten Key Principles of Time Management," should become paragraph III.)

3. After the outline family that now begins "III. The Ten Key Principles of Time Management," insert the following new paragraph:

    VI. Applying the Ten Key Principles

4. After the outline family that begins "V. The Ten Secondary Principles of Time Management," insert the following new paragraph:

    IV. Applying the Ten Secondary Principles

5. After the phrase "The Ten Secondary Principles of Time Management," create a footnote reference. The text of the footnote should be "Adapted from Lester R. Bittel, *Right on Time! The Complete Guide for Time-Pressured Managers,* McGraw-Hill, New York, 1991."

6. At the phrase "Time is Money," create a footnote reference. The text of the footnote should be "Adapted from Stephanie Culp, *How to Get Organized When You Don't Have the Time,* Writer's Digest Books, Cincinnati, 1986."

7. Save the outline as S5TIME.OTL.

8. Print the outline.

3. Report on Using a Word Processor

Write a short report (about 700-1,000 words) on the advantages and disadvantages of using a word processor in writing lengthy reports. In writing your report, do the following:

1. Write an outline before you write the report, then revise the outline after you have completed your report. Submit both versions of the outline to your instructor.

2. Double-space the report.

3. Create a title page that contains the title of your report, your name, the title of your course, the date, and any other information your instructor wants you to include.

4. Include at least two footnotes giving the source of information for your report. Sources of information can be books, articles, or personal communication with family members, teachers, or other students.

5. Include a header and page numbering in the report.

6. Change the location of macro files to your data disk in drive A.

7. Record and use at least two macros to help you write the report. *Hint:* The macros may be recordings of phrases commonly used in the report or of format codes for creating headings or titles. Make sure you copy the macro files onto the disk that you submit to your instructor.

8. Choose **T**ools, **W**riting Tools, **4** (**D**ocument Information) to determine the word count of your report, to make sure you have 700-1,000 words. If necessary edit your document to adjust the word count.

9. Turn on and use hyphenation.

10. Restore the default location of macro files to C:\WP60\MACROS or to the path given by your instructor or technical support person.

11. Save the report as S5WP.REP.

12. Print the report.

Tutorial 6

Merging Documents

Writing a Sales Form Letter

Case: Sanders Imports, Inc.

Immediately after graduating from high school, Whitney Sanders began working as a clerk in an import store owned by International Products, Ltd. (IPL), a large corporation with franchises throughout the United States. During the next six years, Whitney worked her way up to international buyer for IPL. Her job entailed traveling to foreign countries, especially Central and South America, to purchase specialty items, such as rugs, wood carvings, picture frames, ceramics, and cast iron furniture.

Although she enjoyed her job and was successful at it, Whitney wanted to go back to school and earn a degree in business administration. She felt a degree would improve her professional opportunities. So after seven years with IPL, Whitney resigned and went back to school full time. Four years later, she received a B.S. with a major in business administration and a minor in international relations from Howard University in Washington, D.C.

With degree in hand, Whitney started her own import business, called Sanders Imports, Inc. (SII), headquartered in Gaithersburg, Maryland, just outside Washington, D.C. Within 18 months, her business was healthy and growing.

Among Whitney's successes are large contracts with three major discount department stores and more than 20 accounts with specialty shops throughout the United States. Whitney markets to these clients by publishing a quarterly catalog that contains color photographs and descriptions of the items she imports.

Last week Whitney added two major items, Mexican iced tea glass tumblers and Ecuadorian hand-carved chess sets, to her catalog. She is not scheduled to publish another catalog for two months, but she wants to inform her customers immediately about these highly marketable products. She decides to write a letter to her clients (Figure 6-1 on the following page).

OBJECTIVES

In this tutorial you will learn to:

- Create form and data merge files
- Merge files
- Sort a secondary file
- Create address labels

Sanders Imports, Inc.
429 Firstfield Road, Gaithersburg, MD 20878
Phone (301) 590-1000 Fax (301) 590-1825
Orders 1-800-IMPORTS

Date

First Name   Last Name
Company Name
Street Address
City   ,   State   Zip Code

Dear   Salutation Name   :

    I am writing to let you know about two exciting new SII products that I'm certain will appeal to your customers.

    ICED TEA GLASS TUMBLERS, 16 oz., finely painted patterns, imported from Mexico, suggested retail price $24.75 per set of four tumblers, your price $14.80 per set. These drinking glasses have heavy glass bottoms and clear glass sides and come in six different patterns. Sold in attractive cardboard carrying box. Because they are attractive yet inexpensive, these tumblers will sell well.

    HAND-CARVED CHESS SETS, Staunton pattern, weighted and felted bases, detailed knights, natural grain, U.S. Chess Federation approved, imported from Quito, Ecuador, suggested retail price $55.95, your price $28.15 per set. These sets are almost identical in appearance to the sets imported from India that sell for twice this amount.

    I have enclosed photographs of these products.

    Salutation Name   , please call me for more information or to receive samples of either of these items. As always, it is a pleasure doing business with   Company   .

Sincerely yours,

Whitney Sanders

Whitney Sanders
President, SII

Enclosures

Figure 6-1
Whitney's form
letter

Planning the Documents

Whitney wants to write a **form letter**, which is a letter that contains information pertinent to a large number of people (in this case, Whitney's clients) but that also contains information specific to the addressee. The specific information in Whitney's form letter is an inside address and salutation for each client and, in the body of the letter, the client's first name and the company name.

Whitney will use WordPerfect's Merge features to generate her form letters. In general, a **merge** is an operation that combines information from two documents to create many slightly different final documents.

The merge operation employs two separate documents: a form file and a data file. A **form file** is a document — such as a letter or a contract — that, in addition to text, contains merge commands to mark where special information — such as a name or an address — will be inserted. In Whitney's case, the form file will be like Figure 6-1, except that instead of blanks, the document will contain merge commands to mark the location for clients' names, addresses, and other data.

A **data file** is a document that contains information, such as names, street addresses, cities, states, and zip codes, that will be merged into the form file. In Whitney's case, the data file will be an address list similar to Figure 6-2, except that the file will have a slightly different format and will also contain merge commands to help WordPerfect merge the information into the form file.

Malone, Rebecca C. (Becky)
415-825-1585
Compton Novelty Shop
8415 El Arbol Street
Compton, CA 90220

McArdy, Gregory P. (Paul)
719-448-0025
Paul's Imports
854 North Pike's Peak Road
Colorado Springs, CO 80902

Sorenson, Mary Beth (Ms. Sorenson)
218-968-1593
North Star Emporium
51 West Center Street
Bemidji, MN 56601

Pilar, F. Emilio (Emilio)
602-433-8878
Grand Canyon Imports
4851 Caibab Highway Suite 210
Flagstaff, AZ 86001

Gutanov, Mikhail Ivonov (Mike)
404-921-3722
Peachtree Emporium
88 Peachtree Plaza
Atlanta, GA 30304

Figure 6-2
Client information for Whitney's data file

A final document produced by merging information from the data file into the form file is called the **merged document** (Figure 6-3).

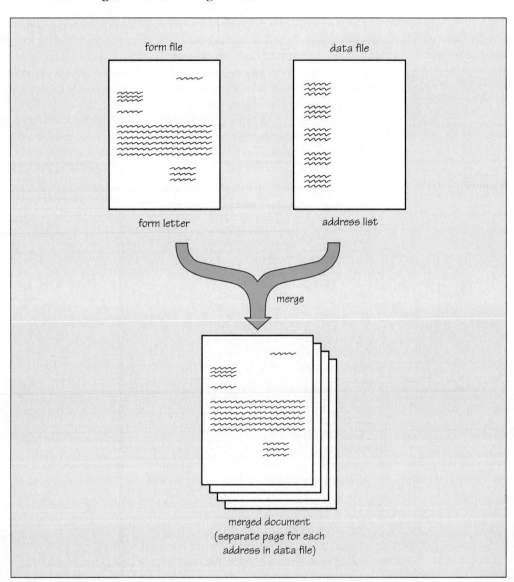

Figure 6-3
Merging a form file
and a data file to
create the merged
document

Merge Operations

During a merge operation, the merge commands in the form file instruct WordPerfect to fetch specific information from the data file. For example, one merge command in the form file might fetch a name, while another merge command might fetch a street address. For each set of data (for instance, a name and address) in the data file, WordPerfect usually creates a separate page in the merged document. Thus, if Whitney's data file has, for example, five sets of names and addresses of clients, the merge will produce five different letters, each with a different name and address and each on a separate page in the merged document (Figure 6-4).

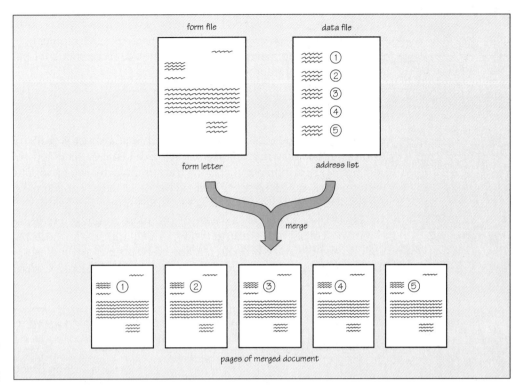

Figure 6-4
Pages of merged
document equal
number of
addresses in
address list

Records and Fields

The set of data on one individual or object in the data file is called a **record**. In Whitney's
data file, each record contains information about one client (Figure 6-5). Each item within a
record is called a **field**. One field might be the client's name, another field the client's street
address, another field the client's city, and so forth. For a merge operation to work properly,
every record must have the same set of fields.

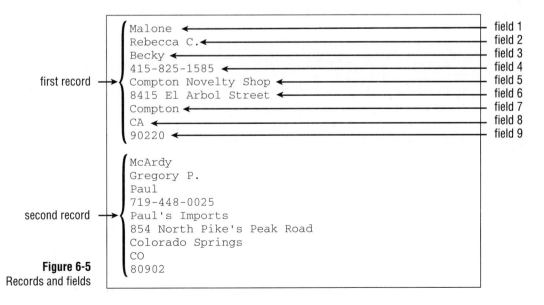

Figure 6-5
Records and fields

Data files are not limited to records about clients. You could create a data file with employee records, records of suppliers, records of equipment, and so forth. Once you understand how to manage and manipulate the records in data files, you'll be able to use them for many different types of applications.

Merge Commands

Form files usually contain merge commands that instruct WordPerfect which fields of each record to fetch and where to place those fields in the merged document. Form files may also contain merge commands that insert the current date, accept input from the keyboard, and perform other functions. Data files, on the other hand, contain merge commands that label the fields in each record, as well as mark the end of each record.

Figure 6-6 is a table of some of the most common merge commands. Each merge command consists of a **merge code**, which appears in the form file or data file as an uppercase, boldface word, often followed by a set of parentheses. You don't actually type the merge command; instead you use WordPerfect's Merge Codes command to insert the command in your form file or data file.

COMMON WORDPERFECT MERGE COMMANDS	
Merge Command	**Action**
DATE	Inserts current date
FIELD(*FieldName*)	Fetches data from field named *FieldName* in data file
FIELDNAMES(*FieldName*); *FieldName2;FieldName3;...*)	Lists names of fields in data file
ENDFIELD	Marks end of the field
ENDRECORD	Marks end of the record

Figure 6-6
Common
WordPerfect merge
commands

Some merge commands require you to supply a parameter. For example, the FIELD command requires a parameter that names a particular field within a record. You type the parameter between parentheses following the name of the command. Hence, a form file containing the merge command FIELD(FirstName) would instruct WordPerfect to fetch the field named "FirstName" from a record in the data file (Figure 6-7). The merge command FIELDNAME(Name;Address;Phone) would instruct WordPerfect to fetch the fields named "Name," "Address," and "Phone" from each record within the data file. The DATE command, which inserts the current date into the document, doesn't require a parameter and therefore appears in a form file without parentheses.

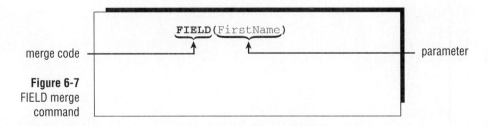

merge code

Figure 6-7
FIELD merge
command

Whitney's form file, including the merge codes, is shown in Figure 6-8. Your task in the following section will be to create this form file.

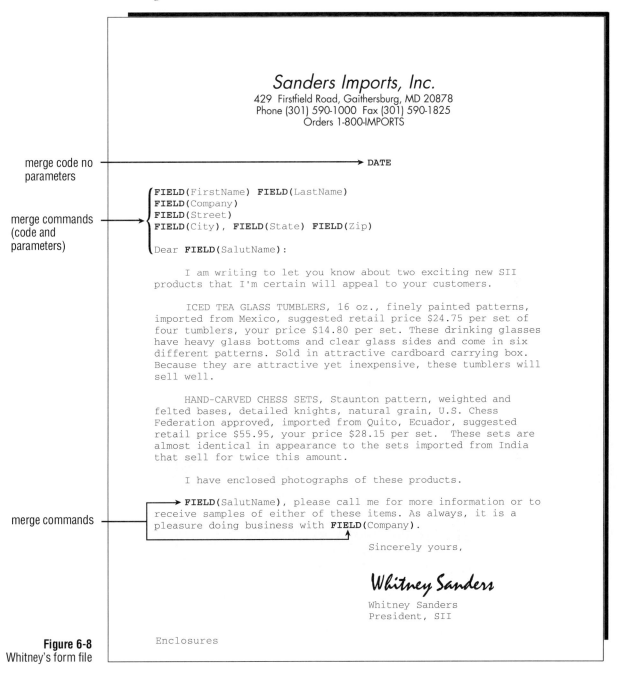

Figure 6-8
Whitney's form file

Creating a Form File

A form file contains text and merge commands. Creating a form file is similar to creating any other type of WordPerfect document, except that you use the Merge Codes command to insert the merge commands into it. You'll begin by inserting the DATE command.

To set up a form file and insert the DATE command:

● Make sure the document window is blank, then press **[Enter]** until the cursor is at Ln 2.5" or lower.

This leaves room for the company letterhead at the top of the page. If your paper doesn't have a letterhead, the blank space will keep the text of the letter from being too high up on the page.

● Press **[Tab]** until the cursor is at Pos 4.5", where Whitney wants the date to appear.

Now you're ready to instruct WordPerfect to set up a form file and insert the DATE command.

● Choose **T**ools, **M**erge, **D**efine or press **[Shift][F9]** (Merge Codes). WordPerfect displays the Merge Codes dialog box, shown in Figure 6-9. Before inserting merge codes, you have to tell WordPerfect what kind of merge file the current document is.

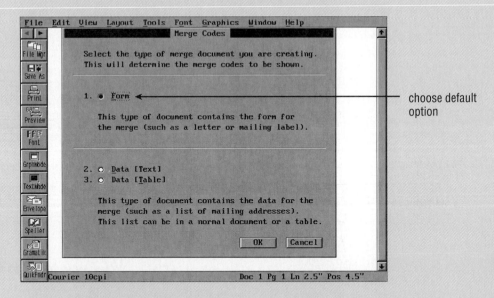

Figure 6-9
Merge Codes
dialog box

● Choose 1 (**F**orm), which is the default, and then choose OK. This informs WordPerfect that the current document is a form file.

Now the Merge Codes (Form File) dialog box appears on the screen. See Figure 6-10. You need to select the merge code to insert the current date. This dialog box lists some common merge codes, but it doesn't list DATE.

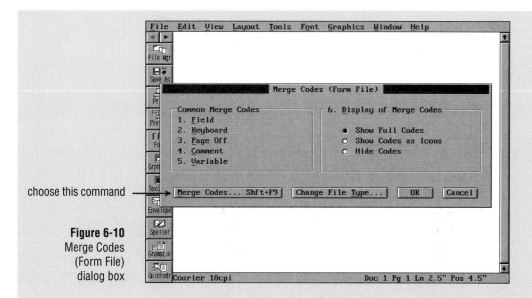

choose this command

Figure 6-10
Merge Codes
(Form File)
dialog box

⑤ Choose **M**erge Codes by pressing **M**, pressing **[Shift][F9]** again, or by clicking the
    Merge Codes button. WordPerfect displays a list of *all* the merge commands in the
    All Merge Codes dialog box. See Figure 6-11. You can use the arrow keys or the
    scroll bar to scroll through the list. You can also type part or all of the name of the
    command into the dialog box.

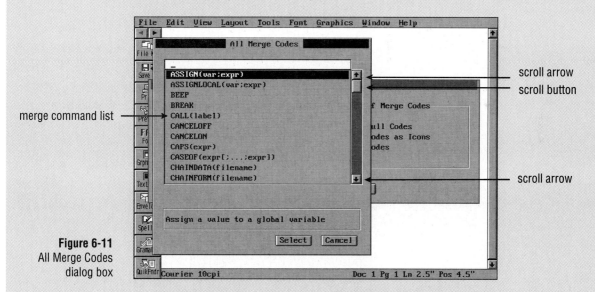

merge command list

scroll arrow
scroll button

scroll arrow

Figure 6-11
All Merge Codes
dialog box

⑥ Start to type **date** until DATE becomes highlighted. (Actually, you'll only have to type
    the "d" to highlight the DATE command.) Alternatively, scroll through the list until
    DATE appears and then highlight it.

⑦ With DATE highlighted, choose Select or press **[Enter]**. The DATE merge code appears in the document window. See Figure 6-12.

merge code

Figure 6-12
Document window
after you insert the
DATE merge code

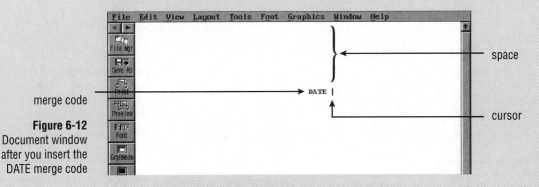

space

cursor

Later, when Whitney executes the merge, WordPerfect will insert the current date at the location of the DATE code on each copy of the letter.

In the following steps, you'll insert the FIELD command into the form file.

To insert the FIELD command into the form file:
① Press **[Enter]** three times to triple space between the date and the inside address.
② Choose **T**ools, M**e**rge, **D**efine or press **[Shift][F9]** to display the Merge Codes (Form File) dialog box.
   The FIELD merge code is listed as a common merge command.
③ Choose **1** (**F**ield). The FIELD merge code requires a parameter, so WordPerfect displays the Parameter Entry dialog box, shown in Figure 6-13.

Figure 6-13
Parameter Entry
dialog box

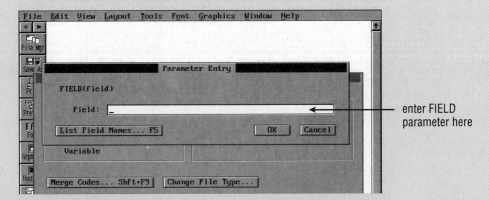

enter FIELD
parameter here

The field name in the form file must correspond to a field name in the data file. Because Whitney hasn't created the data file yet, she can use any field name she wants at this point. She'll have to remember these field names when she creates her data file.

❹ Type **FirstName** and choose OK by pressing **[Enter]** or by clicking the OK button. WordPerfect inserts the FIELD command in the document window and, inside the parentheses, the name of the field. See Figure 6-14.

FIELD command

Figure 6-14
Document window
after you insert the
first FIELD command

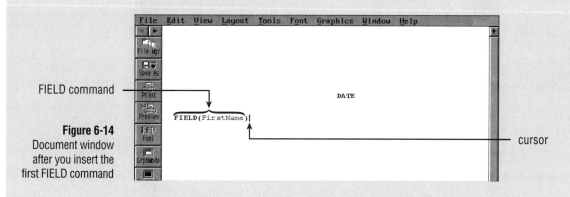

cursor

When Whitney executes the merge, WordPerfect will fetch the first name — which will include the first name and a middle name or a middle initial — from the data file and insert it into the document at that location. Now you're ready to insert the other FIELD commands for the inside address and salutation.

To insert the FIELD commands for the inside address and salutation:

❶ Press **[Spacebar]** to insert a space after the first name.

❷ Choose **T**ools, **M**erge, **D**efine or press **[Shift][F9]** to display the Merge Codes (Form File) dialog box.

❸ Choose **1** (**F**ield) to display the Parameter Entry dialog box.

❹ Type **LastName** and choose OK or press **[Enter]**. Your screen now looks like Figure 6-15.

merge commands

Figure 6-15
Document window
after you insert the
second FIELD
commmand

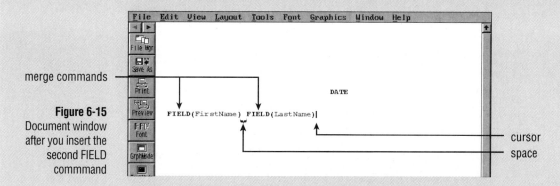

cursor
space

❺ Press **[Enter]** to move the cursor to the next line. Insert the FIELD code with the field name "Company," as shown in Figure 6-8.

❻ Continue typing the merge codes to insert the inside address and the salutation, until your screen looks like Figure 6-16. Remember, never *type* a merge code; always use the Merge Codes command to insert the codes.

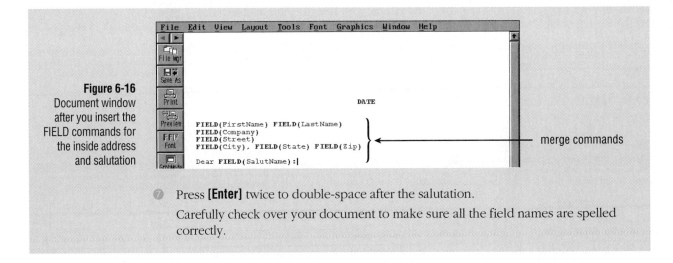

Figure 6-16
Document window
after you insert the
FIELD commands for
the inside address
and salutation

merge commands

⑦ Press **[Enter]** twice to double-space after the salutation.

Carefully check over your document to make sure all the field names are spelled correctly.

The FIELD(SalutName) command in the salutation tells WordPerfect to fetch a name that might be a formal salutation like "Mr. Caballero," a first name, or even a nickname. For example, the data file might list a client's first name as "Rebecca C." but her salutation name (SalutName) as "Becky," because Whitney knows her well.

You'll now retrieve the rest of the form letter (the form file) from the WordPerfect data disk and insert the two merge commands needed to personalize the last paragraph of Whitney's letter.

To retrieve the file:

① Make sure the WordPerfect data disk is in drive A.

Because you will frequently use the disk in drive A to save and open or retrieve files, you will now change the default directory to A:.

② Choose **F**ile, **F**ile Manager or press **[F5]** (File Manager) to display the Specify File Manager List dialog box.

From this dialog box, you now want to display the Change Default Directory dialog box. To do this, you press [=] (equal sign), even though this command is not shown as an option in the current dialog box.

③ Press [=] (equal sign) to display the Change Default Directory dialog box. See Figure 6-17.

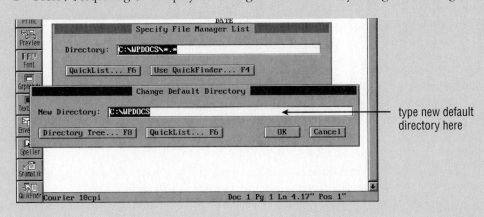

type new default
directory here

Figure 6-17
Change Default
Directory dialog box

④ Type **a:** and choose OK or press **[Enter]**.

⑤ Choose Cancel or press **[Esc]** (Cancel) to cancel the directory listing.

Even though you canceled the directory listing by the File Manager, the default directory is still A:\.

⑥ Choose **F**ile, **R**etrieve or press **[Shift][F10]** twice to display the Retrieve Document dialog box.

⑦ Type **c6file1.dft** and choose OK to retrieve the file from the data disk in drive A.

WordPerfect retrieves the file C6FILE1.DFT into the current document window.

You're now ready to insert the last two FIELD commands into the form letter.

To insert the last two FIELD commands into the form letter:

① Move the cursor to the comma at the beginning of the last paragraph of the letter.

② Insert the command FIELD(SalutName).

③ Move the cursor to the period at the end of the last paragraph.

④ Insert the command FIELD(Company). See Figure 6-18.

Figure 6-18
Document window
after you insert the
last two FIELD
commands

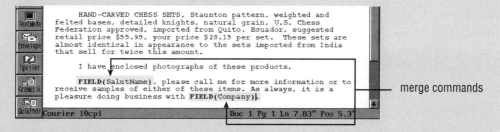

merge commands

The merge commands in the last paragraph of the document will tell WordPerfect to insert the client's salutation name and company name at these locations in the letter.

⑤ Save the file as S6SLSLET.FRM.

The abbreviation "SLSLET" stands for "sales letter," and the filename extension "FRM" stands for "form" to remind you that this is the form file used in a WordPerfect merge operation.

Creating a Data File

As Whitney acquires new and potential clients, she types information about them into a WordPerfect data file. She can then merge the data file with a form file to generate her sales letters.

Figure 6-19 on the following page shows the first five records of Whitney's data file. As you can see, the file contains merge codes that specify the names of the fields and that mark the ends of fields and records.

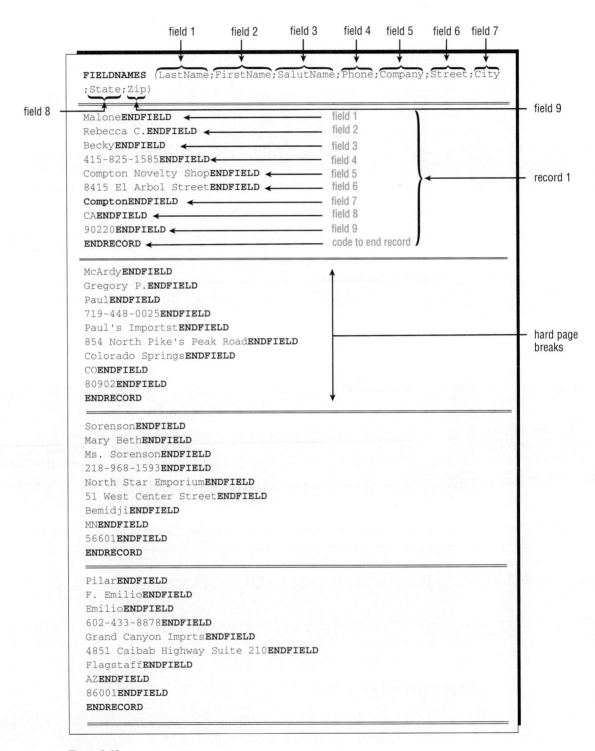

Figure 6-19
Whitney's data file

```
GutanovENDFIELD
Mikhail IvonovENDFIELD
MikeENDFIELD
404-921-3722ENDFIELD
Peachtree EmporiumENDFIELD
88 Peachtree PlazaENDFIELD
AtlantaENDFIELD
GAENDFIELD
30304ENDFIELD
ENDRECORD
```

Figure 6-19
(continued)

To create a data file, you must follow certain procedures:

1. **Name the fields**. WordPerfect internally numbers each field within a record, but to make merge commands easier, you can tell WordPerfect the name of each field. In Figure 6-19, for example, the name of field 1, the first field in each record, is "LastName." Wherever the form file contains the merge command FIELD(LastName), WordPerfect will insert the information from the first field of the data file.

2. **Mark the end of the field names**. After you name all the fields using the FIELDNAME command, WordPerfect automatically inserts the ENDRECORD command (to indicate that there are no more field names) and a hard page break.

3. **Insert data into the data file**. You type the text of a field and then insert the ENDFIELD command to mark the end of the field. You must follow exactly the order you used when you named the fields. For example, the first field of every record must be the last name, the second field of every record must be the first name, and so forth. If you change the order of information in the data file, WordPerfect will insert the wrong information into the document during the merge operation. If the information for a particular field isn't applicable — for example, if a client doesn't use a company name — you must still mark the Company field with the ENDFIELD code. At the end of each record, you must insert the ENDRECORD command.

Let's create the data file of information about Whitney's clients. WordPerfect supports two types of data files: text and table. A **text data file** uses normal text lines to format the records and fields of the data file. A **table data file**, on the other hand, uses a WordPerfect table to format the records and fields. In a table data file, each row of the table is a record, and each cell within a row is a field. In this tutorial, we will create a text data file, but most of the principles covered apply to table data files. First we'll insert the merge command FIELDNAMES, which names the fields.

To create a data file:

❶ Clear the document window.

❷ Choose **T**ools, **M**erge, **D**efine or press **[Shift][F9]** (Merge Codes).

WordPerfect displays the Merge Codes dialog box that you saw earlier. This time, however, you will set up the document as a data file.

❸ Choose **2** (**D**ata [Text]) to specify that this document is a data file using regular text mode to format the records and fields.

The Merge Codes (Text Data File) dialog box appears on the screen. See Figure 6-20.

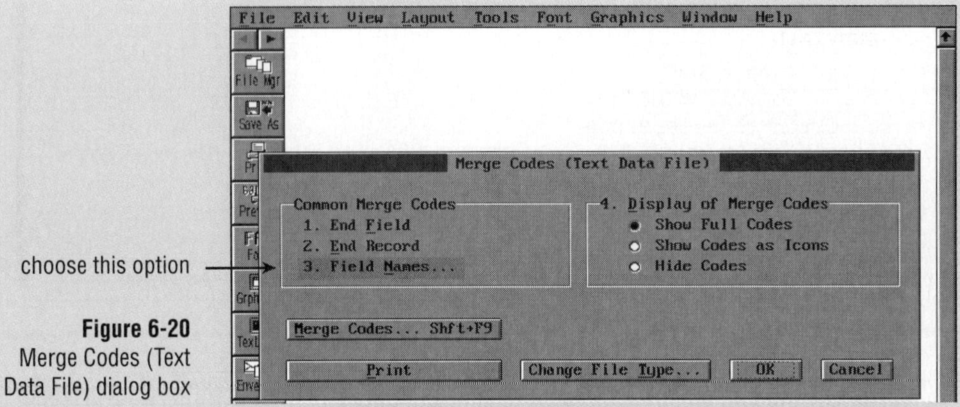

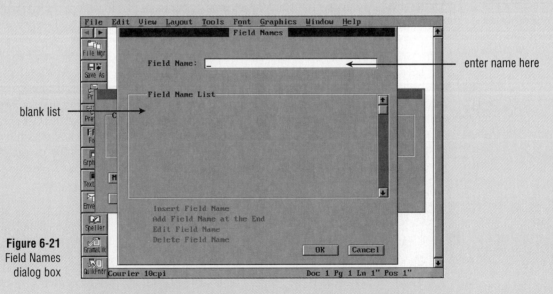

choose this option →

Figure 6-20
Merge Codes (Text
Data File) dialog box

You're now ready to insert the FIELDNAME command to define the names of the fields in each of your records.

To insert the FIELDNAME command into the data file:

● Choose **M**erge Codes by pressing **M**, by pressing **[Shift][F9]**, or by clicking the Merge Codes button.

WordPerfect displays the All Merge Codes dialog box.

● Highlight FIELDNAMES and choose Select or press **[Enter]**. WordPerfect displays the Field Names dialog box, shown in Figure 6-21. The Field Name List is currently blank because you haven't specified any field names yet.

enter name here →

blank list →

Figure 6-21
Field Names
dialog box

● Type **LastName** and press **[Enter]** to specify that the first field in each record will contain the last name of the client.

The field name "LastName" appears in the Field Name List within the dialog box. The Field Names dialog box stays on the screen and prompts you to enter another field name.

④ Type **FirstName** and press **[Enter]** to add the second field name to the list.

⑤ Type **SalutName** and press **[Enter]**. This tells WordPerfect that the third field in each record will contain the name you want to use in the salutation of a letter.

⑥ Type the names of fields 4 through 9 into the dialog box. The field names are "Phone," "Company," "Street," "City," "State," and "Zip." The Field Names dialog box should now look like Figure 6-22.

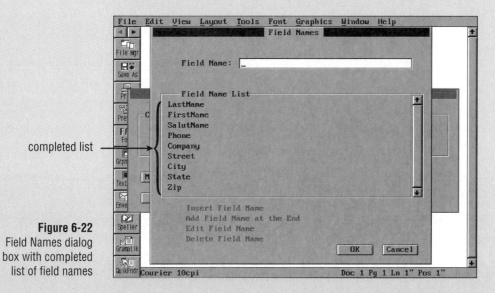

completed list

Figure 6-22
Field Names dialog
box with completed
list of field names

⑦ Choose OK by clicking the OK button or by pressing **[Enter]** twice.

The field names now appear across the top of the screen. See Figure 6-23. The ENDRECORD code and a hard page break appear after the FIELDNAME command. The message "Field: LastName" appears in the status bar, indicating that WordPerfect is waiting for you to enter data for the first field.

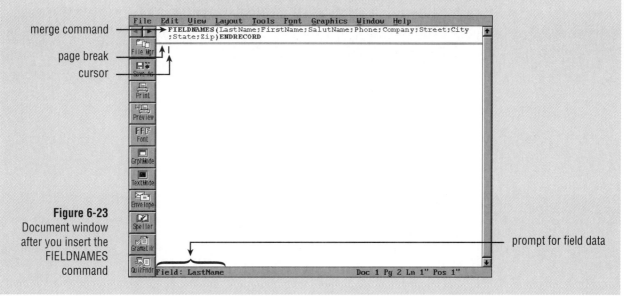

merge command
page break
cursor

prompt for field data

Figure 6-23
Document window
after you insert the
FIELDNAMES
command

If you made a mistake typing a field name, use the regular WordPerfect editing keys to fix the error.

You can now save the file.

⑧ Save this intermediate version of the data file as S6ADDR.INT. "ADDR" indicates that the file contains addresses, and the filename extension "INT" stands for "intermediate version."

The data file you have just created contains no records yet. You'll now enter the data for each record.

Entering Data into a Data File

Whitney is now ready to enter client information into the file, as shown in Figure 6-19. Let's begin by entering data into the first record.

To enter data into a record:

① With the cursor positioned just below the page break, type **Malone.** Do not press [Enter]. This is the last name of the first client.

WordPerfect allows more than one line of text in a field. For example, you may want to include a department name and the company name on two separate lines in the Company field. In this particular file, we will use only one line per field.

② Choose **T**ools, **M**erge, **D**efine, **1** (End **F**ield) or press **[F9]** (End Field). (If you pressed [Enter] instead of [F9], press [Backspace] to delete the invisible [HRt] code.)

Because pressing [F9] is so much easier than using the pull-down menus, we'll tell you to insert the ENDFIELD command by pressing [F9]. If you want to use the pull-down menus, feel free to do so.

WordPerfect inserts the merge code ENDFIELD to the right of "Malone" and automatically inserts a hard return to move the cursor to the next line. The message "Field: FirstName" appears on the status bar, indicating that WordPerfect is waiting for the text of the next field. See Figure 6-24.

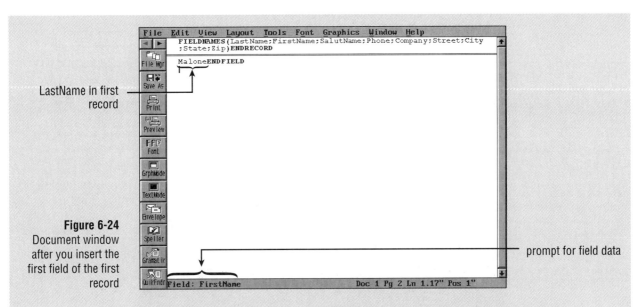

LastName in first record

Figure 6-24
Document window after you insert the first field of the first record

prompt for field data

3 Type **Rebecca C.** and press **[F9]** (End Field) to insert the client's first name. Notice that this field also contains any middle name or middle initial of the client. WordPerfect inserts the ENDFIELD code and a hard return. The message "Field: SalutName" appears on the status bar.

4 Type **Becky** and press **[F9]** (End Field) to insert the client's salutation name. If you know the client well, you would include the first name or a nickname (as you have done here). If you don't know the client well, you would use a more formal salutation name, such as "Ms. Malone."

WordPerfect displays the message "Field: Phone" on the status bar. See Figure 6-25.

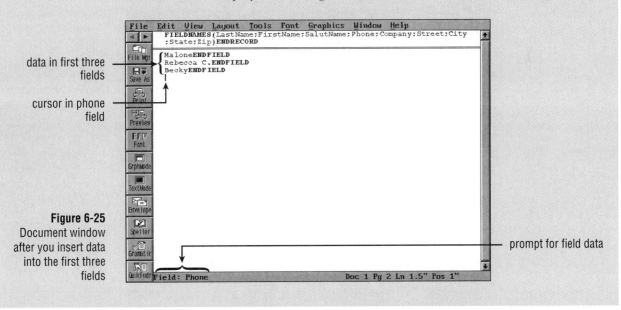

data in first three fields

cursor in phone field

Figure 6-25
Document window after you insert data into the first three fields

prompt for field data

⑤ Type **415-825-1585** and press **[F9]** (End Field) to enter the client's phone number. WordPerfect inserts the ENDFIELD code and displays the message "Field: Company" on the status bar.

⑥ Type **Compton Novelty Shop** and press **[F9]** (End Field) to enter the client's company name and the ENDFIELD code. WordPerfect displays the message "Field: Street" on the status bar.

⑦ Type **8415 El Arbol Street** and press **[F9]** (End Field) to enter the street address and the ENDFIELD code.

⑧ Type **Compton** and press **[F9]** (End Field), type **CA** and press **[F9]** (End Field), and type **90220** and press **[F9]** (End Field) to insert the city, state, and zip code into the record. See Figure 6-26.

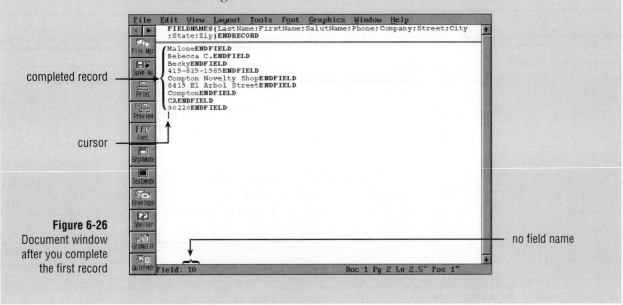

completed record

cursor

Figure 6-26
Document window
after you complete
the first record

no field name

You have now entered all the data for the first record. The status bar displays the message "Field: 10" instead of a field name, because the data file has only nine named fields. You must now mark the end of this record.

To mark the end of a record:

① Choose **T**ools, **M**erge, **D**efine or press **[Shift][F9]** (Merge Codes) to display the Merge Codes (Text Data File) dialog box.

② Choose **2** (**E**nd Record). WordPerfect inserts the ENDRECORD command and a hard page break. See Figure 6-27.

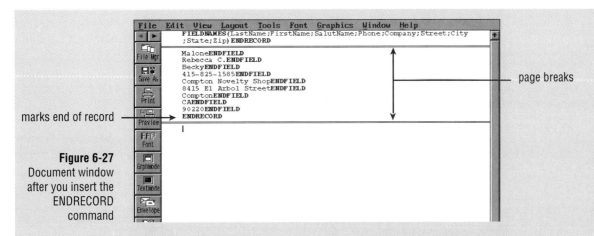

marks end of record →

Figure 6-27
Document window
after you insert the
ENDRECORD
command

→ page breaks

Having created the first record in the data file, you can now enter the next four records of Whitney's client list, as shown in Figure 6-19.

● Finish entering the other four records into the data file. Your screen will look like Figure 6-28.

Figure 6-28
Document window
after you complete
all five records

It's easy to make mistakes as you enter information for each record. Make sure you enter each item (last name, first name, salutation name, phone number, company name, street, city, state, and zip code) into a separate field. Remember to insert the ENDFIELD command at the end of each field and the ENDRECORD command at the end of each record.

After you have entered the final record, WordPerfect prompts you for the last name of another record (Figure 6-28). Ignore this prompt.

● After you have entered the data and double-checked it for accuracy, save the document as S6ADDR.DAT. The filename extension "DAT" stands for "data file."

Although Whitney's data file will eventually contain numerous records (one for each of her many clients), S6ADDR.DAT contains only five records, a sufficient number to demonstrate WordPerfect's merge features.

Merging Form and Data Files

Now that she has created her form letter (form file) and her address list (data file), Whitney is ready to merge the two files to create personalized letters to send to her clients. Let's merge S6SLSLET.FRM (the form file) with S6ADDR.DAT (the data file).

To merge a form file and a data file:

① Clear the document window.

Because WordPerfect creates the merged file in an empty document window, this step is not essential.

② Choose **T**ools, **M**erge, **R**un. Alternatively, press **[Ctrl][F9]** (Merge/Sort) to display the Merge/Sort dialog box (see Figure 6-29), then choose **1** (**M**erge).

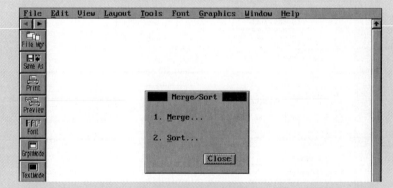

Figure 6-29
Merge/Sort dialog box

The Run Merge dialog box appears on the screen. See Figure 6-30.

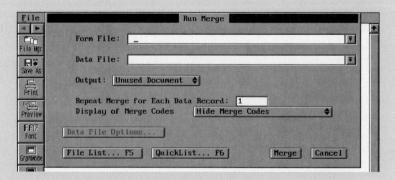

Figure 6-30
Run Merge dialog box

③ In the Form File text box, type **s6slslet.frm** and press **[Tab]** or **[Enter]**. This is Whitney's form file, which contains her form letter.

④ Type **s6addr.dat** and press **[Enter]**. This is Whitney's data file, which contains her address list. The Run Merge dialog box should now look like Figure 6-31.

Figure 6-31
Run Merge dialog box after you enter the filenames

```
┌──────────────────────────────────────────────────────────────────────┐
│ File  ┌──────────────────────  Run Merge  ──────────────────────────┐ │
│ ◄ ►   │                                                              │ │
│ 🖿     │  1. Form File:   s6slslet.frm                          ▼   │ │
│ File Mgr│                                                            │ │
│ 🖫     │  2. Data File:   s6addr.dat                            ▼   │ │
│ Save As │                                                            │ │
│ 🖨     │  3. Output:  Current Document ♦                            │ │
│ Print   │                                                            │ │
│ 🖳     │  4. Repeat Merge for Each Data Record: 1                   │ │
│ Preview │  5. Display of Merge Codes      Hide Merge Codes      ♦   │ │
│ FFP    │                                                            │ │
│ Font   │  Data File Options...                                      │ │
│ ▢      │                                                            │ │
│ GrphMode│ File List... F5   QuickList... F6       Merge   Cancel    │ │
│       └──────────────────────────────────────────────────────────────┘ │
└──────────────────────────────────────────────────────────────────────┘
```

⑤ Choose Merge by pressing **[Enter]** or by clicking the Merge button.

WordPerfect merges the form and data files to create the merged document.

The end of the merged document now appears in the document window. See Figure 6-32.

data fetched from last record of data file

Figure 6-32
Document window after you merge the form and data files

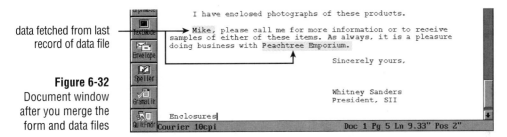

```
I have enclosed photographs of these products.

Mike, please call me for more information or to receive
samples of either of these items. As always, it is a pleasure
doing business with Peachtree Emporium.

                              Sincerely yours,


                              Whitney Sanders
                              President, SII

Enclosures
Courier 10cpi                          Doc 1 Pg 5 Ln 9.33" Pos 2"
```

During the merge operation, WordPerfect retrieved information from the data file — one record at a time — and inserted it into the form file according to the merge commands to create five letters. After each letter, WordPerfect inserted a hard page break, so that each letter will print on a separate page. You can use the cursor-movement keys to move through the resulting merged document. As you can see, it contains five pages, one page for each of the five records in the form file. The first page of the merged document, the letter to Rebecca Malone, appears in Figure 6-33 on the following page.

This will not be on
your document →

Sanders Imports, Inc.
429 Firstfield Road, Gaithersburg, MD 20878
Phone (301) 590-1000 Fax (301) 590-1825
Orders 1-800-IMPORTS

July 29, 1994

Rebecca C. Malone
Compton Novelty Shop
8415 El Arbol Street
Compton, CA 90220

Dear Becky:

I am writing to let you know about two exciting new SII
products that I'm certain will appeal to your customers.

ICED TEA GLASS TUMBLERS, 16 oz., finely painted patterns,
imported from Mexico, suggested retail price $24.75 per set of
four tumblers, your price $14.80 per set. These drinking glasses
have heavy glass bottoms and clear glass sides and come in six
different patterns. Sold in attractive cardboard carrying box.
Because they are attractive yet inexpensive, these tumblers will
sell well.

HAND-CARVED CHESS SETS, Staunton pattern, weighted and
felted bases, detailed knights, natural grain, U.S. Chess
Federation approved, imported from Quito, Ecuador, suggested
retail price $55.95, your price $28.15 per set. These sets are
almost identical in appearance to the sets imported from India
that sell for twice this amount.

I have enclosed photographs of these products.

Becky, please call me for more information or to receive
samples of either of these items. As always, it is a pleasure
doing business with Compton Novelty Shop.

Sincerely yours,

Whitney Sanders

Whitney Sanders
President, SII

Enclosures

Figure 6-33
First page of
merged document
with merged data
highlighted

Sorting a Data File

As Whitney looks through the merged document containing the letters to her clients, she observes one problem. She is going to use bulk mailing rates to send her letters, but the U.S. Postal Service requires bulk mailings to be divided into groups according to zip code. Currently the letters are in the order in which she added the client information to her data file. She must, therefore, sort the data file by zip code.

In WordPerfect, to **sort** means to arrange a list or a document in some specified order. WordPerfect allows you to perform three types of sort: merge, line, and paragraph. A **merge sort** allows you to sort the records in a data file, as you'll see shortly. A **line sort** allows you to sort lines within any type of document (Figure 6-34). A **paragraph sort** allows you to sort the paragraphs within any type of document. You have to tell WordPerfect which type of sort you want to carry out.

lines in document before line sort

lines in document after alphabetic line sort

Figure 6-34
Sorting lines in a document

You also need to tell WordPerfect whether the sort involves only numbers, called a **numeric sort**, or numbers and letters, called an **alphanumeric sort**. For a merge sort, you need to instruct WordPerfect to sort by last name, by company name, by zip code, or by any one of the other fields in the data file. You also need to tell WordPerfect which word in the field to sort by. For example, if Whitney wanted to sort her data file by each client's first name, she must tell WordPerfect to sort using the first word in the FirstName field rather than using any other word in the field (the middle names or initials).

Whitney decides that before printing the letters, she will sort the data file by zip code and then execute the merge again so that the letters appear in order according to their zip codes. Let's do that now.

To sort the data file:

① Clear the merged document from the document window without saving it and open S6ADDR.DAT, the data file containing the client information.

② Choose **T**ools, So**r**t or press **[Ctrl][F9]** (Merge/Sort) and choose **2** (**S**ort).

WordPerfect displays the Sort (Source and Destination) dialog box shown in Figure 6-35 on the following page. Notice that the Document on Screen checkbox is selected for both the From (Source) file and the To (Destination) file. Because we want to sort the file on the screen (S6ADDR.DAT) and have the results written back to the current document window, we accept the default settings.

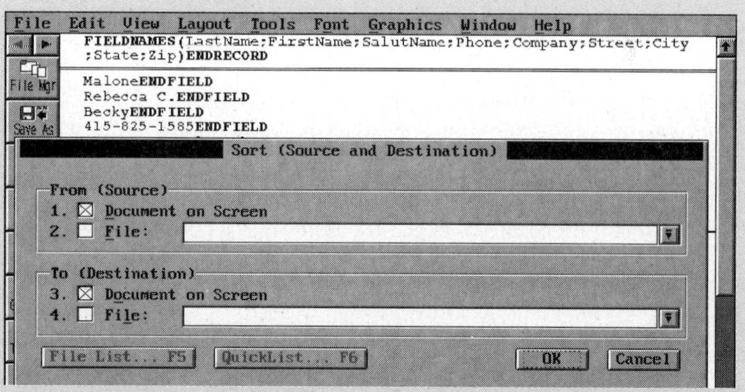

Figure 6-35
Sort (Source and
Destination) dialog
box

③ Choose OK. WordPerfect displays the Sort window on the bottom half of the screen. See Figure 6-36. You will use this menu to specify how you want WordPerfect to sort the data file.

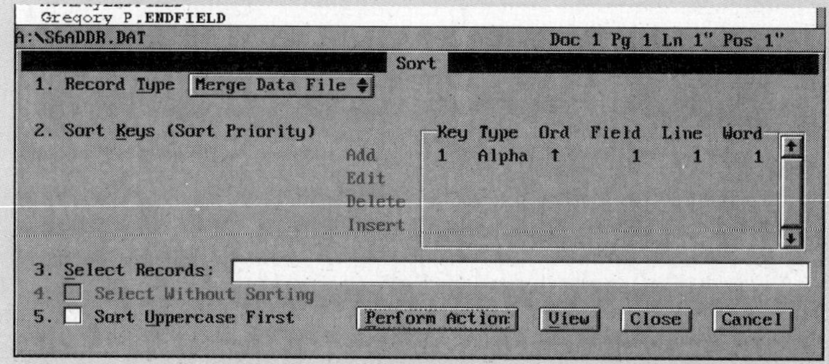

Figure 6-36
Sort window

Notice that option 1 (Record **T**ype) is set to Merge Data File. WordPerfect recognized the document on the screen as a data file and therefore sets the proper default record type.

You'll now tell WordPerfect how you want to carry out the sort. This information is communicated to WordPerfect via the **sort keys**. Sort keys allow you to specify whether the sort is alphanumeric or numeric and also to specify the field and word by which you want to sort. Let's use a sort key to tell WordPerfect that we want to sort by field 9 ("Zip").

④ Choose **2** (Sort **K**eys). The Sort Keys region of the Sort dialog box becomes selected, and the current sort key becomes highlighted. See Figure 6-37. Let's edit this sort key.

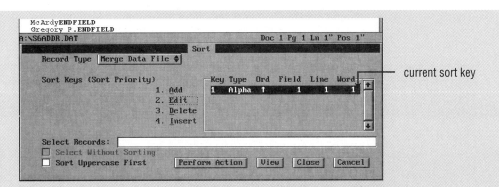

current sort key

Figure 6-37
Sort window with
sort key highlighted

⑤ Choose **2** (**E**dit) to display the Edit Sort Key dialog box. See Figure 6-38.

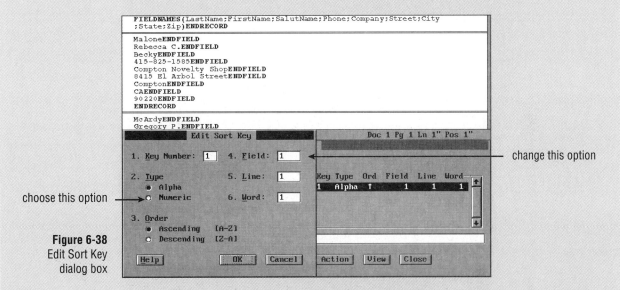

change this option

choose this option

Figure 6-38
Edit Sort Key
dialog box

Option 1 (Key Number) is number 1, which means that WordPerfect will use this sort key as the first priority in the sort. If two records have the same information (in our case, the same zip code) for the first sort key (key 1), then WordPerfect will go to key 2 to decide which of the two records will appear first in the sorted output file. Because you want to sort according to a number — the zip code — you'll tell WordPerfect to carry out a numeric sort rather than an alphanumeric sort.

⑥ Choose **2** (**T**ype) and then **2** (**N**umeric) or click the mouse pointer on the circle next to Numeric.

You don't need to change option 3, the Order of the sort, because you want the records sorted by ascending values of the zip codes, and Ascending is the default. You do, however, want to change option 4, the sort Field. The default sort field is 1, which in our case is the last name. Let's change that to field 9, the zip code.

⑦ Choose **4** (**F**ield), type **9**, and press **[Enter]**.

Because the Zip field in Whitney's data file is a number, you don't need to specify a line or a word within the field. The Edit Sort Key dialog box is therefore complete, as shown in Figure 6-39.

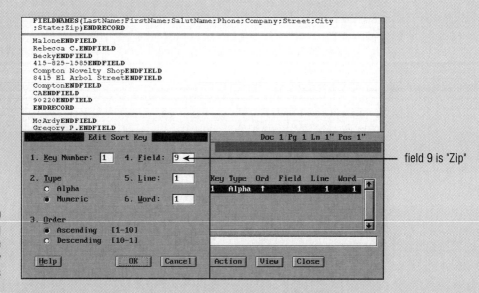

Figure 6-39
Edit Sort Key dialog
box after you make
the necessary
changes

field 9 is "Zip"

⑧ Choose OK to return to the Sort dialog box.

You have now set sort key 1. WordPerfect allows you to set up to nine sort keys. In Whitney's data file, however, the order of the records having the same zip code doesn't matter, so she doesn't set any other sort keys. You are now ready to execute the sort and perform the merge.

To sort the records of the data file and perform the merge:

① From the Sort dialog box, choose Perform Action.

WordPerfect sorts the data file, outputs the results to the document window, exits the Sort menu, and returns the cursor to the document window. The screen contains the data file, with its records sorted according to zip code. See Figure 6-40. Use your cursor keys to move through the document to see that the first record is Mikhail Gutanov, with a zip code of 30304 (Georgia), and that the last record is Rebecca Malone, with a zip code of 90220 (California). You should now save the sorted data file.

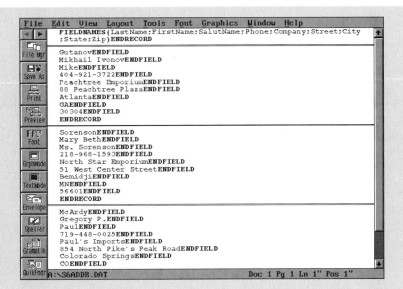

Figure 6-40
Document window
after you sort the
records in the data
file

② Save the data file as S6ADDR2.DAT to your data disk.

③ Clear the document window.

④ Choose **T**ools, **M**erge, **R**un or press **[Ctrl][F9]** (Merge/Sort) and choose **1** (**M**erge) to display the Run Merge dialog box.

The previous names of the form and data files appear in the dialog box. You don't want to change the name of the form file, but you do the data file.

⑤ Choose **2** (**D**ata File), type **s6addr2.dat,** and press **[Enter]**.

⑥ Choose Merge to merge the two files.

WordPerfect merges the files. Now the first letter in the merged document is to Mikhail Ivonov Gutanov, and the last letter is to Rebecca C. Malone.

You can now save and print the merged document.

To save and print the merged document:

① Save the merged document as S6MERGED.DOC.

② Print all five pages of the merged document.

As you can see, the letters print in order according to their zip codes, starting with the letter to Mike Gutanov, whose zip code is 30304, and ending with Becky Malone, whose zip code is 90220.

Printing Address Labels

Whitney wants to mail the form letters and accompanying photographs in 9-by-12-inch manila envelopes. Rather than typing the address on each envelope, she will use WordPerfect's labels and merge features to create mailing labels.

Creating the Labels Form File

Whitney's first task is to create a form file that specifies the format of the mailing label. The contents of her labels form file is shown in Figure 6-41. As you can see, this form file contains FIELD commands similar to those in Whitney's form letter. Let's create the labels form file.

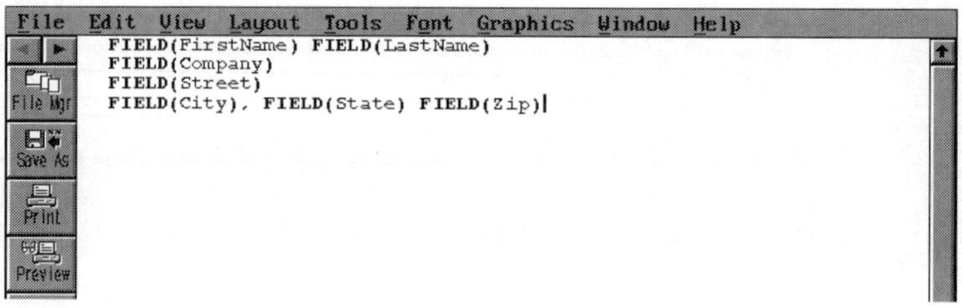

Figure 6-41
Document window
with the form file for
labels

To create a form file for labels:

① Clear the document window.

② Choose **T**ools, **M**erge, **D**efine or press **[Shift][F9]** (Merge Codes) to display the Merge Codes dialog box.

③ Make sure that option 1 (Form) is selected and choose OK.

④ Choose **1** (Field), type **FirstName**, and choose OK.

⑤ Press **[Spacebar]** and insert the next FIELD command, as shown in Figure 6-41.

⑥ Continue inserting the FIELD commands and formatting the label exactly as shown in Figure 6-41.

⑦ Save the file using the filename S6LABELS.FRM.

Because the mailing labels contain only the names and addresses of the clients, this labels form file includes no text except spaces, hard returns, and a comma.

Merging the Labels Form File with the Address List

Whitney's next task is to merge the labels form file she has just created with the data file (the client list) she created earlier.

To merge the files:

① Clear the document window.

② Choose **T**ools, **M**erge, **R**un or press **[Ctrl][F9]** (Merge/Sort) and choose **1** (**M**erge).

③ Type **s6labels.frm** and press **[Enter]** to specify the name of the form file.

④ If necessary, type **s6addr2.dat** and press **[Enter]** to specify the name of the data file.

⑤ Choose Merge to merge the form and data files.

WordPerfect merges the form and data files to yield the five documents shown in Figure 6-42, with one page for each record in the data file.

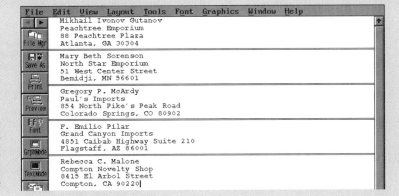

Figure 6-42
Document window
after you merge the
labels form file with
the data file

Creating the Labels Document

If Whitney were to print the merged labels document as it appears now, she would get one address in the upper-left corner of each printed page. Instead, she wants the addresses to be printed on a standard sheet of gummed labels. Fortunately, WordPerfect provides a method for printing on gummed labels.

To format the merged document for labels, you need to change the page definition. WordPerfect's **page definition** is a set of instructions that specify the page type and page size of the printed document. By telling WordPerfect that you are printing labels and by specifying certain measurements about those labels, you can create a page definition for printing them successfully.

Whitney has purchased Avery Laser Printer Labels number 5161, in sheets, from a local office supply store. Each label measures 4 inches by 1 inch, as shown in Figure 6-43. Each sheet has ten rows of labels, with two labels in each row, for a total of twenty labels per sheet. (See Figure 6-44.) WordPerfect supports most types of commercial label sheets. If you use a different type of gummed label from the one illustrated here, you will set up your merged document for that type.

You're now ready to tell WordPerfect the type of gummed labels you're using.

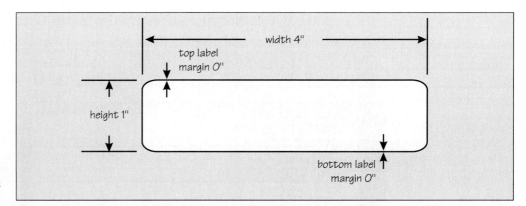

Figure 6-43
Dimensions for a
typical label

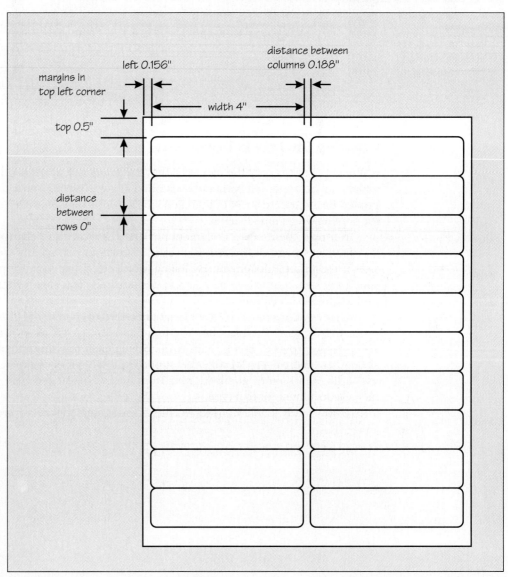

Figure 6-44
Dimensions for a
typical labels page

To set up the merged document for gummed labels:

1. Move the cursor to the very beginning of the merged labels document, before any format codes except [Open Style:InitialCodes].

2. Choose **L**ayout, **P**age or press **[Shift][F8]** (Format) and choose **3** (**P**age) to display the Page Format dialog box. See Figure 6-45.

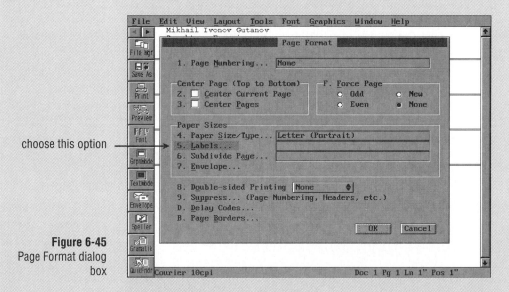

choose this option

Figure 6-45
Page Format dialog box

3. Choose **5** (**L**abels) to display the Labels dialog box. See Figure 6-46.

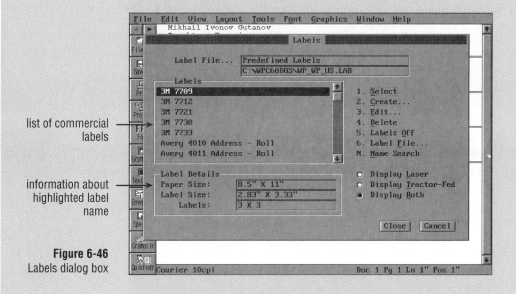

list of commercial labels

information about highlighted label name

Figure 6-46
Labels dialog box

The dialog box gives a list of commercial printer labels.

④ Scroll through the Labels list until you find the name of your labels, for example, Avery 5162 Address.

If your brand of labels isn't in the list, choose a brand that closely matches the sheet size (usually 8.5 by 11 inches), the label size, and the number of labels on a page — for example, 2 by 10, which means 10 rows of 2 labels each. You would then choose the Edit command from the Labels dialog box and edit the detailed dimensions of your labels. In this example, we will assume that your labels are on the list.

⑤ Highlight the name of your printer labels (for example, Avery 5162 Address) and choose **1** (**S**elect). WordPerfect displays the Labels Printer Info dialog box. See Figure 6-47.

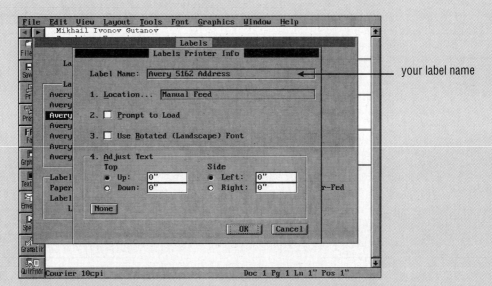

your label name

Figure 6-47
Labels Printer Info
dialog box

This dialog box gives the name of the labels, the location of the labels in the printer (Continuous or Manual feed), and other information. You should accept the default settings in this dialog box unless your instructor or technical support person tells you otherwise.

⑥ Choose OK or Close until you exit all the dialog boxes and return to the document window.

Your screen should now look like Figure 6-48. If the characters in the text appear unusually large, do the following:

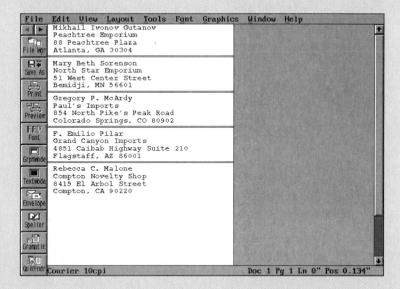

Figure 6-48
Document window
after you set the
page to labels

⑦ Choose **V**iew, **Z**oom, 100**%** to set the screen view to actual size.

You can now view the labels document to see how it will look before you print it. Then save the document and print it.

To view, save, and print the labels document:

❶ Choose **F**ile, Print Pre**v**iew, or press **[Shift][F7]** (Print/Fax) and choose **7** (Print Pre**v**iew), or click the Preview button.

❷ If necessary, choose **V**iew, **1**00% View or click the Zoom 100% button to display the document at full size.

The Print Preview screen looks like Figure 6-49, unless you used a different type of printer labels.

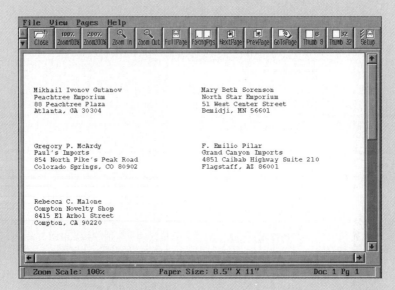

Figure 6-49
Print Preview of
labels document

- After viewing the document, choose **F**ile, **C**lose or press **[F7]** (Exit) to return to the document window.
- Save the document as S6LABELS.DOC.

  If you don't have a sheet of labels, you can print the labels document on an ordinary sheet of paper. If you're using a sheet of labels, consult your instructor or technical support person about how to feed the sheet into the printer.
- Print the labels document.

With the letters and labels printed, Whitney is now ready to send out her mailing. She attaches the gummed labels to manila envelopes, inserts the sales letters and product photographs, and mails them.

■   ■   ■

Exercises

1. Define or describe each of the
   a. form file
   b. data file
   c. merge code
   d. record
   e. field
   f. sort key
   g. merged document

2. Explain how you would insert the FIELDNAMES merge command into a form file.

3. What is the purpose of the FIELDNAMES merge code in a data file?

4. Suppose during a merge you wanted to insert a field named "Company" into a form file. Explain how you would do this.

5. When entering data into a data file, how do you mark the end of a field? the end of a record?

6. How would you initiate a merge between a form file and a data file?

7. How would you sort a data file using the zip code as the sort key? Assume the zip code is Field 6, named "Zip," in the data file.

8. Explain in general (without listing keystrokes) how you would use a data file to create mailing labels.

Tutorial Assignments

Open the file T6FILE1.DFT and do the following:

1. To the right of "MEMO TO:," press **[Tab]** and then insert the FIELD merge commands for the fields "First" (for the first name) and "Last" (for the last name).

2. To the right of "DATE:" in the memo, press **[Tab]** and insert the DATE merge code.

3. At the beginning of the body of the memo, before the word "here," insert the FIELD code for the field "First," followed by a comma and a space.

4. Save the file as S6MEMO.FRM.

Clear the document window and do the following:

5. Insert the FIELDNAMES merge code to create the following field names: "Last", "First", and "HomePhone".

6. Create a record for each of the following Sanders Imports employees. Enter the records in the order given:
    Zapata, Guillermo E., 286-1121
    Lim, Ching, 286-8442
    Mustoe, Geoffrey, 285-9142
    Apgood, Arnold, 285-3435
    Trifiletti, Samuel, 287-4501
    Qiad, Ke, 285-3318

7. Save the file as S6EMPL1.DAT.

8. Sort the file by last name.

9. Save the sorted file as S6EMPL2.DAT.

Clear the screen and do the following:

10. Merge the files S6MEMO.FRM and S6EMPL2.DAT.

11. Save the merged document as S6MEMO.MRG.

12. Print the file S6MEMO.MRG.

Open the file T6FILE2.DFT and do the following:

13. On the second line of the document, below the title, insert the DATE merge code, centered between the left and right margins.

14. Move the cursor to the right of "Product Name:," press **[Tab]** to move the cursor to position 4", and insert the FIELD command using the field name "ProductName."

15. Move the cursor to the right of "Suggested Retail Price:," press **[Tab]** to move the cursor to position 4", and insert the FIELD command using the field name "RetailPrice."

16. Continue inserting a tab and a FIELD command after each of the items in the document, using the field names "WholesalePrice," "Country," and "QuantInStock."

17. Save the file as S6PRODS.FRM.

Clear the document window and do the following:

18. Insert the FIELDNAMES merge code to create the following field names: "ProductName", "RetailPrice", "WholesalePrice", "Country", and "QuantInStock".

19. Create a record for each of the following products. Enter the records in the order given. In the list below, each line is a record. Fields in each record are separated by semicolons. (Don't include the semicolons in your data file record.)
    Teapot, Irish; 48.98; 28.80; Ireland; 258
    Rug, Alpaca; 185.95; 105.40; Peru; 188
    Mug, Designer Ceramic; 6.49; 3.20; Taiwan; 467
    Sweater, Turtleneck; 38.95, 20.60; Germany; 1,285
    Bowl, Wooden; 25.95, 15.80; Ecuador, 858

20. Save the file as S6PRODS.DAT.

21.   Sort the file by product name.

22.   Save the sorted file as S6PRODS2.DAT.

Clear the screen and do the following:

23.   Merge the files S6PRODS.FRM and S6PRODS2.DAT.

24.   Save the merged document as S6MEMO.MRG.

25.   Print the file S6PRODS.MRG.

Case Problems

1.   Form Letter to Small-Business Review Panel

Robyn Palkki is managing director of the National Entrepreneurial Foundation (NEF), headquartered in Denver, Colorado. She receives grant proposals from entrepreneurs who have innovative ideas for developing and marketing new products. The NEF funds several of these ideas each year. The proposals are reviewed by a panel of small-business experts. Ms. Palkki is preparing a data file of the current members of the review panel and a form letter to accompany a set of proposals.

Do the following:

1.   Create a data file with the following field names: "Name", "NickName", "Title", "Company", "Street", "City", "State", and "Zip".

2.   Enter the following records into the data file. Each paragraph below is one record. The fields in each record are separated by semicolons. (Don't include the semicolons in the records.)
      Michael Richardson; Mike; President; R&U Toy Company; 1630 Chicago Avenue; Evanston; IL; 60201
      Lisa C. Holmes; Lisa; Employment Manager; The David J. Wang Company; 300 Pike Street; Cincinnati; OH; 45202
      Susan Whitman; Sue; Chief Financial Officer; The Glidden Company; 925 Euclid Avenue; Cleveland; OH; 44115
      Elizabeth Kreischer; Liz; Director, Research and Development; Kwasha Lipton, Inc.; 2100 North Central Road; Fort Lee; NJ; 07024

3.   Save the data file as S6PANEL.DAT.

4.   Open the document P6PANEL.DFT, which is the body of the letter to the review panel.

5.   Insert blank spaces at the beginning of the document to allow room for the letterhead. The cursor should be below Ln 2".

6.   Insert the DATE merge command and press **[Enter]** three times to leave blank lines between the date and the inside address.

7. Insert FIELD commands for the complete inside address. Include fields for each panel member's name, title, company, street, city, state, and zip code.

8. Insert a blank line below the fields for the inside address and create the salutation of the letter. Use the field name "NickName" in the salutation. Insert another blank line between the salutation and the body of the letter.

9. Before the comma at the beginning of the second paragraph, insert the NickName field again.

10. Save the document as S6PANEL.FRM.

11. Sort the data file S6PANEL.DAT by company name.

12. Save the sorted file as S6PANEL2.DAT.

13. Merge the form file and the sorted data file to create a set of letters to the review panel.

14. Save the letters file as S6PANEL.MRG.

15. Print the first two letters.

16. Create a file of mailing labels for the panel members. Use Avery 5162 Address labels.

17. Save the labels file as S6PANEL.LBL.

18. Print the labels file onto a plain sheet of paper.

2. Form Letter to Announce a Class Reunion

Do the following:

1. Write a one-page form letter describing a high school class reunion that you are helping to organize. Include the following in the letter:
    a. Merge code for the current date.
    b. FIELD merge codes for the inside address and salutation of the letter.
    c. At least one FIELD merge within the body of the letter.
    d. Information to classmates about the cost, time, date, and location of the reunion.

2. Save the form file as S6REUN.FRM.

3. Create a data file containing the names and address of at least five classmates. You can use fictitious names and addresses.

4. Sort the file alphabetically by classmate's last name.

5. Save the data file as S6REUN.DAT.

6. Merge the form file and the data file.

7. Save the merged document as S6REUN.MRG.

8. Print the first two pages (letters) of the merged document.

9. Create a labels form file. You can use any printer label type you like, as long as each name and address fits on one label and all the labels fit on one page.

10. Save the labels file as S6REUN.LBL.

11. Print the labels file onto a plain sheet of paper.

3. Managing Computer Supplies

Bruce Warrenton is the administrative assistant to the office manager of Valtech International. One of his duties is to keep track of computer supplies at corporate headquarters. Bruce decides to do this using WordPerfect's merge feature. He decides to generate a merged document that lists the current inventory and the cost of each item.

Do the following:

1. Create a form file with the following features:
   a. The title "COMPUTER SUPPLIES" centered at the top of the page.
   b. The DATE merge code centered below the title.
   c. A line with the text "Type of item:" for the type of office supply. Item types will include such items as disks, laser paper, toner cartridges, software, and so forth.
   d. A line with the text "Product Name:" for the name of the product. For example, if the type of item is software, the product name might be "WordPerfect," "Microsoft DOS 6.0," or "Lotus 1-2-3."
   e. A line with the text "Number in stock:" for the quantity of that particular item on hand.
   f. A line with the text "Cost per item:" for the cost of each item.
   g. To the right of each of the above lines of text, insert a [Tab] and a FIELD merge command with the field names "Type", "Name", "Stock", and "Cost".

2. Save the form file as S6SUPPL.FRM.

3. Create a data file with the field names "Type", "Name", "Copies", and "Cost".

4. In your data file, include at least ten records of office supply items. Names, quantities, and costs can be fictitious.

5. Sort the data file by the cost per item, from most expensive to least expensive.

6. Save the sorted data file as S6SUPPL.DAT.

7. Merge the form and the data files.

8. Save the merged document as S6SUPPL.MRG.

9. Print the first two pages of the merged document.

WordPerfect Index

modes. See also graphics mode; text mode; typeover
  mode
    currently active   WP 23
    insert mode   WP 84-85
    Outline Edit mode   WP 204-205, WP 208
    switching between   WP 23
modifier keys   WP 15
mouse. *See also* drag (a mouse)
    entering text using   WP 10
    using button bar with   WP 16, WP 22
    using scroll bar with   WP 60-61
    using with pull-down menus   WP 14
mouse pointer   WP 10
move box   WP 134
moving
    cursor. *See* cursor movement
    footnotes   WP 229
    highlight bar   WP 18
    outline family   WP 206-208
    between pull-down menus   WP 12
    between screens   WP 58, WP 59, WP 210-214
    text   WP 128-131, WP 134-135   WP 211-212
multiple document window   WP 210-212

N

named macros
    defined   WP 215
    executing   WP 221
    recording   WP 220
[NUM LOCK] key   WP 10, WP 58
numbering
    footnotes   WP 226, WP 227
    pages. *See* page numbers
    paragraphs in outline. *See* paragraphs
numeric sort   WP 263

O

OK, choosing   WP 21
open style   WP 164
opening/retrieving
    document files   WP 40-42, WP 56, WP 111-112
    form files   WP 250-251
options, choosing   WP 16
organization of document   WP 5, WP 54, WP 110,
    WP 144, WP 192
orphans
    defined   WP 180
    protection from   WP 180-181
Outline Bar
    defined   WP 17
    turning off   WP 208
    using   WP 202-203

Outline Edit mode   WP 204-205
    exiting   WP 208
outline families
    defined   WP 204
    editing   WP 204-206
    moving   WP 206-208
Outline feature   WP 192-198
    turning off   WP 209
outlines
    creating   WP 192-198
    cursor movement through   WP 196, WP 199
    editing   WP 200-208
    inserting new paragraph numbers   WP 200-201

P

page breaks. *See also* hard page breaks
    soft   WP 79
    in tables   WP 175
page definition   WP 269
page numbers
    default setting   WP 11
    defined   WP 9
    in headers/footers   WP 158
    setting, WP 154-155, WP 159-160
    suppressing   WP 158-159
Page Suppress feature   WP 158-159
pages
    centering top to bottom   WP 147-150
    conditional end of   WP 177-180
    numbering. *See* page numbers
    title   WP 147-150
paper size   WP 11
paragraph sort   WP 263
paragraph style   WP 164
paragraphs
    copying   WP 132-133
    deleting   WP 133-134
    hard return to mark   WP 31
    indenting   WP 77-79
    numbers in outlines   WP 192-193, WP 195,
        WP 197-198, WP 200-201
parameters   WP 244, WP 245
parentheses ( )   WP 244
[PgDn] key   WP 59
[PgUp] key   WP 59
planning documents   WP 4-6, WP 36-37, WP 43,
    WP 54, WP 74, WP 99-101, WP 234
plus sign (+) button/key   WP 58, WP 206
position number   WP 9-10
previewing printing. *See* Print Preview
Print/Fax options   WP 38, WP 102, WP 150, WP 273
Print Preview
    address labels   WP 273-274
    centered text   WP 150
    documents   WP 37-38, WP 160-161

WORDPERFECT 6.0 COMMAND REFERENCE

Command	Function Keys	Pull-Down Menus	Button Bar
Block On/Off	[Alt][F4] or [F12]	Edit, Block	
Bold	[F6]	Font, Bold	
Bookmark	[Shift][F12]	Edit, Bookmark	
Center	[Shift][F6]	Layout, Alignment, Center	
Columns/Tables	[Alt][F7]	Layout, Columns or Tables	
Date	[Shift][F5]	Tools, Date	
Decimal Tab	[Ctrl][F6]	Layout, Align, Decimal Tab	
End Field	[F9]	Tools, Merge, End Field	
Envelope	[Alt][F12]	Layout, Envelope	Envelope
Exit	[F7]	File, Exit	
File Manager	[F5]	File, File Manager	File Mgr
Flush Right	[Alt][F6]	Layout, Align, Flush Right	
Font	[Ctrl][F8]	Font, Font	Font
Format	[Shift][F8]	Layout	
Graphics	[Alt][F9]	Graphics	
Help	[F1]	Help	
Indent, Left	[F4]	Layout, Alignment, Indent	
Indent, Left/Right	[Shift][F4]	Layout, Alignment, Indent	
Mark Text	[Alt][F5]	Tools	
Merge Codes	[Shift][F9]	Tools, Merge, Define	
Merge/Sort	[Ctrl][F9]	Tools, Sort or Tools, Merge, Run	
Move	[Ctrl][F4]	Edit, Select	
Notes	[Ctrl][F7]	Layout, Footnote or Endnote	
Open/Retrieve	[Shift][F10]	File, Open or Retrieve	Open
Outline	[Ctrl][F5]	Tools, Outline	
Play Macro	[Alt][F10]	Tools, Macro, Play	
Print/Fax	[Shift][F7]	File, Print/Fax	Print, Preview
Record Macro	[Ctrl][F10]	Tools, Macro, Record	
Reveal Codes	[Alt][F3] or [F11]	View, Reveal Codes	
Save	[Ctrl][F12]	File, Save	
Save As	[F10]	File, Save As	Save As
Screen	[Ctrl][F3]	View	GrphMode, Text Mode
Search	[F2]	Edit, Search	
Search and Replace	[Alt][F2]	Edit, Replace	
Search Backward	[Shift][F2]	Edit, Search	
Setup	[Shift][F1]	File, Setup	
Shell	[Ctrl][F1]	File, Go to Shell	
Speller	[Ctrl][F2]	Tools, Writing Tools, Speller	Speller
Styles	[Alt][F8]	Layout, Styles	
Switch Document	[Shift][F3]	Window, Switch	
Switch to Document	[F3]	Window, Switch to	
Tab Set	[Ctrl][F11]	Layout, Tab Set	
Table Edit	[Alt][F11]	Layout, Table, Edit	
Underline	[F8]	Font, Underline	
WP Characters	[Shift][F11]	Font, WP Characters	
Writing Tools	[Alt][F1]	Tools, Writing Tools	Speller, Grammatik